Whither the Early Republic

Whither the Early Republic

A Forum on the Future of the Field

EDITED BY JOHN LAURITZ LARSON
AND MICHAEL A. MORRISON

PENN

University of Pennsylvania Press

Philadelphia

10   9   8   7   6   5   4   3   2   1

Published by
University of Pennsylvania Press
Philadelphia, Pennsylvania 19104-4112

Library of Congress Cataloging-in-Publication Data

Whither the early republic : a forum on the future of the field / edited by
John Larson and Michael Morrison.
    p.   cm.
  Includes bibliographical references and index.
  ISBN-13: 978-0-8122-1932-6 (pbk. : acid-free paper)
  ISBN-10: 0-8122-1932-5 (pbk. : acid-free paper)
  1. United States—Civilization—1783–1865—Historiogaphy.   2. United
States—Civilization—To 1783—Historiography.   3. United States—
History—1783–1865—Historiography.   I. Larson, John Lauritz, 1950–
II. Morrison, Michael A., 1948–
  E164.W57   2005
  973′.072′073—dc22

                                                        2005041827

Contents

Introduction: What Is This Book?

BY JOHN LAURITZ LARSON AND MICHAEL A. MORRISON

The Invitation

After fourteen and ten years respectively in the editorial chairs at the *Journal of the Early Republic*, the editors of this collection, Morrison and Larson, gave up the ghost and returned to the splendid insignificance of public university employment. Our years with the journal were marked (we like to think) by a successful enlargement of the scope and range of scholarship appearing in those pages concerning the history and culture of the early American republic. Like rodeo cowboys, we often feared that the mount had control of the rider, not the other way around; still, in all, we found it enormously rewarding, intellectually enriching, and personally very satisfying to try to stay conversant with the explosion of scholarly activities that have marked our field in the last decade or so. The extent to which we actually succeeded will be best known to readers of the journal, but our intentions were honorable and catholic, whatever limitations may have kept us from being truly open-minded.

John Lauritz Larson is Professor of History at Purdue University. For ten years he was an editor at the *Journal of the Early Republic*. He is author of *Internal Improvement: National Public Works and the Promise of Popular Government in the Early United States* (2001), and editor of a forthcoming special issue of the OAH *Magazine of History* on the market revolution in America. His current project is a study of environmental factors and the rise of capitalism in the early United States.

Michael A. Morrison is Associate Professor of History at Purdue University. For fourteen years he was an editor at the *Journal of the Early Republic*. He is author of *Slavery and the American West: The Eclipse of Manifest Destiny and the Coming of the Civil War* (1999) and numerous collections of essays. He is currently writing a book on the Mexican-American War and the transformation of American political culture.

As a parting gift to the journal and its readers, we wanted to assemble a final collection of essays that somehow took measure of the state of the field. First thoughts suggested a retrospective evaluation, but looking backward did not suit us. Furthermore, detailed historiographical summations are getting harder and harder to come by. The literature is bursting forth in all directions, segmenting as it goes into sub-conversations, and threatening always to erupt in open schism between rival interest groups. Sensible historians are reluctant to take the kind of risks Robert Shalhope so generously did in his two masterful assessments of the "republicanism" literature some years ago. It was our gut sense that the scholars we would want to construct such summaries were smart enough to refuse, while those who might be willing probably had some ax to grind that would make us wish we had not asked.

In the end we settled on an idea that followed no familiar model. Why not set down four or five general areas that seemed to be on the cutting edge of where the field was currently tending? Find the leading voices in those innovative conversations and ask them who is doing new and exciting work on the frontiers they know best. Then recruit from among those innovative practitioners essays meditating on the future of the field as seen from these outer edges. Our invitation to these authors, ultimately, was to reflect forward (as much as that is possible) and consider where the interest and excitement is *going to lie* for the generation of historians who are currently entering graduate school. For each topical unit we assigned a senior scholar (the original "leading voice") the role of organizer and commentator. The exact approach, division of labor, and selection of contributors depended largely on each part organizer's suggestions and the universe of possibilities—which varied widely from topic to topic. As a result, the parts that follow in this collection are not exactly parallel except in the structural sense that each starts with three original essays and ends with a fourth commentary that to some extent looks back on the three.

The result of this experiment in group print conversation is, we think, provocative, refreshing, entertaining, and hopefully instructive. The collection first appeared in the *Journal of the Early Republic* in the summer of 2004, and it was the subject of a very lively, well-attended session at the SHEAR Conference that July in Providence, Rhode Island. Given the "buzz" generated by the special issue, we believed the collection might prove useful, especially in senior or graduate seminars, for colleagues trying to introduce a new generation of would-be historians to the nature of our field and the almost infinite possibilities that lie in the future for scholars of this fascinating period. Hence the present volume: WHITHER THE EARLY REPUBLIC: A FORUM ON THE FUTURE OF THE FIELD.

The Plan of the Work
Our collection is arranged around the following topics:

- **Continental possessions:** *encompassing the all struggles for control of North America that finally helped shape the culture of the early United States.*
- **Pursuing happiness:** *concerning the economic culture of the United States that created and distributed wealth and in the process reshaped the culture.*
- **Interactive landscapes:** *embracing those aspects of environmental history that expose the interactions of human beings with climate, plants, animals, and germs.*
- **Commodification of people:** *in which people are bought and sold or otherwise reduced to ciphers in a marketplace increasingly structured by capitalist principles.*
- **Private, public, and spirit worlds:** *at the intersections of which, we think, culture is constructed, contested, and negotiated.*

Our first part, "Continental Possessions," reflects a deepening and radical trend in early American scholarship to think, not backward from the United States, but forward from the perspective of the place—North America—and the contests for possession that dominated its history between 1500 and the middle of the nineteenth century. Nobody knows the problem better than Alan Taylor, whose recent survey, *American Colonies* (2001), completes a process begun somewhat haltingly two generations ago by the "imperial school" of colonial historians (Andrews and Osgood) to place the privileged "original thirteen" in the context of Europe's expansion into the Americas. Atlantic and Caribbean historians have been after us for years to notice Greenland, Barbados, and the whole West Indian colonial project along with the mainland colonies; more recent scholars have forced our attention into the northern, southern, and western lands bordering Great Britain's mainland colonies. As a result, the story of North America in the era of colonization turns into a saga of invasions and rivalries far more complicated than any simple narrative of the "discovery" of a "lost" wilderness ever could explain. Alan recruited Andrés Reséndez, Elizabeth Fenn, and James F. Brooks to share their thoughts on the problem of comprehending the story of continental possession in America. Their essays, together with Alan's comment, throw down a challenge that both specialists and teachers of the general American survey course that will ignore, we believe, at their peril.

Property—getting, holding, and spending it, a primeval ambition central both to Locke's schematic formulations and the actual experience of Americans of all descriptions—focuses our second part, "Pursuing Happiness." Economic history has been in something of a doldrums lately, nudged off the stage of scholarship by sex and violence among other things. The fault lies not with historians alone: Bitter quarrels in the 1960s and 1970s over quantification and economic theory (whether footnotes without limit functions counted as documentation) helped drive "mathematically challenged" students from the study of economic life. Our friends at the Program for Early American Economy and Society (PEAES) in Philadelphia, led by Cathy Matson and The Library Company of Philadelphia, have done much to correct this situation, and in a small corner of the field there is enormously important and interesting work being done. Still, it seems odd to us that a period in which one central framing device is called the "market revolution" should see so little action in the field of economic history. James L. Huston, one of the best writers on political economy in the early American republic agreed to organize this part and recommended focusing on three special links between economic life and (1) religion, (2) rural life, and (3) the business of private enterprise. Stewart Davenport, Christopher Clark, and Barbara Tucker and Kenneth Tucker take up these assignments in stimulating summaries of the problems they see remaining in our field, and Jim follows with a brief for the reunification of a concept that has been sundered by modern statistical analysis: "political economy."

America itself, the land, landscape, and all that made up what we now call the "environment," is the subject of part three, "Interactive Landscapes." In times past historians paid more attention to weather, landscape, and "major crops and exports" (remember, it was U. B. Phillips, not M. C. Hammer, who first sang "Hot and Wet"). Historical geographers such as Carville Earle and Donald W. Meinig continued to coach us from the geography departments, but only in the last generation has environmental history surged in interest, driven by the extraordinary work of new Western historians and also the rising interest of colonial and early republic scholars in the wake of William Cronon's enormously successful *Changes in the Land* (1983). Theodore Steinberg stands as one of the leading voices in the environmental history community, and one of the leading scholars whose work is *not* primarily anchored in the western United States. With powerful studies of New England water, natural disasters, and a new survey textbook to his credit, Ted seemed like the ideal person to gather for our benefit specialists who work on the environment and its place in the early United States. The topic being unavoidably place-specific, he chose to recruit contributors according to a regional template: Brian Donahue for New England, Mart Stewart for the antebellum South, Conevery Valencius for the early West (that is, the humid antebellum frontiers before John Muir became famous or Walter Webb introduced the six-gun, barbed-wire, and windmill formula for understanding frontier history). Their provocative essays and Steinberg's summary reflections explore what may prove to be one of the more open and promising areas of study in the decade or two ahead.

Slavery endures as a problem for Americans, American historians, and nearly everybody else who studies human interactions in the past and the present. Recent scholarship seems to be escaping the bounds once set down by Marxist scholars to distinguish slave labor from free. Influenced by cultural studies and more complicated templates concerning domination and subjection, historians of slavery seem determined to push the conceptual envelope both toward a core concept of commodification and toward a more inclusive understanding of all kinds of power relations that convert persons into fungible property. Having recently published a remarkable cultural study of slave buying and selling, slave making, and slaveholder making, *Soul by Soul: Life Inside the Antebellum Slave Market* (1999), Walter Johnson seemed perfectly situated to help us find the future of this still critical field. At his invitation David Waldstreicher, Amy Dru Stanley, and Stephanie Smallwood contribute three very different and very challenging essays designed to unsettle whatever we think we know about slavery, freedom, paternalism, and exploitation. Johnson then returns our attention to Marx's original struggle with the conceptual boundary between capitalism and slavery.

Finally, we wanted to explore the rich outpouring of cultural studies in a part titled "Public, Private, and Spirit Worlds." Historians once naively thought of cultural history as the spread of arts and letters into the Ohio Valley (remember Louis B. Wright, *Culture on a Moving Frontier?* [1955]). Well, now cultural history is everywhere, and it is "*not* your father's Oldsmobile." Close readings of all kinds of "texts" (no transparent documents here) has resulted in interpretive performances that sometimes seem incomprehensible to historians. Yet this scholarship has so effectively disoriented our fundamental notions of documents, evidence, analysis, and narration that we cannot afford to ignore it. David S. Shields accepted responsibility for provoking our readers in this direction. Patricia Cline Cohen looks at sex and sexuality; Bernard Herman analyses space itself—social, racial, political, and geographical; and Leigh Schmidt complicates the already difficult area of religion by suggesting that *all* religions contributed to the cultural matrix even at times when hardly any Americans acknowledged them. Apparently decentered by his own recruits' success at complicating our perspectives, Shields himself retreats into a fascinating list of questions for the coming generation to ponder.

How to Read this Book

Left to right and front to back is always good advice. But seriously, we would like readers to begin with a sense that this is a free-flowing conversation and not a series of final pronouncements. The reason we append this long introduction is to bring readers up to speed on the nature of the assignments that went out to our authors. Nobody was expected to present new research—although some did so and all clearly depend on the rich scholarly engagement of the authors. Nobody was required to include historiographical notes or bibliography—which, again, some did anyway although illustratively and never with the intention of completeness. The five parts stand in no particular order and are not intended to accumulate sequentially: feel free to read or discuss them in any order. Similarly, the five parts suggest but by no means exhaust the exploratory avenues along which current scholarship is moving. We have no doubt that a lively conversation would repay the question: What other parts ought to have been included?

It seems to us, both veterans of many a graduate seminar, that the ideal way to approach this collection is not the standard "what-is-wrong-with-these-essays" approach but something more akin to a free-association exercise in which colleagues and students interact (perhaps chaotically) with the central question: Where are we going? It is a question that empowers the newer voices, because what interests and energizes them is what will dictate the future of the field. It is a question that unsettles the elders because it makes possible, maybe even invites, not a refutation of explanations we have long messaged to perfection, but a casual dismissal of our preoccupations as boring and old-fashioned. The resulting tension—perhaps a reversal of the vectors of authority that typically structure a seminar setting—ought to be great fun. If it proves not to be, then we have verified what we suspected when we decided to retire from the journal: put a fork in these two, they're done.

PART I

Continental Possessions

. . . encompassing all the struggles for control of North America that finally helped shape the culture of the early United States.

ALAN TAYLOR, CHAIR

Our first part reflects a deepening and radical trend in early American scholarship to think, not backwards from the United States but forwards from the perspective of the place—North America—and the contests for possession that dominated its history between about 1500 and the middle of the nineteenth century. Nobody knows the problem better than Alan Taylor, whose recent survey, American Colonies *(2001), completes a process begun somewhat haltingly two generations ago by the "imperial school" of colonial historians (Andrews and Osgood) to place the privileged "original thirteen" in the context of Europe's expansion into the Americas. While Atlantic and Caribbean historians have taught us to notice Greenland and Barbados along with the mainland colonies, more recent scholars have forced our attention into the northern, southern, and western borderlands, until the story of North America in the era of colonization looks more like an invasion of aggressive outsiders than the discovery of lost continents. Alan recruited Andrés Reséndez, Elizabeth Fenn, and James F. Brooks to share their thoughts on the problem of comprehending the story of continental possession in America, after which Alan reflects on the issues raised and the profits to be gained from this angle of perspective.*

Continental Possessions—Three Deepening Trends

ANDRÉS RESÉNDEZ

It may well be embarrasing, perhaps downright painful, to come back to this fortune-telling exercise twenty-five years from now. My only defense is that the vision of the future presented in these pages is inevitably mixed with my own wishful thinking. Without further apologies, I predict (and wish) that three trends—already noticeable in the scholarship—will continue to unfold and deepen as scholars concerned with the struggles for control of North America forge ahead in the course of the next generation. These three trends are: 1) Indigenous societies will continue to move toward the center of the imperial story of North America; 2) historians will continue to broaden their understangings of imperial and colonial relationships through the prism of understudied sites where relations of power were negotiatied; and 3) North America will go global as scholars compare colonialism, imperialism, nationalism, frontiers, and other processes in Asia, Africa, Latin America, Europe, and North America.

>‑◆›‑O‑‹◆‑‑◄

Recent scholarly emphasis on colonial and national diversity may lead one to believe that the trend to center or privilege Native-American stories is about to—or has already—run its course. There is little need to belabor this point. Scholarship on colonial North America (British, French, and Spanish) as well as works stemming from the now aging

Andrés Reséndez is an assistant professor at the University of California, Davis, and author of *Changing National Identities at the Frontier: Texas and New Mexico, 1800–1850* (2005).

"New Western history" have made great progress in shedding light on the roles played by various groups that had been short-shrifted in past historical treatments, especially native peoples. Indeed, some recent efforts to reclaim native agency may well have pushed the pendulum too far in the other direction, resulting in an underestimation of the influence of Europeans both in terms of their stated goals and—more importantly perhaps—the unintended consequences of their presence and actions. My prediction is that the next generation of scholars will probe more deeply into how indigenous societies understood, coped with, took advantage of, and ultimately succumbed to the imperial designs of the various European powers. Europeans were not only conquerors and colonists bent on rolling back indigenous influence, they also were bearers of important resources that some Native Americans were able to marshall and deploy in their own struggles for control. As Thomas Kavanagh has pointed out—to cite the most obvious example—the kaleidoscopic Comanche political organizations were simply on-the-ground manifestations of cultural structures meant to exploit particular resources ranging from hunting buffalo and conducting peaceful exchanges with Euroamerica communities to waging war on other Native Americans and thriving on an economy that included widespread raiding on native and non-native settlements.[1]

This exploration of how indigenous aims and strategies intersected with the unfolding imperial designs of Europeans will happen for multiple reasons and will run along parallel lines. Most obviously, indigenous sources in the form of winter counts, oral traditions, published accounts, periodicals, and others sources written by Indian authors will be reassessed critically and more thoroughly mined than they have been thus far.[2] Moreover, as historians increasingly train their sights on non-textual realms of inquiry—dress habits, food preferences, medical practices, civil celebrations, sexual mores, patterns of exchange, musical traditions, etc.—the imbalance between European and Indian sources will become less pronounced. Non-textual evidence will show the different ways in which Native Americans both selectively adapted European items and preserved their own mores, institutions, and beliefs.

---

1. Thomas W. Kavanagh, *The Comanches: A History 1706–1875* (Lincoln, 1996), *passim*.

2. Cheryl Walker, *Indian Nation: Native American Literature and Nineteenth-Century Nationalism* (Durham, 1997), *passim*.

Finally, a better understanding of the origins, spatial distribution, and relative influence of different indigenous groups will come about as various disciplines, especially DNA studies and linguistics, yield information that will further elucidate ethnohistorical and archeological sources. This will be particularly important when dealing with indigenous groups in a greater time horizon. DNA evidence already has been successfully used to track population movements and to establish degrees of relatedness among different indigenous societies where no other evidence is available.[3] While genetic evidence tells a story of biological mixing, linguistic information constitutes an independent source that has more to do with prestige, influence, and relationships of domination/subjugation.[4] All of this new information will necessarily lead to an overall reassessment of the native world of North America and the ways in which the arrival of different groups of Europeans altered this human landscape.

>–·‹›·–O·–‹›·–‹

Of course, the appearance of rival groups generated conflicts and negotiations for power. Any student of empire, colonialism, and nationalism would readily admit that the formal acquisition of territory and its political administration represented only one facet—albeit a crucial one—of the story. Empire (or nation) also was about consumption patterns, medical practices, print cultures, clothing fashions, civic celebrations, musical traditions, marriage practices, food and drink, leisure and work habits, child-rearing activities, and so forth. One or two generations ago scholars still privileged formal power exchanges carried out by leaders and sanctioned in treaties and agreements, but in the last decades there has been an explosion of works focusing on more mundane layers of power negotiation like the ones described above. Nevertheless, there is a long way to go in studying these sites of power negotiation, especially across imperial, colonial, and national boundaries.

Let me offer two examples of such sites of power negotiation along the United States-Mexico frontier area. Important work has been done on medicine and medical practices in colonial/national America and in

---

3. Ripan S. Malhi, *et al.*, "Native American mtDNA Prehistory in the American Southwest," in *American Journal of Physical Anthropology*, 120 (2003): 108–24.

4. Jane H. Hill, "Proto-Uto-Aztecan: A Community of Cultivators in Central Mexico?" in *American Anthropologist*, 103 (2001): 219–32.

New Spain/Mexico.[5] From these and other texts it is clear that the residents of places like Texas, New Mexico, and California witnessed a medical exchange of major proportions during the early-to-mid-nineteenth century as diseased members of all ethnicities, in their quest for health, experimented with all medical traditions available to them. We still know precious little about how these medical encounters took place, how a hierarchy of medical cultures came into being in the region, and why frontier inhabitants so readily embraced Euroamerican pharmacopeia in spite of the fact that its most popular medicines and medical procedures—mercury-based pills and the use of the lancet for venesections—were just as ineffectual as the other healing methods.

Similarly, historians have done insightful work on drinking habits in colonial and early national Mexico and in the United States.[6] As Mexicans and Anglo-Americans along the frontier came to terms with each other in the 1820s–1840s, these different drinking cultures affected one another and had profound repercussions on the indigenous societies of the area. Again, we know relatively little about how drinking patterns changed in the area, how and why rum came to replace a host of other alcoholic beverages previously consumed in the area including wine, brandy, and pulque, and what meanings were attached to drinking and drunkeness in the various drinking cultures that coexisted along the frontier. This is especially relevant given that increased levels of production and consumption of alcohol were at the root of at least some of the interethnic animosities in Texas and New Mexico in the years leading up to the Mexican-American War.[7]

There is a real risk of fragmentation as this exploration of multiple

5. See Luz María Hernández Sáenz, *Learning to Heal: The Medical Profession in Colonial Mexico, 1767–1831* (New York, 1997). Works dealing with the medical establishment in Texas and New Mexico include Sylvia Van Voast Ferris, *Scalpels and Sabers: Nineteenth Century Medicine in Texas* (Austin, 1985).

6. William B. Taylor, *Drinking, Homicide, and Rebellion in Colonial Mexican Villages* (Stanford, 1979); W. J. Rorabaugh, *The Alcoholic Republic: An American Tradition* (New York, 1979), *passim*.

7. I have dealt with this subject rather summarily in "Getting Cured and Getting Drunk: State versus Market in Texas and New Mexico, 1800-1850" *Journal of the Early Republic*, 22 (2002): 77–103; and also in my book *Changing National Identities at the Frontier: Texas and New Mexico, 1800–1850* (New York, 2004), *passim*.

sites of imperial, colonial, and national negotiation unfolds and deepens in the years ahead. The accumulation of works on each of these sites will necessarily lead to subspecialties and perhaps even to thematic islands and ghettoes. It is my belief, however, that the most ambitious of these works will cull information from different and unexpected realms of human experience to construct compelling arguments about the workings of colonialism, imperialism, expansionism, frontier dynamics, and others.

My third prediction is that North America will go global as scholars compare colonialism, imperialism, nationalism, frontiers, and other processes in Asia, Africa, Latin America, Europe, and North America. Such a research agenda has been long in the making, although up to now it has been unable to make much headway because most working historians are still trained in one or at most two areas of the world. Recent scholarly attention on world history, greater reliance on collaborative work, and a rediscovery of the virtues of the comparative method may well lead to significant progress in the decades ahead. It is impossible to predict just which institutions or processes will be most fruitfully compared and studied in settings around the world. The obstacles remain formidable, but recent scholarly trends suggest that there is reason for hope.

Let me offer the case of frontiers and identities by way of example. In a work published 25 years ago devoted to comparing the frontiers of South Africa and the United States, Howard Lamar and Leonard Thompson proposed an ambitious agenda that one day would culminate in a grand synthesis—along the lines of the literature on comparative slavery—informed by frontier experiences drawn from around the world.[8] Their vision has yet to come to fruition, but recent research on frontiers and identities along the Pyrenees, on the Ghana-Togo frontier, along the medieval Irish frontier, or in the Ohio Valley—just to name a few—gives us a better sense of both commonalities and variation through time and space.[9]

---

8. Howard Lamar and Leonard Thompson, eds., *The Frontier in History: North America and Southern Africa Compared* (New Haven, 1981), 5–6.

9. Peter Sahlins, *Boundaries: The Making of France and Spain in the Pyrenees* (Berkeley, 1989); Paul Nugent, *Smugglers, Secessionists & Loyal Citizens on the Ghana-Togo Frontier: Life on the Borderlands since 1914* (Athens, OH, 2002); James Muldoon, *Identity on the Medieval Irish Frontier: Degenerate Englishmen, Wild Irishmen, Middle Nations* (Gainesville, 2003); and Kim M. Gruenwald, *River*

If we begin by just limiting ourselves to the western world, we discover that for a thousand years or so European Christian society has expanded outward in all directions, venturing beyond its original heartland roughly coinciding with the contours of the Carolingian Empire. This millennium of relentless European expansion (with occasional retrenchments) has given rise to numerous frontiers in the most diverse settings, bringing together multifarious peoples. Scholars working on European frontiers during the medieval and early modern period have stressed the centrality of Christianity, a shared religious culture, as an anchor of European identity and as a key determinant in their relations with peoples beyond the Mediterranean/Christian world.[10]

The consolidation of national-states beginning in the seventeenth century marked a new plateau in the frontier experience. Modern nations emerged only when centralized states were strong enough to launch a process of institutional and cultural integration that resulted in higher levels of effective control of national frontiers than had been possible before. Peter Sahlins's insightful study of the Spanish-French frontier along the Pyrenees from the seventeenth through the nineteenth centuries describes the frontier experience in the modern era, highlighting that although boundaries may have been at first arbitrary state impositions, frontier peoples in certain instances found it convenient to uphold and maintain such demarcations in order to further their own interests.[11] The activism of nation-states in asserting their territorial claims led to the intensification of frontier clashes and negotiation of identities not only in Europe but in frontiers around the world as independent nations in Latin America, Asia, and Africa sought to uphold, resist, or change old colonial boundaries.

At the same time that nation-states consolidated their power, the market economy has spread since the eighteenth century. Many frontier studies reveal the paramount importance of economic transactions in shaping borders and identities. Paul Nugent's recent work on the Ghana-Togo frontier, for instance, shows the extent to which the exploitation of cocoa has affected the mental geography of Togolanders and how

---

of Enterprise: The Commercial Origins of Regional Identity in the Ohio Valley, 1790–1850 (Bloomington, 2002).

10. Muldoon, *Identity on the Medieval Irish Frontier*, xii, 13–14.

11. Sahlins, *Boundaries, passim.*

smuggling—and state efforts to stop this practice—has given meaning and concreteness to the border.[12] Similarly, Kim M. Gruenwald has shown the inextricable linkage between the commercial development of the Ohio Valley since the late eighteenth century and peoples' understandings of the region and its role in the larger national context.[13]

The consolidation of state power and the intensification of capitalism occurred at different rates in different parts of the world thus giving rise to encounters in which frontier residents counted on widely different levels of state and market resources. In this regard, the United States-Mexican borderlands may well constitute the paradigmatic example of this frontier type. But it is hardly the only case. In South America, similar frontier circumstances arose in the Atacama Desert where Bolivia's claims were thwarted by Chile's expanding nitrate industry. Even in Europe, so neatly parceled out among nations, we can find areas like Alsace-Lorraine formally administered by one nation (France) but economically integrated to another one (Germany). Given that we now have monographs of various frontiers around the world, and given also that scholars have been able to identify different frontier dynamics, the field seems ripe for more comparative work. And in this brave new world, the United States-Mexican borderlands—as well as other frontier areas and other institutions and processes throughout North America—will play important roles.

In addition to frontiers, many other institutions and processes have been compared and will increasingly be placed in a global context including imperial competition, colonialism, industrialization, and so forth. Indeed, it is easy to see that these phenomena, long forced into national or sub-national straitjackets, are more naturally conceived as spanning the world. Scholars also will fruitfully compare more discrete sites like the ones described in section two of this essay. In fact, such comparisons are the ones that can be more insightfully and realistically carried out. It is one thing to compare the workings of the British Empire in India and the Spanish Empire in New Spain, and quite another to study child-rearing practices in both places. The upshot of all of this is that future scholars, working along several parallel lines, will succeed in placing the history of North America on a global context.

---

12. Nugent, *Smugglers, Secessionists & Loyal Citizens,* chaps. 2 and 3.
13. Gruenwald, *River of Enterprise, passim.*

Whither the Rest of the Continent?

ELIZABETH A. FENN

Late fall is a difficult time to travel on America's northern prairies. In a warm spell, the sun might draw daytime temperatures into the 50s, but more typically they hover around the freezing mark. Even in October, the weather can turn bitter. Pools of standing water freeze solid at night, the Missouri River ices over entirely, and relentless northwest winds carry with them the first real snows of winter.[1]

It was nevertheless in the late fall of 1738 that an unlikely party of travelers meandered southwestward across these interior grasslands. The party came from modern-day Manitoba; its destination was modern-day North Dakota. Among its members were some twenty-odd Frenchmen, at least one Native-American slave, and 142 families of Assiniboine Indians. In all, there were more than of six hundred people. They proceeded on foot, marching Indian style in three columns that wound serpent-like through undulating waves of grass.[2]

Elizabeth A. Fenn is an Assistant Professor of History at Duke University. She is the author of *Pox Americana: The Great Smallpox Epidemic of 1775–82* (2001) and the coauthor, with Peter H. Wood, of *Natives & Newcomers: The Way We Lived in North Carolina before 1770* (1983). She is currently working on a book on the rise and fall of the Mandan nation, 1738–1837.

1. On October 31, 1804, north of present-day Bismarck, North Dakota, William Clark and Meriwether Lewis reported the Missouri "very low and the season so far advanced that it frequently shuts up with ice in this climate." The expedition thus established winter quarters among the Mandans. Gary E. Moulton, ed., *The Definitive Journals of Lewis & Clark* (10 vols., Lincoln, 2002–03), 3:219.

2. G. Hubert Smith, *The Explorations of the La Vérendryes in the Northern Plains, 1738–1743*, ed. W. Raymond Wood (Lincoln, 1980), 47–50. This work contains the most recent and trustworthy translation of La Vérendrye's journal.

At the head of the Frenchmen was a fur trader–explorer named Pierre Gaultier de Varennes, Sieur de la Vérendrye. His intent was to find the Indians he called the "Mantannes," or Mandans, and to learn from them the route to the long-sought Sea of the West. The Sea of the West was a myth, a creation of wishful imagination on the part of the French, whose pursuit of it mirrored the contemporaneous English hunt for a Northwest Passage. For La Vérendrye, this quest, along with the gathering of furs, was his life's mission. He understood from Indian stories that the fabled sea could be reached by way of the Mandans. And he likewise believed that once he found it, the sea would lead him to the Pacific Ocean.[3]

With this goal in mind, the French explorers followed their Assiniboine guides across what La Vérendrye termed "magnificent plains." Each step they took extended the bounds of the European known world. When they finally arrived among the Mandans on December 3, an enormous crowd greeted them. The Frenchmen were the first Europeans ever to set foot in the tidy streets and massive earth lodges these Indians called home.[4]

But the edge of the world for the French constituted the very center of the world for the Mandans. Indeed, these corn- and bean-growing farmers occupied a country quite close to the middle of the North American continent.[5] Their settlements felt impressively urban to the French newcomers. Fortified by ditches and great wooden palisades, each contained hundreds—even thousands—of people. La Verendrye counted "as many as 130" lodges in the village where he halted his journey. So numerous and so indistinguishable were the dwellings that the visitors "often lost their way among them."[6]

La Vérendrye reported a total of five Mandan "forts" within a day's journey of the one where he stopped. These were almost certainly the villages clustered on both sides of the Missouri River near modern-day Bismarck and Mandan, North Dakota, where the Heart River flows in from the west. There may have been other Mandan settlements as well,

---

3. *Ibid.*, 20–22.

4. *Ibid.*, 50, 59.

5. Today, the town of Rugby, North Dakota, roughly ninety miles from the former site of the Heart River villages, stakes a contentious claim to this honor.

6. Smith, *Explorations of the La Vérendryes*, 59.

beyond the six that La Vérendrye recorded.[7] Taken together, these Indian towns housed at least six thousand people.[8]

The Mandan villages pose a problem for historians of early America. Here was a densely settled community of 6,000 or more Americans, prospering at hunting, farming, and commerce in the late 1730s. Numerically, the Mandans constituted a population smaller than that of Philadelphia (around 8,800) yet larger than that of the Georgia colony (1,110) at the same time.[9] But unlike the inhabitants of Philadelphia and the

---

7. The town where La Vérendrye stopped may have been Menoken village (not its original name), roughly sixteen miles east of the Missouri and the Heart River settlements. The evidence, however, is more suggestive than conclusive. For a thorough discussion of this and other possibilities, see *ibid.*, 89. Although Henry Schoolcraft said that there were as many as thirteen Mandan villages, Raymond Wood (using evidence from David Thompson) has suggested that at least three of these must have been Hidatsa, not Mandan. W. Raymond Wood, *An Interpretation of Mandan Culture History*, vol. 25 of *Reprints in Anthropology* (1967 rep.; Lincoln, 1982), 140.

8. Population estimates are extrapolated from several sources. Donald Lehmer has posited a Mandan population of "about 6000" before the smallpox epidemic of 1781. The number is clearly an estimate, and if anything, it would have been larger, not smaller, in 1738. Donald J. Lehmer, "Epidemics among Indians of the Upper Missouri," in *Selected Writings of Donald J. Lehmer*, ed. W. Raymond Wood, vol. 8 of *Reprints in Anthropology* (Lincoln, 1977), 107. More recently, in his 1985 Ph.D. dissertation, Michael Trimble has suggested that at the time of La Vérendrye's journey there were six to eight villages, each containing approximately 130 lodges. (The estimate of lodges may be low. It comes from La Vérendrye's appraisal of the first village he visited, which he said was smaller than the others.) If each lodge contained eight people, as David Thompson observed in the winter of 1797–98, then the population of the Heart River towns would have been from 6,240 to 9,360 at the time of La Vérendrye's visit. Michael K. Trimble, "Epidemiology on the Northern Plains: A Cultural Perspective" (Ph.D. diss., University of Missouri, Columbia, 1985), 158; David Thompson, *David Thompson's Narrative 1784–1812*, ed. Richard Glover (Toronto, 1962), 173. W. Raymond Wood analyzes Thompson's data in some detail in his discussion of Thompson's journal in David Thompson, "David Thompson at the Mandan-Hidatsa Villages, 1797–1798: The Original Journals," ed. W. Raymond Wood, *Ethnohistory*, 24 (1977): 329–42.

9. On Philadelphia, see Gary B. Nash, *The Urban Crucible: Social Change, Political Consciousness, and the Origins of the American Revolution* (Cambridge, MA, 1979), 402. The Georgia statistics are for the colony itself, exclusive of Creek and Cherokee territory. See Robert V. Wells, *The Population of the British Colonies in America before 1776: A Survey of Census Data* (Princeton, 1975), 170; and

Georgia colony, these Indians rarely appear in our history books until the nineteenth century, when a series of famous visitors, including Lewis and Clark, George Catlin, Prince Maximilian von Weid, and John James Audubon made them noteworthy in the eyes of historians.[10] By this time, however, the Mandans were a mere shadow of their former selves. The Heart River towns had been abandoned, their occupants had relocated, and only a fraction of the nation survived.

Where do the Mandans fit in North American history? Why is their story (and that of the Tlingits and Paiutes and Cree and many others) not an integral part of the American narrative? The answer surely has many dimensions. The familiar seems safe and comfortable, while the unfamiliar seems risky and unsettling. For English speakers, Spanish and French sources can be daunting, and Lakota and Mandan evidence can be more so. For bi-coastal historians accustomed to transcontinental air travel, the geography alone can pose difficulties.

But the crux of the problem is the early republic itself. As the central organizing entity of American history, the early republic is fundamentally flawed. By its very nature, this focus narrows our gaze to the United States (however constituted at any given time) and to the thirteen colonies that gave birth to it. As a consequence, we lose sight of the millions of Americans who lived beyond the confines of this nation-state and its political antecedents. Only when their homelands are absorbed into the expanding republic do the descendants of these Americans finally become eligible for participation in the traditional narrative.

Demographic uncertainties facilitate our omissions. Perhaps no other realm of early American history remains as contested and in such need of serious attention. After 1607, we know with some precision how many people, white and black, occupied the thirteen Anglo-American colonies that later became the United States.[11] We likewise know how many colo-

---

Peter H. Wood, "The Changing Population of the Colonial South: An Overview by Race and Region, 1685–1790," in Peter H. Wood, Gregory A. Waselkov, and M. Thomas Hatley, eds., *Powhatan's Mantle: Indians in the Colonial Southeast* (Lincoln, 1989), 56–66.

10. For a recent and noteworthy exception to this pattern, see Alan Taylor, *American Colonies* (New York, 2001), 418–19.

11. Wells, *Population of the British Colonies.*

nists lived in New Spain and New France (and later Canada).[12] But until sometime in the eighteenth century, fewer than half of the people living north of Mexico resided in these colonies.

How many people inhabited North America, from the Rio Grande to Hudson Bay, at the time of European contact? In 3000 BCE, at the dawn of maize agriculture? In 1776, at the time of Anglo-American independence? Astonishingly, we don't know, and we may never know with any certainty. "High Counters" such as Henry Dobyns and the nineteenth-century painter George Catlin put the population of North America in 1492 as high as 18,000,000 and 16,000,000 respectively.[13] "Low Counters" such as Douglas Ubelaker and Alfred Kroeber put the same population as low as 1,894,350 and 900,000 respectively.[14] Only one absurd conclusion is possible: The true answer lies either between or beyond these parameters. Most likely it is somewhere in between.

Luckily we do not need certainty to understand the essential problem presented here, because even the "Low Count" numbers suggest that colonial populations did not surpass indigenous populations until some-

---

12. The quickest route to such population figures is the index to Taylor, *American Colonies*. Additional statistics can be found in David J. Weber, *The Spanish Frontier in North America* (New Haven, 1994), 183–86, 193–95, 322; Daniel H. Usner Jr., *Indians, Settlers, & Slaves in a Frontier Exchange Economy: The Lower Mississippi Valley before 1783* (Chapel Hill, 1992), 48–49, 114–15; and W. J. Eccles, *France in America* (New York, 1972), 120 and *passim*. For a fascinating attempt to estimate the *total* population of Spain's northern frontier, see Peter Gerhard, *The North Frontier of New Spain* (Princeton, 1982), 24–25.

13. When I use the term "North America" here, I am referring to America north of present-day Mexico. Henry F. Dobyns, with the assistance of William R. Swagerty, *Their Number Become Thinned: Native Population Dynamics in Eastern North America* (Knoxville, 1983), 42; and George Catlin, *Letters and Notes on the North American Indians* (North Dighton, MA, 1995), 6.

14. We might add "Non Counter" David Henige to the mix as well. David P. Henige, *Numbers from Nowhere: The American Indian Contact Population Debate* (Norman, 1998); Douglas H. Ubelaker, "North American Indian Population Size: Changing Perspectives," in John W. Verano and Douglas H. Ubelaker, eds., *Disease and Demography in the Americas* (Washington, DC, 1992), 171–74; and Alfred L. Kroeber, *Cultural and Natural Areas of Native North America*, vol. 38 of *University of California Publications in American Archaeology and Ethnology* (Berkeley, 1939), 166.

time in the eighteenth century.[15] Their sheer existence should command
our attention, pointing not to alternative narratives but to parallel ones,
intertwined in a long, braided strand. Who were these people? What
were they doing? How did they shape their own lives and the nature of
the larger strand itself?

In the last generation, two new strains of scholarship have added im-
mensely to our understanding of early America, and their success has
hinged on inclusiveness. One strain reaches deeply into the social and
cultural milieu of Anglo-America, showing how slaves, women, Native
Americans, and the white working classes all shaped early American history in important ways. We have learned not just that these people were
there but also that they *mattered*, that they influenced historical outcomes
in ways that challenge prior assumptions and conclusions alike.

The second strain operates more broadly, literally across the Atlantic
Ocean. This scholarship has opened our eyes to the ways in which
coastal societies in Europe, West Africa, and the Americas participated
in a broader Atlantic World, a world that in some ways challenged the
organizing principle of the early republic and in other ways explained it,
contained it, and even made it possible. The insights yielded by this
scholarship relate not just to social and cultural diasporas but also to the
economic and political developments that created them.

All of this work has emphasized inclusiveness not for its own sake but
because it has genuine explanatory power. Think, for example, of teaching the American Revolution without reference to the trans-Atlantic ideological heritage illuminated by Bernard Bailyn or the social and economic
pressures uncovered by Woody Holton.[16] But even Atlantic World
scholarship, focusing on one ocean and its littoral, has done little to
illuminate the lives of those beyond the Atlantic fall line and the Appala-
chian frontier.

Present scholarship is poised on the brink: Will we retreat to the
familiar? Or will we expand what we claim as familiar (in the true family
sense), drawing the Pacific World and the pre-Anglo West into the story-
line of American history? A formidable array of historians have already

---

15. Ubelaker, "North American Indian Population Size," 173.
16. Bernard Bailyn, *The Ideological Origins of the American Revolution* (1967;
enlarged ed., Cambridge, MA, 1992); and Woody Holton, *Forced Founders: Indians, Debtors, Slaves, and the Making of the American Revolution in Virginia*
(Chapel Hill, 1999).

tried: Francis Parkman, Herbert Bolton, John Francis Bannon, Louise Phelps Kellogg, Reuben Gold Thwaites, W. J. Eccles, Elizabeth A. H. John, and even the anti-continentalist Harold Innis all expanded our understanding of the North American West before Lewis and Clark. But with the exception of Parkman, these authors struggled to gain acceptance among American historians writ large and usually remained relegated to various historiographical "borderlands" that are not integrated into our mainstream narrative.

The question is whether this will continue to be the case in the future. At the moment, there is cause for optimism. The 1991 publication of Richard White's *The Middle Ground* marked a turning point of sorts. In graduate programs across the country, professors assigned *The Middle Ground* not just to Native-American seminars but to early American seminars as well. White's *Middle Ground* hardly spanned the Mississippi River, even if it did drain into it. But it did do something else: it described American history from an entirely new vantage point, that of the peoples of the *pays d'en haut*. And it did so in a way that got the attention of American historians.

The widespread influence of *The Middle Ground* marked the emergence of a new cutting edge in early American scholarship, a cutting edge that took as its starting point not the organizational exigencies of the early republic but the geography and demography of the North American continent. Other watershed books accompanied *The Middle Ground* or came close on its heels: Ramón Gutiérrez's controversial work on marriage in New Mexico (1991); Daniel Usner's work on the cultural milieu of early Louisiana (1992); Gary Clayton Anderson's work on the ethnogenesis of the Indian Southwest (1999). Even David Weber's masterful *Spanish Frontier in North America* (1992), more of a survey than the others, represented a concerted effort to recast the customary American narrative.[17] The accumulated weight of this scholarship was growing, inching its way toward acceptance.

---

17. Ramón A. Gutiérrez, *When Jesus Came, the Corn Mothers Went Away: Marriage, Sexuality, and Power* (Stanford, 1991); Usner, *Indians, Settlers, & Slaves*; Gary Clayton Anderson, *The Indian Southwest, 1580–1830: Ethnogenesis and Reinvention* (Norman, 1999); Weber, *Spanish Frontier*. Similarly important works appeared in the 1970s and 1980s, but mainstream acceptance was more limited. Worth mentioning in this regard are Arthur J. Ray, *Indians in the Fur Trade: Their Role As Hunters, Trappers and Middlemen in the Lands Southwest of*

If these monographs opened the door, we may well have crossed the threshold in 2001, with the publication of Alan Taylor's *American Colonies*. Taylor's book is the first truly continental history of early North America. The Puritans are there, but alongside them we find Caddo hunters, French *engagés*, African field laborers, Russian *promyshlenniki*, and Hawaiian fishermen, all deftly interwoven into a singularly convincing narrative. Daniel Richter's *Facing East from Indian Country*, another book published in 2001, likewise signals a shifting historical vantage point. Indeed, there may be no more powerful sign of the vitality of this approach than the events of 2003. First came the stunning success of James Brooks's *Captives and Cousins*, a masterful study of captivity, kinship, and colonization in the Southwest that garnered prestigious prizes not just in western history, ethnohistory, and the history of slavery but in American history as well. Then came the publication of Colin Calloway's *One Vast Winter Count*, a magnificent survey of the West before Lewis and Clark.[18]

The groundwork is clearly in place. But will the next generation of scholars choose to build on it? Doing so will mean insisting that the pre-1800 West is American history, not just western history. It will also mean going where early American historians are often loath to go. It will mean going beyond the English colonies and even beyond the colonies of France and Spain. It will mean reading new kinds of evidence, revisiting the work of archaeologists, and teasing out possibilities as well as certainties. It will mean recognizing that ethnohistory is *our* history, and it will mean incorporating that history into our history in a readable form. It will mean that Americans such as the Mandans, who constitute

Hudson Bay, 1660–1870 (Toronto, 1974); Arthur J. Ray and Donald Freeman, *"Give Us Good Measure": An Economic Analysis of Relations between the Indians and the Hudson's Bay Company before 1763* (Toronto, 1978); Calvin Martin, *Keepers of the Game: Indian-Animal Relationships and the Fur Trade* (Berkeley, 1978); and Gary Clayton Anderson, *Kinsmen of Another Kind: Dakota-White Relations in the Upper Mississippi Valley, 1650–1862* (Lincoln, 1984).

18. Taylor, *American Colonies*; Daniel K. Richter, *Facing East from Indian Country: A Native History of Early America* (Cambridge, 2001). See also James F. Brooks, *Captives & Cousins: Slavery, Kinship, and Community in the Southwest Borderlands* (Chapel Hill, 2002); and Colin Calloway, *One Vast Winter Count: The Native American West before Lewis and Clark* (Lincoln, 2003). Published in 2002, Brooks's book received the prizes I refer to in 2003.

most of the population over most of the period we teach and study, really count. And it will mean a new generation of scholarship every bit as compelling as the pioneering generation of social history and Atlantic history that preceded it.

After his long plains crossing, La Vérendrye stayed put among the Mandans for ten days. But while he stayed behind, Mandan escorts took his son and several other Frenchmen for a short visit to another settlement nearby. This town was on the banks of the Missouri itself. It was twice as large as the first, and the visitors found "the open places and streets" to be "very fine and clean."[19] Indeed, the Frenchmen reported that in all their villages, the Mandans had great stores of supplies, including "corn, meat, fat, dressed robes, and bearskins."[20]

Abundance, however, was not what La Vérendrye sought. His goal was the Sea of the West, and it was now December. Without a translator or sufficient trade goods to last the winter, his explorations could proceed no further.[21] If the Frenchmen wintered among the Mandans, sodden ground and high water might hinder their trek back to Canada in the spring. Reluctantly, as it was "the most inclement season of the year," La Vérendrye decided not to wait.[22] Instead, sickly and cold, he returned northward across the prairies toward Manitoba, finally arriving at his Fort La Reine departure point on February 10, 1739.

From the perspective of the French, the expedition's outcome was disappointing: La Vérendrye had found the meandering oxbows of the Missouri River, but he had not found the much-sought Sea of the West, now more elusive than ever. For early American historians, he offers much more: a glimpse of the world from the center of the continent, an opportunity to reconsider our assumptions and our starting points. For the Mandan people, the prospects were less promising. For better or worse, they now had a secure place on eighteenth-century European maps. The question today is when they will find their way into early American history.

---

19. Smith, *Explorations of the La Vérendryes*, 60.

20. *Ibid.*, 59.

21. A substantial portion of La Vérendrye's supplies was stolen from him as he drew near to the first Mandan village. His interpreter, a Cree man who spoke Assiniboine (which some Mandans also spoke), left the Frenchman in pursuit of an Assiniboine woman who refused to remain until the man was no longer needed. *Ibid.*, 54–56.

22. *Ibid.*, 61.

Continental Drifts

JAMES F. BROOKS

Not long ago I looked out from a 10th floor hotel window in
Riverside, California, and enjoyed one of those everyday epiphanies that
remind me just how parochial is my mastery of continental North
America in the early national era—despite all attempts to extend my analytical reach. Below me spiked the tops of palm trees, only slightly
shrouded this day with in-blown Los Angeles smog and the residues of
the recently dampened San Bernardino mountain fires. Abruptly ahead
rose a hill, heavily bouldered and spotted with chaparral, that the hotel's
Information for Visitors marked as "Mount Robidoux (1,399 feet)." As
someone who had worked the history of colonial and nineteenth century
New Mexico, the name struck a familiar note, being that of a French fur
trading family that became prominent in Santa Fe and regions northwest
in the 1820s and 1830s. But it seemed out of place here, on the palm-
and-orange grove frontier.

A visit to the Riverside Municipal Museum alerted me to the thinness
of my knowledge and drove me back to readings overlooked or long
forgotten. Louis Robidoux had arrived in this Santa Ana river valley in
1844, with a party that included his younger brother, Antoine, with
whom he had formerly operated a store in Santa Fe and a fur trapping
operation along the Uncompahgre River in the Utah and Colorado. The
Robidoux settled on the Robidoux Rancho San Timoteo and began a
new career in the livestock and mercantile business. Indeed, Louis may

James F. Brooks is a member of the research faculty and director of SAR Press
at the School of American Research in Santa Fe, New Mexico. He is author of
*Captives & Cousins: Slavery, Kinship, and Community in the Southwest Border-
lands* (2002) and is at work on a new book entitled *Mesa of Sorrows: Archaeology,
Purity, and Prophetic Violence in the American Southwest.*

have authored one of the earliest pieces of boosterism for the valley (and triggered interregional resentments that persist to this day), when he wrote to a friend in New Mexico that "I compare the people of New Mexico to ants, who shut themselves in during the winter to eat what they have worked so hard for all summer." California's valleys were not "ungrateful like the land of New Mexico . . . [but rather were] the promised land where the arroyos run with virgin honey and milk." In a final (perhaps prescient) metaphor, he declared California "another Texas." Yet as we shall see, the Robidoux family as much fled New Mexico as did they seek a new Canaan.[1]

Today—when New Mexico's arroyos run, if not with honey and milk, with the din of vacationing Texans' ATVs and the footfalls of relocated Californians questing for high desert health and cosmic correction—we do well to remind ourselves that cultural crisis, dissatisfaction, and resettlement have a deep history in the region. Long bedeviled by scarce resources, even its pre-Columbian indigenous peoples found that survival depended upon migrations and negotiated encounters with strangers. Making new places meant engaging new neighbors, a process barely understood in the archaeological record. Indeed, one of the great interpretive injustices wreaked upon southwestern indigenes was the conjunction of the Spanish term "pueblo" with anthropological taxonomy of "sedentism," which froze the Ancestral Pueblo peoples of the region in villages that had, in practice, always been but "temporary homelands." Their seeming permanence on the archaeological landscape belies the fact that many Ancestral Pueblo villages were occupied for little more than two generations. After maize farming depleted nitrogen from the soil and hunting exhausted local game, their residents sought new homeplaces across a vast, yet familiar, landscape. Perhaps the most recurrent thematic strain in Tewa ontological narratives involves the invocation "We were wanderers again."[2]

Baseline aridity and cycles of drought, coupled with the very human penchant for cultural restlessness and capacity for violence, produced a

---

1. David J. Weber, ed. and trans., "Louis Robidoux: Two Letters from California, 1848," *Southern California Quarterly*, 54 (Summer 1972): 109, 110.

2. Patrick D. Lyons, *Ancestral Hopi Migrations* (Tucson, 2003); Douglas W. Schwartz, *Temporary Homeland: The Life & Death of an Ancient Pueblo* (Santa Fe, forthcoming); James F. Brooks, "Violence, Exchange, and Renewal in the American Southwest," *Ethnohistory*, 49 (2002): 205–18.

history that links—in yet-to-be understood dialectics—mobility and the making of place over many millennia across the Southwest. The advent of Spanish colonialism traumatically intensified patterns of migration and displacement, but in ways not necessarily entirely new to Pueblo peoples. The whole of the Colorado Plateau seems to have suffered population decline in the thirteenth and fourteenth centuries, a crisis that the emergence of the Katsina religion addressed by validating aggregation and communalism in many fewer, but larger, pueblos in the greater Rio Grande valley where, in the sixteenth century, Spanish intruders found them. Thus, the severe depopulation and relocations of the colonial era, while unprecedented in scale, were not without the range of Pueblo peoples to address in culturally sophisticated ways. Ironically, their greatest challenge may have come in Bourdon-era New Mexico (1760–1810), when a modernizing economy and growth in Spanish population disrupted daily face-to-face social and labor relations between Pueblos and Spaniards and forced Pueblo retrenchment within now-immovable land-grant based villages. The spatial flexibility and multi-linguality that characterized the pre-Hispanic and early colonial periods faded, leaving an archipelagic cultural landscape that later ethnographers would misread as residual of a timeless past.[3]

Embracing the tension between movement and place-making as our focus for further research suggests we need to come unbound from conventional periodizations, to release the history of the continent from, in Michel-Rolph Trouillot's phrase, "the fixity of pastness." Although the events and issues of the early national period certainly deserve our serious attention, the *processes* and *meanings* that preceded and postdated them must also be figured into their narrative deployment. One need only encounter, on the rimrock mesas of the Pajarito Plateau, freshly placed *pahos* (prayer sticks) next to fourteenth-century petroglyphs to know that the indigenous peoples of the Rio Grande valley never "abandoned" the villages they left behind on their urgent migrations, and that

3. Steven A. LeBlanc, *Prehistoric Warfare in the American Southwest* (Salt Lake City, 1999); Michelle Hegmon, ed., *The Archaeology of Regional Interaction: Religion, Warfare, and Exchange Across the American Southwest and Beyond* (Boulder, 2000); Ross Frank, *From Settler to Citizen: New Mexican Economic Development and the Creation of Vecino Society, 1750–1820* (Berkeley, 2000), esp. 209–22.

the "presence of the past" remains very much alive in their landscape today.[4]

Louis Robidoux reenacted more than resettlement when he made trail for California. Movement for the Robidoux brothers meant, as it did for centuries of wanderers before and after, the interpenetration of peoples and the cognitive mixing of places. Louis brought his Mexican wife, Guadalupe Garcia of Santa Fe, their children, and dependent servants to join him at Rancho San Timoteo. His offspring from several unions with Indian women "in the custom of the country" presumably remained with their mothers' people in the mountains of Colorado. Louis may have been more circumspect than his younger brother, who unabashedly listed "José my Payute Boy" among those agents he sent on trading ventures, but the Robidoux outposts in Utah and Colorado were enmeshed in an increasingly vigorous Great Basin slave trade that targeted Paiutes for resale in New Mexico. In fact, Indian anger to the Robidoux's involvement in slave trafficking hastened Louis's relocation to California, since angry Utes had destroyed Fort Uncompahgre in the autumn of 1844. Yet with a commerce in New Mexican sheep and (often stolen) Californian horses moving briskly along the Old Spanish Trail by the 1840s, Robidoux may have played a part in introducing California Indians to the flow of indigenous slaves that arrived in Hispano households in the San Luis valley of northern New Mexico and southern Colorado. We know little of how dependent kin, servants, and slaves experienced and made sense of the new places and people among whom they found themselves mixed.[5]

---

4. Michel-Rolph Trouillot, *Silencing the Past: Power and the Production of History* (Boston, 1995), 152; Steven Feld and Keith Basso, *Senses of Place* (Santa Fe, 1996).

5. Janet Lecompte, *Pueblo, Hardscrabble, and Greenhorn: Society on the High Plains, 1832–1856* (Norman, 1978), 137–38; 301n; Sondra Jones, *The Trial of don Pedro León Luján: The Attack against Indian Slavery and Mexican Traders in Utah* (Salt Lake City, 2000); Andrew Hernandez, "The Indian Slave Trade in New Mexico" (Ph.D. diss., University of New Mexico, 2003); Ned Blackhawk, *Violence Over the Land: Colonial Encounters in the American Great Basin* (Cambridge, MA, forthcoming); for at least one California Indian woman in a San Luis valley household in 1865, see Appendix D, in Frank McNitt, *Navajo Wars: Military Campaigns, Slave Raids, and Reprisals* (Albuquerque, 1972), 444; James F. Brooks, *Captives & Cousins: Slavery, Kinship, and Community in the Southwest Borderlands* (Chapel Hill, 2002), 300–01.

Is there a presence in this past? Hauntingly so. In the 1930s "salvage ethnographers" from the Federal Writer's Project interviewed Hispano families in the region and noted the presence of "pseudo kinspeople" in many San Luis Valley households. Claimed as adoptive members of the families, they did not, however, seem to the interviewers to be fully enfranchised in these families. Assigned the most arduous work in an already harsh farming and ranching economy, and their children bypassed for educational opportunity or inheritance, these shadow kin raise painful questions about the persistence of human bondage in the Southwest well into the twentieth century. New Mexico state historian Estévan Rael-Gálvez has traced dozens of these peripheral family members to Indian slaves who appear in nineteenth-century baptismal and census records, and detailed the intricate stories woven by their host families to explain their presence therein. Suppressed by his parents' generation, kept quietly alive by his grandmother, and reawakened in his own generation, the peoples of mixed descent today are working toward a new politics of identity. His work reminds us that the construction of masters, servants, memory, and emergent identities are as much the work of the present as they are sedimented in the past.[6]

The San Luis valley is but a microcosm of the mixed societies that formed, fought, and scattered across the continent during the 18th and 19th centuries, and we might take its enigmatic condition today as a cue for more expansive questioning. The residents and satellite communities around Bent's Fort (est. 1834) on the Arkansas River hailed from French, Spanish, Mexican, German, English, American, Blackfoot, Assiniboine, Arikara, Sioux, Arapahoe, Cheyenne, Pawnee, Shoshone, Sanpete, and Chinook roots. They bore offspring by the score, and it stands to reason that there linger in the blood and family memory faint traces with the potential to force us to rethink the modern meaning of those "national" affiliations. So too for the coerced intermixing of peoples among the indigenous practitioners of the southwestern slave system: how did some Mexican, Paiute, Apache, and Ute captives *become* Navajo and Comanche in their hearts and minds, and how did others fail to do so? What does it mean for the twenty-first-century descendants of those victims,

---

6. Estévan Rael-Gálvez, "Identifying Captivity and Capturing Identity: Contested Narratives of Indian Servitude in New Mexican/Colorado Households" (Ph. D. diss., University of Michigan, 2002).

and for the descendants of their masters, to confront a past so at odds with the federally imposed biological determinants of political identities? The ongoing struggle by Seminole Freedmen to claim a role in the Seminole Tribe—at once a matter of historical justice and a crisis for contemporary notions of tribal sovereignty—demonstrates the legacy of dueling ideas about "belonging." Strom Thurmond's family has recently confronted their own history of involuntary union and shadow kinship, with the claim that their tardy recognition might foster "racial healing." One thinks it may prove more difficult than they wish.[7]

The complications of writing these stories suggest we must replace subject-centered histories with process driven narratives. The urgency that underlies human history on the continent is reflected in nearly constant movement. Movement then, or the historical anthropology of movement, is one unresolved legacy of the continent. These dynamic webs of volatile, often violent, cultural exchange expanded and intensified across time to shape the essential core of regional interactions in the twenty-first century. With each historical epoch new peoples brought additional layers of intricacy to the region's human mosaic, and each new group laid claim to its placedness through stories. Within a few years of his arrival in California, Louis Robidoux, of French descent, Mexican nationality, an Indian affine, and a *nuevo californio*, sided with the Americans in their conquest. As justice of the peace of the San Bernardino District in the 1850s, he became a wealthy boor who lulled visitors to sleep with his tales of his Anglo-Norman ancestry and exploits as an Indian fighter. Somewhere else dwell the stories of his descendants, and of the Sonoran Indian boy who toiled in the kitchen at Rancho San Timoteo.[8]

---

7. Brooks, *Captives & Cousins*, 228–34; Andrew Metz, "A Nation Divided: Seminole Rift More than a Nation Divided," *Newsday*, Dec. 23, 2003.

8. Major Horace Bell, *Reminiscences of a Ranger: or, Early Times in Southern California* (Santa Barbara, 1927), 283.

Continental Crossings

ALAN TAYLOR

During the summer of 1793 Alexander Mackenzie led a small expedition of Indians and French Canadians westward up the rocky and rapid Peace River into the Canadian Rockies. Born in Scotland, Mackenzie had emigrated as a boy with his family to the Mohawk Valley in New York in 1774. Remaining loyal to the Union of the Empire, the Mackenzies rejected the Revolution by fleeing northward to British-held Canada. At the age of fifteen, Alexander joined one of the Montreal firms engaged in the fur trade with Indians beyond the Great Lakes. During the 1780s he developed an expertise in the waterways, forests, and natives of the Athabasca region deep in the continent's northern interior. In 1789 he first sought a route to the Pacific, but instead reached the Arctic. Learning from his mistakes, Mackenzie tried again in 1793.[1]

Mackenzie knew his desired destination through the writings of British mariners who, beginning with Captain James Cook in 1778, had probed the Northwest coast, opening a profitable trade with the native peoples, exchanging manufactured metal goods for sea otter pelts. Proceeding on to China with those pelts, the mariners purchased porcelain, tea, spices, and silks for conveyance and sale in Europe—completing circumnavigations that lasted over two years. In 1793, Mackenzie sought an overland route across Canada to gain a share in that profitable trade for Montreal's

Alan Taylor is Professor of History at the University of California at Davis and a contributing editor to *The New Republic*. He is the author of *Liberty Men and Great Proprietors* (1990), *William Cooper's Town* (1995), *American Colonies* (2001), *Writing Early American History* (2005), and *The Divided Ground: The Northern Borderland of the American Revolution* (forthcoming in 2006).

1. Barry Gough, *First Across the Continent: Sir Alexander Mackenzie* (Norman, 1997), 67–98; W. Kaye Lamp, "Sir Alexander Mackenzie," *Dictionary of Canadian Biography*, 5:537–38.

Northwest Company. Rather than haul sea otter pelts eastward via Montreal to London, the Montreal men hoped to send British manufactures westward over land to the continent's west coast to procure sea otter pelts and build ships to traverse the Pacific to China.[2]

The overland passage proved arduous and confusing as the mountains became higher, wider, and more complex than anticipated—leading Mackenzie's party into steep cul-de-sacs. Ultimately Mackenzie found his way with the help of British manufactured goods, which had reached the Sekani peoples of the mountains. Just a month before a British maritime expedition led by Captain George Vancouver, a protégé of Cook, had visited the Northwest coast. While trading with the natives, one of Vancouver's men, Thomas Manby, astutely observed,

As neither Land [n]or Water, stops the car[r]ier of commerce, I dare say, many of our articles have by this time, nearly approached, the opposite side of the Continent, as a continual chain of barter, exists between Tribe and Tribe, through this amazing track of Country, which in time, will no doubt, find their way, to our factories in Canada, or the back settlements of Hudson's bay.

Indeed, Indians had long traversed the mountains that were so mysterious, complicated, and daunting to Mackenzie. Upon spying the metal goods among the Sekani, Mackenzie explained that he set out to "pursue that chain of connexion by which these people obtain their ironwork." Once Mackenzie reached the Nuxalk people on the Bella Coola River, those trade goods proliferated, confirming his proximity to the coast— which the party reached on July 19. The emerging Pacific world of trade that was Mackenzie's goal also generated the tangible clues that drew his party to its destination. The eastward and overland passage of those clues revealed a long-standing web of intertribal connections otherwise opaque to the explorer.[3]

In 1793, three centuries after Columbus, most of North America remained Indian country, as European colonization had become consolidated only in Mexico and along the Atlantic Seaboard and in pockets

---

2. Gough, *First Across the Continent*, 105–06; James P. Ronda, *Astoria & Empire* (Lincoln, 1990), 15–18.

3. Thomas Manby quoted in Elizabeth A. Fenn, *Pox Americana: The Great Smallpox Epidemic of 1775–82* (New York, 2001), 251; Gough, *First Across the Continent*, 105–23, 128 (Mackenzie quotation).

along the St. Lawrence, Mississippi, and Rio Grande valleys. And yet, as Mackenzie discovered, the European invasion of the continent had already affected almost every corner of that vast Indian America. In addition to trade goods, disease pathogens had passed far beyond European hands through Indian intermediaries. That summer along the Northwest coast, Vancouver found the signs of a massive smallpox epidemic: abandoned villages, bleaching skeletons scattered on the beaches, and native survivors with grim stories and pocked faces. Consumers of trade goods and survivors of imported epidemics, native peoples still possessed a mastery of most of the geography, belying the discoveries of the lost, like Alexander Mackenzie. In investigating the history of the continent, its immense space and diverse peoples, we encounter a world both beyond the control of empires and, yet, deeply influenced by them.

It is difficult scholarly terrain for historians reliant on the paper trail left by the colonizers—who but imperfectly and irregularly understood the native world at a distance from the major settlements and trading posts. But we have extraordinary new guides in the recent work by James Brooks, Elizabeth Fenn, and Andrés Reséndez. By ranging across cultural and national boundaries to examine processes of exchange, all three "decenter" the traditional nationalist narrative of the United States. They focus on complex processes of human interaction rather than on bounded categories—such as a particular tribe, nation, empire, or republic. Although this work has been called "continentalist," it is primarily about the movement of peoples and the fluidity of identity which extends beyond as well as within North America.[4]

>━━◆>━○━◆━━◁

In *Captives & Cousins: Slavery, Kinship, and Community in the Southwest Borderlands* (2002), James Brooks draws readers into an apparently chaotic world of intercultural violence on the northern frontier of New Spain (later Mexico) and, still later, the southwestern borderland of the

---

4. For invocations to transnational history, see David Thelen, ed., "The Nation and Beyond: Transnational Perspectives on United States History," *Journal of American History*, 86 (1999): 965–1307; and Ian Tyrrell, "American Exceptionalism in an Age of International History," *American Historical Review*, 96 (1991): 1031–55. For a static definition of "continentalist" history, see Joyce E. Chaplin, "Expansion and Exceptionalism in Early American History," *Journal of American History*, 40 (2003), 15.

expanding United States. Challenging traditional dualities of native versus colonist or Hispanic versus Anglo, Brooks examines the processes of exchange—sometimes violent, sometimes peaceful—of women and children taken and lost by all the groups uneasily sharing a beautiful land of scarcities. Within the conspicuous conflicts that have dominated past study, Brooks finds processes of demographic and cultural creativity in the long-term and collective effects of captive taking and absorption. To an array of identities—Apachean, Hispanic, Puebloan, Shoshonean—Brooks brings a new clarity by focusing on recurrent patterns of raiding, trading, the incorporation of new peoples, and the redefinition of cultural and status difference—patterns that uneasily united them all. Attentive to the power of language in past texts, and in his own narrative, Brooks weaves a cogent analysis into compelling stories of collective rituals and individual lives. Sometimes those stories are grim, occasionally redemptive, but always humane in their attention to both suffering and creativity.[5]

>—·—·>—·O—·<—·—·<

In *Pox Americana: The Great Smallpox Epidemic of 1775–82* (2001), Elizabeth Fenn operates on a still larger scale, introducing readers to the subtle interconnections that integrated the continent beneath the level of imperial projects. We tend to think of eighteenth-century North America as a set of distinct and isolated regions—a mismatched set of Spanish, French, Dutch, British, and even Russian colonies. Clustered along distant coasts, these colonies have seemed isolated by a broad and vague interior then still possessed by diverse Indian peoples. Consequently, historians of the early American republic rarely venture beyond the new states along the Atlantic Seaboard and immediately west of the Appalachians. By tracking a massive smallpox epidemic across colonial boundaries throughout North America, Fenn recovers the larger picture that we have long missed. Like a marker in the bloodstream, smallpox generated far-flung documents, exposing the networks of human contact and exchange that criss-crossed the continent, from Quebec to New Orleans, from Mexico City to Hudson Bay, and from South Carolina to the Pacific Northwest. The spreading epidemic demonstrated that war and trade

---

5. James F. Brooks, *Captives & Cousins: Slavery, Kinship, and Community in the Southwest Borderlands* (Chapel Hill, 2002).

had already interlocked the lives and fates of native and colonial peoples throughout the continent. In recent years, scholars have called for a more transnational approach to American history; Fenn reveals how it can be done and the benefits of trying.[6]

In *Changing National Identities at the Frontier: Texas and New Mexico, 1800–1850* (2004) Andrés Reséndez qualifies the traditional narrative of American national expansion: a story of unification initiated and sustained by a political elite at the geographic core of the United States. He tells the other, neglected half of that story: the compromises compelled, or the collaboration launched, by groups at the boundaries. Examining two quite distinct provinces on Mexico's northern frontier, Reséndez examines local negotiations that cut across neat ethnic categories of "American" or "Mexican" to reveal provincial *tejano* and *nuevomexicano* elites engaged in "cross-cultural and cross-class alliances and counteralliances." During the 1820s and 1830s provincial entrepreneurs pursued new trade links with Anglo-Americans to the unease of Mexico's national leaders. In the end, United States expansion owed as much to the weakness of Mexican national identity on the periphery as to the strength of the American ideology of "Manifest Destiny."[7]

But how, readers may fairly ask, can this continental approach contribute to the field of the early republic, where most scholars necessarily remain focused on the United States. This essay began with a Scots-born Loyalist leading French Canadians and Indians deep into Indian country in the Canadian Rockies in hopes of connecting to the China Trade. Only the year, 1793, seems to pertain to "the early republic." Moreover, how inconvenient that a Canadian crossed the continent a decade before Meriwether Lewis and William Clark—and far more easily, cheaply, and quickly (and no one knows how many natives had done so without any

---

6. Fenn, *Pox Americana*.

7. Andrés Reséndez, *Changing National Identities at the Frontier: Texas and New Mexico, 1800–1850* (New York, 2004). See also Andrés Reséndez, "National Identity on a Shifting Border: Texas and New Mexico in the Age of Transition, 1821–1848," *Journal of American History*, 86 (1999): 668–88, quote on 670; Andrés Reséndez, "Getting Cured and Getting Drunk: State versus Market in Texas and New Mexico, 1800–1850," *Journal of the Eary Republic*, 22 (2002): 77–103.

record or parade). In historical allegiance to our own explorers, how can we linger over their foreign predecessor?

But events and influences did not remain so easily bounded by nations and empires as our historical narratives often imply. In 1801 in London, Mackenzie published his journals of exploration, causing a sensation on both sides of the English Channel and of the Atlantic Ocean. He urged the British government to establish fortified posts in the Pacific Northwest, to command the native peoples and the sea otter trade. According to Mackenzie, the stakes were global:

By opening this intercourse between the Atlantic and Pacific Oceans and forming regular establishments through the interior, at both extremes, as well as along the coasts and islands, the entire command of the fur trade of North America might be obtained. . . . To this might be added the fishing in both seas and the markets of the four quarters of the globe.

Otherwise, he warned, the Americans would occupy both. Lacking the men and the money, the British government demurred. Ironically, Mackenzie proved most persuasive with an American reader, President Thomas Jefferson, who procured a copy of the journals in 1802. Ever fearful of British intentions, Jefferson concluded that British officials would, of course, embrace Mackenzie's scheme to fortify posts in the Pacific Northwest just to spite him and the United States. To counter that fantastic danger, Jefferson began preparing the Lewis and Clark expedition to replicate Mackenzie's achievement but within the latitudes of the United States.[8]

And after Lewis and Clark returned, the Jefferson administration supported the fortified trading post proposed by a New York City fur merchant, John Jacob Astor, who had learned western geography and commercial prospects during dealings with the Northwest Company in Montreal. In 1811 two parties of Astor's men—one by sea and the other by land—established a stockaded post named "Astoria," near the mouth

---

8. Gough, *First Across the Continent*, 170–86, 205 (Mackenzie quotation); Peter S. Onuf, *Jefferson's Empire: The Language of American Nationhood* (Charlottesville, 2000), 100; Robert W. Tucker and David C. Hendrickson, *Empire of Liberty: The Statecraft of Thomas Jefferson* (New York, 1990), 42–43, 62.

of the Columbia: the first American establishment on the West Coast, thereby preempting Mackenzie's proposal.[9]

In consequence, Mackenzie's journey was not so peripheral to that preoccupation of United States history: "our" expansion to the Pacific. The preceding essays by Reséndez, Fenn, and Brooks also suggest how we can study the early republic as entangled in continental, indeed global relations of commerce, migration, disease, and identity. In broadening our geographic stage, and questioning the stability of ethnic and national categories of identity, this new scholarship weakens the usual stark distinction between core and periphery in our historical geography—but it does not abolish them. By opening up old boundaries, these three historians invite other scholars to find the diverse Americans of the early republic (and outside it) engaged across a continent and through the world's oceans in negotiations with an array of others. And in the process, they all continuously remade that early republic.

9. Donald D. Jackson, *Thomas Jefferson & the Stony Mountains: Expanding the West from Monticello*, 280–81 (Jefferson to Astor, Apr. 13, 1808, quoted on 281); Ronda, *Astoria & Empire*, 38–50.

PART II

Pursuing Happiness

. . . concerning the economic culture of the United States that created and distributed wealth and in the process reshaped the culture.

JAMES L. HUSTON, CHAIR

Economic history has been in something of a doldrums lately, nudged off the stage of scholarship (and television) by sex and violence among other things. Our friends at the Program for Early American Economy and Society (PEAES) in Philadelphia, led by long-time SHEAR stalwart Cathy Matson and new SHEAR sponsor, The Library Company of Philadelphia, have done their best to correct this situation, and in a small corner of the field there is enormously important and interesting work being done. Meanwhile, out in the wilds of Oklahoma, James L. Huston turns out volume after volume on political economy in the early United States, a prodigious outpouring of scholarship that gives most of us pause when we look at our own lists of publications. Jim graciously agreed to chair a section addressing the intersections between economic history and other issues in the early republic. He specifically wished to focus on links with religion, rural life, and the business of private enterprise. Below Stewart Davenport, Christopher Clark, and Barbara Tucker and Kenneth Tucker take up his challenge with stimulating summaries of the problems they see remaining in our field, and Jim follows with a summary comment.

Liberal America/Christian America
Another Conflict or Consensus?

STEWART DAVENPORT

Scholars love paradoxes. They give us problems on which we can spin our intellectual wheels almost interminably. Thus—to say the least—historians of the early republic are some of the luckiest scholars around. The time and place that we have chosen to make our specialty is absolutely brimming with logical contradictions, tortured internal conflicts, and base hypocrisies. How can America hold within itself the ideal of liberty and the institution of slavery? Was Thomas Jefferson first and foremost a virtue-obsessed romantic, or a commerce-driven pragmatist? And what about Jackson? Was he the people's best defense against emerging capitalism, or the people's capitalist?

To all of these questions I would like to add another. Why has America always been one of the most voluntarily religious nations in the world, as well as—far and away—the most grossly materialistic? Another way of putting this would be to say that Americans simultaneously and paradoxically subscribe to both the Christian ethic of humility and selflessness, and the American liberal-capitalist ethic of competition, success, and self-promotion. From the very beginning, many Americans have gone about trying to understand themselves and their world with the Bible in one hand and John Locke in the other.

Reconciling the two, however, has never been an easy task. "We are, if I may say so, in an unfortunate dilemma," Orville Dewey lamented in 1838. "Our political civilization has opened the way for multitudes to

Stewart Davenport is Assistant Professor of American History at Pepperdine University. He is currently working on a book-length study of religion and economics in the early republic, tentatively entitled "'Friends of the Unrighteous Mammon': Northern Christians and Market Capitalism, 1815–1860."

wealth, and created an insatiable desire for it." Greed, luxury, selfishness, and a mean spirit of competitiveness were all apparently on the rise in the young American republic. Most observers, of course, recognized that these impulses were not new. "The passions of men are, at the present moment, the same as they have ever been," wrote Francis Wayland. But they were also aware that something was new in the economic structure of things that was having an impact in the hearts of Americans. The "case with us, now," Dewey wrote, "is different. . . . The pursuit of property, and that in no moderate amount, has acquired at once an unprecedented activity and universality."[1]

John Patrick Diggins is the only scholar I know of who has investigated the paradox of liberal America/Christian America, and his book, *The Lost Soul of American Politics: Virtue, Self-Interest, and the Foundations of Liberalism*, deserves greater attention, especially as we consider what might come next in early-American scholarship. As he explains it: "Liberalism is the intellectual pride of conquering the resistance of nature, Christianity, the humility of the heart. One demands success, the other sacrifice." This partnership obviously has not been without its tensions, and it is precisely these tensions that have made the American story so interesting. But for various reason, three of which I will now try to explain, historians on the whole have failed to notice this conflict and its centrality both to American history in general, and to the history of the early republic in particular.[2]

The first reason scholars fail to see this paradox is because—believe it or not—they still cannot get out of the intellectual orbit of Hartz, Hofstadter, Beard, and Schlesinger. In part this is because scholarship is always a cumulative process with later writers paying due reverence to those who came before them; but it is also because these early historians dared to ask some of the biggest questions possible in American history.

---

1. Orville Dewey, "Discourses on Commerce and Business," in *Works of Orville Dewey, D. D.* (2 vols., New York, 1848), 2: 248, 219. Originally published as *Moral Views of Commerce, Society, and Politics, in Twelve Discourses* (New York, 1838). Francis Wayland, *A Discourse delivered in the First Baptist Church, Providence, R.I. on the Day of the Public Thanksgiving, July 21, 1842* (Providence, 1842), 18.

2. John Patrick Diggins, *The Lost Soul of American Politics: Virtue, Self-Interest, and the Foundations of Liberalism* (Chicago, 1984), 325–26.

What is up for grabs, as Charles Sellers puts it, is nothing less than the nature of "American identity and destiny."[3]

When it comes to religion, however, it is not so much that scholars fail to see it but that they do not know what to do with it. They know that religion matters, but they don't know how to make this foreign set of ideas and institutions fit in with the other powerful forces at work in the early republic. This latter explanation is the second reason why historians do not pay much attention to the paradoxical coexistence of American liberalism and American Christianity. Simply put—and this relates to the first reason—religion destabilizes the tidy bipolar categories of the progressive/consensus debate. In America there is capitalism and democracy. When you add a third party, religion, to this Cold-War like scenario, things start to get messy.

The best example of this messier, but still old-school progressive-bound scholarship is Charles Sellers's magnum opus, *The Market Revolution: Jacksonian America, 1815–1846*. In his narrative, the market revolution unfolds as a virtually unstoppable force that squashed every form of resistance that dared challenge it. By 1846 the "calculating elites" of the market revolution had succeeded totally in establishing their hegemony over the now powerless American people. And for Sellers, religion played its part in helping establish this hegemony.[4]

Much to his credit, Sellers actually makes religion an important part of his narrative. In one response he even wrote: "To me, the Protestant tension between antinomianism and arminianism was *the* central tension in early American life." But ultimately his Gramscian commitments lead him to perceive a more calculating side to the religious revivals of the Second Great Awakening. This is somewhat sad, actually, because Sellers should be praised for daring to pick up the subject of religion and bring it into what has been discussed most often by political historians without much reference to religion. In fact, he seems almost proud of

3. Charles Sellers, "Capitalism and Democracy in American Historical Mythology," in Melvyn Stokes, and Stephen Conway, eds., *The Market Revolution in America: Social, Political, and Religious Expressions, 1800–1880* (Charlottesville, 1996), 312.

4. Charles Sellers, *The Market Revolution: Jacksonian America, 1815–1846* (New York, 1991), 297.

himself for making what he calls "the shorn lambs of a secular age" pay attention to the ideas and activities of religious people.[5]

The result is an ambitious and impressive book but one that illustrates well these earlier two points. Sellers is fascinated by religion and admirably adds it to the traditional progressive narrative, but ultimately he is unable to break away from that paradigm. He succeeds at making this narrative messier—and his critics would say he makes it unnecessarily complicated because he does not fully understand the religious beliefs of which he speaks; but when faced with the destabilization that this third force creates, he simply folds it back into the older categories of capitalism versus democracy, and unfortunately religion seems to have joined forces with the bad guys.[6]

The longevity and (for many) the inescapability of the progressive/consensus debate, even when bringing religious life into the mix, testifies to how much the debate still matters, both for America's past and its present. But it is time to shift our scholarly attention to a related but different problem. Instead of Sellers's "American identity and destiny . . . contested between capitalism and democracy," I would propose it is time to take a closer look at Diggins's war "for the soul of America." Conflict is still the central theme, obviously, but Diggins wants to shift the focus to the struggles that took place within individuals in the early republic, rather than the struggles among them.[7]

The internal, and in some ways invisible, nature of this conflict is the third and final reason why it has not received more scholarly attention. Traditional "history" is the place where we see the material interests and political factions that Madison described in *Federalist #10* contend against one another, sometimes violently. But the conflicts inherent in liberal America/Christian America manifested themselves most often within a single body, not the body politic.

---

5. Charles Sellers, "Charles Sellers's Response," *Journal of the Early Republic*, 12 (1992), 473. Emphasis mine.

6. For criticisms of Sellers's understanding of religious terminology and theology see: Daniel Walker Howe, "The Market Revolution and the Shaping of American Identity in Whig-Jacksonian America," and Richard Carwardine, "'Antinomians' and 'Arminians': Methodists and the Market Revolution," in Stokes and Conway, eds., *The Market Revolution in America: Social, Political, and Religious Expressions, 1800–1880*, 259–81, 282–310.

7. Sellers, "Capitalism and Democracy," 312; Diggins, *Lost Soul*, 326.

Ironically for Diggins though, shifting attention to the internal conflicts of early Americans brings up the debates over ideological republicanism that both he and Sellers loathe. Sellers dislikes republicanism
for the same reason that he dislikes most intellectual history—because it
diminishes the causal importance of class and class conflict. For Diggins,
the intellectual historian, the rationale is more complicated. While loving
ideas, he believes that Calvinist theology, and not classical republicanism, was the real antithesis to liberalism in early America. He is also
skeptical of the causal power of political ideology in the first place, seeing
it instead as a reflection of material reality, not a shaper of it.

As a possible way forward in the scholarship of the early republic, I
would like to suggest a couple of things related to these two earlier scholarly paradigms. The general point is that we need to shift to a different
conflict. Instead of reviving the old progressive/consensus debate, we
need to take a closer look at the paradox of liberal America/Christian
America. John Diggins recognizes the centrality of this paradox to early
American history; Charles Sellers does not. The related point is that the
objections of both Diggins and Sellers to the republicanism/liberalism
debate need to be over-ruled, and the discussion needs to continue. In
my opinion, sustained attention to republicanism actually can help us
better understand the paradox of liberal America/Christian America; but
this republicanism needs to be understood as an evolving Christian republicanism.

As Mark Noll has reminded us, early Americans could hold ideas
together that modern historians find incompatible. Thus we should not
be looking for intellectual consistency where it did not exist. Neither
should we try to squeeze people into airtight ideological definitions. The
historical fact of the matter is that in the early republic ideologies were
exceedingly plastic. Sometimes people synthesized presumably incompatible schools of thought, like Christianity and republicanism.[8] Other
times, opposing forces and ideologies balanced each other out. The writers of the Constitution famously understood the reality of competing
interests and the necessity of checks and balances. The properly functioning government, in their opinion, would neither deny nor seek to

---

8. Mark A. Noll, *America's God: From Jonathan Edwards to Abraham Lincoln*
(New York, 2002), 73.

destroy those interests, but harness the competitive energy among them for political stability and economic productivity.[9]

The coexistence of Christian republicanism and Lockean liberalism likewise created an energetic tension that led to political stability and economic productivity. This tension existed almost exclusively within single persons, not between persons in the body politic. What were contradictory impulses within an individual (love your neighbor/compete with your neighbor) nevertheless made that individual an ideal citizen of the new republic, as long as he or she knew when to act on which impulse. Such a person was hard-headed enough to appreciate the reality of competition and self-promotion in a liberal society but at the same time soft-hearted enough to love his competitor, employee, or patron as himself.

Unfortunately few sources address these tensions specifically, but what sources do exist make these same points explicitly. "We are indeed to do to others as we would have them do to us," wrote Orville Dewey in his publication, *Moral Views of Commerce Society and Politics*. But there was nothing "in Scripture," he went on to argue, "or in the laws of human brotherhood, that forbids this honest, not fraudulent, but honest competition between men's exertions, faculties and wits." Such was life in a liberal society. An economic revolution, Henry Boardman wrote, had "come over the world within the last half-century. . . . Whether this revolution could have been prevented, or whether it is not on the whole beneficial," he continued, "is not a question now before us." To these northern Christians, it was simply useless to criticize the system itself, or long for a now-lost social order. The current structure of American civilization was generally good and was not going to go away.[10]

The same was true of the slave South. When it came to internal con-

9. Noll, *America's God*, 211. See also the works he references: Daniel Walker Howe, *Making the American Self: Jonathan Edwards to Abraham Lincoln* (Cambridge, MA, 1997), 10–17; and John M. Murrin, "Escaping Perfidious Albion: Federalism, Fear or Aristocracy, and the Democratization of Corruption in Postrevolutionary America," in Richard K. Matthews, ed., *Virtue, Corruption, and Self-Interest: Political Values in the Eighteenth Century* (Bethlehem, PA, 1994), 138–39.

10. Dewey, "Discourses on Commerce and Business," 160–61. Henry A. Boardman, *The Bible in the Counting House: A Course of Lectures to Merchants* (Philadelphia, 1853), 14–15.

flicts, slaveholders in no way differed from economically influential Christians in the North. They had exactly the same conservative commitment to a market mechanism (although more international than national) and an even greater awareness that it was people who kept the economic machine running. Paternalism still is a controversial topic, but it does seem that in America the large population of resident masters, who were even more Christianized after the Second Great Awakening, would allow for the creation of such a tension-filled culture. Southern slaveowners were supposed to love their slaves; and at the same time they could use them like tools for their individual pursuits of happiness. Thus the South was no great exception to the paradox of liberal America/Christian America. In fact it fits perfectly with what John Diggins calls "the liberalism peculiar to us, a liberalism that embraces radical means to achieve conservative ends." Secession in 1861 is perhaps the greatest example of this.

Most of American history between the Revolution and the Civil War, however, is decidedly less dramatic. I would argue that this is because most conflicts took place on what Charles Sellers calls "the private battlegrounds of every human relationship," as well as the battlegrounds that existed within individual minds. I would also argue that these conflicts were the manifestations of the paradoxes inherent in early American life that were necessary for America to work. All of the paradoxes mentioned at the beginning of this essay were created to serve the ultimate American god of pragmatism. Why slavery in the land of liberty? Edmund S. Morgan has famously answered that it was racial slavery that created the possibility of liberty, and allowed the republic to come into being in the first place. Why were Jefferson's and Jackson's policies so contradictory? They wanted to keep the national ship afloat as long as they could, and they would do whatever it took, no matter how inconsistent it might be.[11]

Similarly, how could Americans pursue both happiness and holiness at the same time? The answer, again, is because it allowed the young American republic to work. Although full of private tensions the liberal Christian was the perfect republican, and his much-used system of internal checks and balances allowed the nascent American government precious time to work out the many kinks inherent in its own constitution.

---

11. Sellers, *Market Revolution*, 31.

It is here that I would like to conclude and point to the future possibilities for the scholarship of the early republic. I believe that our work needs to follow Diggins and concentrate on the conflicts within early Americans rather than the conflicts among them. Excellent biographies and community-studies, of course, already have been done, but these unfortunately do not always take religion as seriously as it should be taken. Allen Guelzo's new biography of Abraham Lincoln is a notable recent exception and a model for the future. Plus there are other leading Americans who thought about as well as lived the tension-filled American dream: Francis Wayland, Orestes Brownson, Arthur and Lewis Tappan, Calvin Colton, Joseph Smith, Gerrit Smith, Charles Grandison Finney, and many others.[12] By themselves their lives are merely biographies, somewhat in the tradition of Horatio Alger stories. Taken together, however, it is obvious that this generation of Americans shared important common problems that they dealt with privately—first among them being the challenge of personal integrity, which was nearly impossible in liberal America/Christian America. But much, especially consistency, was sacrificed at the altar of American pragmatism, and we need to take a closer look at the era when those sacrifices began.

---

12. Allen C. Guelzo, *Abraham Lincoln: Redeemer President* (Grand Rapids, 1999).

The View from the Farmhouse

Rural Lives in the Early Republic

CHRISTOPHER CLARK

It is a truth universally acknowledged that the early United States was overwhelmingly a rural society, and that this remained so well beyond the mid-nineteenth century. Yet in the early years of the new social history in the 1970s many historians regarded rural people and their experience as rather peripheral to the main patterns of American growth and development. Early social historians of the nineteenth century adapted community studies from the colonial period, but they tended to regard rural societies as residual phenomena, about to be overtaken by urbanization and industrialization. The exceptions to this tendency did not undermine it. The frontier and "westward expansion" were still discussed within a framework set out by Frederick Jackson Turner and his Progressive-era colleagues and were largely ignored at first by "new" social historians. Slavery and the rural South, while the subjects of pioneering historical methods, were still portrayed as aspects of the old, rather than the new. Adherence to agriculture and reliance on slave labor were badges of the South's backwardness, preludes to defeat in the Civil War and to continued poverty and underdevelopment thereafter. Rural America seemed marginal to important currents of change, and the victim rather than the progenitor of changes that came about.

During the *Journal of the Early Republic*'s lifespan this perspective on rural history has been altered significantly. The invitation to reflect here

Christopher Clark was for many years Professor of North American History at the University of Warwick, UK, and in 2005 will assume an appointment at the University of Connecticut. His books include *The Roots of Rural Capitalism: Western Massachusetts, 1780–1860* (1990). He is currently completing a short social history of the United States from the Revolution to the Civil War period.

on the dimensions of rural peoples' lives between 1783 and 1850 offers a chance to draw attention to this shift of emphasis and to suggest ways in which future research might carry it further. As the field of labor history went into decline, many social historians redirected their traditional focus on industrial workers. The rise of women's history led to the recognition and use of fresh source material, much of it relating to rural women.[1] European historians' interest in cottage industry and "protoindustrialization" suggested that the countryside might be a source of economic and social trends, not just their recipient. Scholars of the slave South questioned the assumption that the region was economically backward, and stressed the efforts of many southern farmers and planters to adopt agricultural improvements and new methods of production.[2] Rural societies moved towards the center of attention. In 1840 agriculture remained the predominant economic activity; only in Rhode Island was it no longer the leading occupation, and in the nation as a whole agricultural employment exceeded manufacturing employment by more than four to one. Freehold farming ensured that the proportion of property holders in the population was high by international standards. As a group the richest antebellum Americans were the large plantation owners of the South, whose control and exploitation of slaves more literally made them Robber Barons than their successors among the merchants, industrialists, and financiers of the Gilded Age.

Recognition of rural societies' scale and scope accompanied a fresh understanding of rural peoples' roles in key processes of change, starting with the American Revolution itself, which one recent historian has dubbed "the farmers' war."[3] In New England resistance to Britain turned into revolution only when rural folk joined the disputes initiated by their

---

1. Among pioneering works here was Joan M. Jensen, *Loosening the Bonds: Mid-Atlantic Farm Women, 1750–1850* (New Haven, 1986).

2. Recent examples include Mark M. Smith, *Mastered by the Clock: Time, Slavery, and Freedom in the American South* (Chapel Hill, 1997), and dissertations that will soon be revised for publication: Richard J. Follett, "The Sugar Masters: Slavery, Economic Development, and Modernization on Louisiana Sugar Plantations, 1820–1860" (Ph.D. diss., Louisiana State University, 1998), and Adam Rothman, "The Expansion of Slavery in the Deep South, 1790–1820" (Ph.D. diss., Columbia University, 2000).

3. Allan Kulikoff, *From British Peasants to American Colonial Farmers* (Chapel Hill, 2000), 255–88.

urban cousins. In Virginia the planter gentry and yeomen farmers headed the movement for independence. Rural communities provided most of the war's soldiers, and most of its food and other supplies. Rural peoples' demands for land and migration to new regions had helped foster tensions between the colonies and Britain in the first place and provided the driving force behind the expansion of white settlement beyond the original thirteen states after independence. As historians have explored the early republic's rural societies in more detail, they have recognized them as sources of the important economic and social changes of the nineteenth century. Migration, urbanization, and industrialization had vital roots in the countryside.

Most rural history has been studied at the local level, because many sources can be found there and such studies are manageable. But if community studies have remained important, historians have come to a new sense of their connections to a wider whole.[4] The accumulation of evidence on many topics, from crop regimes and gender roles at work to labor systems and demographic patterns, has emphasized the importance of regional variations, and the difficulty of establishing single instances as representative of national patterns or trends.[5] Though this might lead to an irreparable fragmentation that could marginalize the field again, historians are starting to regard regional differences as components of a mosaic that made up a larger picture. In this way evidence about rural individuals and families will be deployed to elucidate and explain wider patterns.[6] Laurel Thatcher Ulrich, for example, noted that earlier scholars had dismissed as "trivia" much of the detail in the remarkable diary

4. Orville Vernon Burton, "Reaping What We Sow: Community and Rural History," *Agricultural History*, 76 (2002): 630–58.

5. Many works in rural history are local or regional in scope, but among those that draw attention to the significance of regional differences are Carville Earle and Ronald Hoffman, "The Foundation of the Modern Economy: Agriculture and the Costs of Labor in the United States and England, 1800–1860," *American Historical Review*, 85 (1980): 1055–94; Thomas M. Doerflinger, "Rural Capitalism in Iron Country: Staffing a Forest Factory, 1808—1815," *William and Mary Quarterly*, 59 (2002): 3–38; Adrienne D. Hood, *The Weaver's Craft: Cloth, Commerce, and Industry in Early Pennsylvania* (Philadelphia, 2003), 13–14, 140–75.

6. Edward L. Ayers, *et al.*, *All over the Map: Rethinking American Regions* (Baltimore, 1996); Marc Egnal, *Divergent Paths: How Culture and Institutions have Shaped North American Growth* (New York, 1996).

of the late-eighteenth-century Maine midwife Martha Ballard.[7] Ulrich and others have shown how careful detective work can reveal the significance of even the smallest fragments of text or material, shedding light on issues of broad significance. If we can recover and interpret it, the view from the farmhouse holds a key to understanding much that was important to early America's growth and development.

Though recent historiography has placed rural people at the center of change, it has reached no consensus as to the direction change was taking. The most prominent synthesis, Charles Sellers's *The Market Revolution* (1991), argued that there was a significant shift from pre-market to market-dominated economic patterns, and a persistent confrontation between farmers settled on the land and the agents of a market economy.[8] This "market revolution" thesis has had a mixed reception. Many colonialists and scholars of the early republic have taken Sellers to task for underestimating the range and significance of markets in the eighteenth-century rural economy and for misinterpreting political and religious tensions in the nineteenth. On the other hand, the "market revolution" has been the framework within which a considerable number of younger scholars have conducted fresh research.[9] At the very least, it challenges historians to consider how the processes of participation in economic activity must have looked to the farm families and their members who inhabited rural regions in the period of the early republic.

Models that suggest transition "from" one pattern of activity "to" another may be inadequate to address the complexity of change at farm level during this period. The notion of farm "self-sufficiency," a conceptual legacy from the Progressive era, has proved exceptionally resistant

---

7. Laurel Thatcher Ulrich, *A Midwife's Tale: The Life of Martha Ballard, Based on her Diary, 1785–1812* (New York, 1990), 9.

8. Charles Sellers, *The Market Revolution: Jacksonian America, 1815–1846* (New York, 1991).

9. Daniel Feller, "The Market Revolution Ate My Homework," *Reviews in American History*, 25 (1997): 408–15; some critical essays are among those collected in Melvyn Stokes and Stephen Conway, eds., *The Market Revolution in America: Social, Political, and Religious Expressions, 1800–1880* (Charlottesville, VA, 1996). The "America: History and Life" database lists eighteen books, dissertations, and articles (other than reviews or review essays) published since 1992 with "Market Revolution" in the title; many others have adopted or at least addressed the concept.

to attempts at eradication. Some confusion arises because the dichotomy that has often been assumed between "self-sufficiency" and reliance on the market is too simple to express the range of production strategies and exchange relationships that were open to early American farmers. One solution, suggested by Richard L. Bushman, has been to emphasize that many farm families conducted both production for use and production for sale, running what he terms "composite farms."[10] My own preference has been to explore not just what farm families used and what they sold, but what social relationships they employed to conduct their various activities and transactions. More research needs to be done on this, not least because no clear vocabulary has yet emerged to embrace the complex mix of familial, kin, neighborhood, mercantile, "barter," cash, and credit arrangements that ensured farmers' livelihoods.[11]

The understanding that farms and plantations were essentially households acting in the economy has revolutionized our interpretations of the dimensions of rural experience. It has drawn attention to the interactions among men, women, and children in farm production, to the economic importance of domestic as well as field-based activities, and to the array of relationships between family members and other laborers: slaves, servants, the "borrowed" children of neighbors or kin, hired workers, or neighbors " 'changing works."[12] The focus on farms as locations of household production has provided an overall framework for analysis that nevertheless embraces regional and local variations. It helps explain the replication of agricultural and cultural patterns as farm families moved to new areas in the nineteenth century, and also—as Stephanie McCurry argued in an important book—the shared identity of southern

10. Richard Lyman Bushman, "Markets and Composite Farms in Early America," *William and Mary Quarterly*, 55 (1998): 351–74.

11. Christopher Clark, *The Roots of Rural Capitalism: Western Massachusetts, 1780–1860* (Ithaca, 1990), 23–38, 64–93. For an alternative view, see Winifred B. Rothenberg, *From Market-Places to a Market Economy: The Transformation of Rural Massachusetts, 1750–1850* (Chicago, 1992).

12. Jeanne Boydston, *Home and Work: Housework, Wages, and the Ideology of Labor in the Early Republic* (New York, 1990); see also *idem*, "The Woman who wasn't there: Women's Market Labor and the Transition to Capitalism in the United States," *Journal of the Early Republic*, 16 (1996): 183–206; Barry Levy, "Girls and Boys: Poor Children and the Labor Market in Colonial Massachusetts," *Pennsylvania History*, 64 (1997): 287–307.

planters and yeoman farmers that underpinned their antebellum political alliances against the critique of slavery.[13] But historians also have realized that households should be the focus of critical examination. Work patterns and gender roles, tensions between spouses, and between parents and children, and the relationships among different households all formed part of the fabric that shaped the character of rural lives and also influenced the directions in which they changed.[14]

Much work remains to be done to reconstruct this fabric. The history of food, for example, and its implications for rural people is still in relative infancy. Not only are there rich possibilities for the exploration of social, symbolic, and nutritional aspects of food production and consumption in farm households, but more work is needed on the connections between food creation and wider demographic developments. Some time ago, John Komlos speculated that dietary changes contributed to the fall in life expectancy Americans experienced across the first half of the nineteenth century.[15] Recent developments in the wider history of consumption patterns also have important implications for rural historians of the early republic. Substantial work is required to correlate the great amount of evidence we now have about late colonial consumption with our understanding of nineteenth-century changes, because rural consumption patterns in the first half of the new century remain largely to be traced.[16] That process will also involve more than enumerating

13. Stephanie McCurry, *Masters of Small Worlds: Yeoman Households, Gender Relations, and the Political Culture of the Antebellum South Carolina Low Country* (New York, 1995).

14. Nancy Grey Osterud, *Bonds of Community: The Lives of Farm Women in Nineteenth-Century New York* (Ithaca, 1991); Karen V. Hansen, *A Very Social Time: Crafting Community in Antebellum New England* (Berkeley, 1994).

15. Sarah F. McMahon, "'All Things in their Proper Season': Seasonal Rhythms of Diet in Nineteenth Century New England," *Agricultural History*, 63 (1989): 130–51; John Komlos, "The Height and Weight of West Point Cadets: Dietary Change in Antebellum America," *Journal of Economic History*, 47 (1987): 897–927; see also Peter A. Coclanis, "Food Chains: The Burdens of the (Re)-Past," *Agricultural History*, 72 (1998): 660–74.

16. Among important studies of eighteenth-century consumption are Cary Carson, "The Consumer Revolution in Colonial British America: Why Demand?" in Cary Carson, Ronald Hoffman, and Peter J. Albert, eds., *Of Consuming Interests: The Style of Life in the Eighteenth Century* (Charlottesville, VA, 1994), 483–697; T. H. Breen, "The Narrative of Commercial Life: Consumption, Ideology, and Community on the Eve of the American Revolution," *William and Mary*

goods; it will need to consider how households adapted their use of family labor, kin, and various patterns of exchange to adjust to the availability of consumption items. Writing of the eighteenth century, Daniel Vickers has pointed out that locally based and kin-based systems of exchange both provided security and imposed restraints on farmers and their households.[17] When and to what extent did they try to move beyond them?

Though the focus on farms as household units is essential for understanding the dimensions of rural lives, note must also be taken of the array of different labor systems that were in use in post-revolutionary America, and the differences these made in practical realities. Expanding onto new land entailed a substantial deployment of labor, and early American landowners made extensive use of coerced or compelled labor to accomplish this work. In addition to slavery, they used apprenticeships, indenture, tenancy, and other forms of bound labor. The family itself, above all, served as an agency of compulsion, both in the cooperative sense that its members had obligations to one another, and in the hierarchical sense that wives had legal duties to husbands and children legal obligations to parents. We still need to know more than we do about the cooperative and coercive aspects of household work and decision-making, and to establish how far the differential burdens of men's and women's contributions to rural households shaped their strategies in relation to home production, migration, outside work, and consumption patterns.[18]

In many parts of the North, formally coerced labor other than that within families was in decline during the early nineteenth century. By 1850 much of the region was becoming a conscious exponent of the ideology of "free labor."[19] The South, instead, refused to abandon coer-

Quarterly, 50 (1993): 471–501; Gloria L. Main, *Peoples of a Spacious Land: Families and Cultures in Colonial New England* (Cambridge, MA, 2001); and many of the works of Lorena S. Walsh.

17. Daniel Vickers, "Competency and Competition: Economic Culture in Early America," *William and Mary Quarterly*, 47 (1990): 3–29.

18. Martin Bruegel, "Work, Gender, and Authority on the Farm: The Hudson Valley Countryside, 1790s-1850s," *Agricultural History*, 76 (2002): 1–27. On the importance of rural women's innovativeness, see B. Zorina Khan, "'Not for Ornament': Patenting Activity by Nineteenth-Century Women Inventors," *Journal of Interdisciplinary History*, 31 (Autumn 2000): 159–95.

19. Robert J. Steinfeld, *Coercion, Contract, and Free Labor in the Nineteenth Century* (Cambridge, UK, 2001), 1–28, 253–89.

cion, and began to contemplate severe measures to sustain it. Until the advent of large-scale immigration in the 1840s, however, the northern shift towards free labor appeared as something of a paradox. Significant expansion across the land, coupled with substantial industrial developments and urban growth in certain regions, created intense demand for labor for which various forms of coercion might seem to have been an answer. An explanation for the paradox lies in the character of household work and relationships. The farm household could be the emblem of "free labor" on "free soil" because the authority that compelled work from women and children was not subjected to scrutiny. Before 1850 John C. Calhoun and other defenders of slavery began to attack the northern reliance on "wage slaves"; but only a few radical abolitionists publicly denounced the disturbing parallel they noticed between chattel slavery and marriage as agencies for compelling labor and obedience.[20] "Free labor" was rooted in the not entirely free character of the farm household.

Nor should a focus on households deflect attention from the exploration of inequalities and class differences in rural societies. One characteristic of rural poverty was difficulty functioning in integrated households, while a characteristic of "success" for a farm household was an ability to accumulate means of reproducing secure conditions for offspring.[21] By the middle of the century, some successful farmers were also able to adopt cultural and consumption patterns comparable with those of the urban middle class.[22] There had always been a distinction between what one historian has called "subsistence" and "substance," but it will be

---

20. Amy Dru Stanley, *From Bondage to Contract: Wage Labor, Marriage, and the Market in the Age of Slave Emancipation* (Cambridge, UK, 1998).

21. Ruth Wallis Herndon, *Unwelcome Americans: Living on the Margins in Early New England* (Philadelphia, 2001); Charles C. Bolton, *Poor Whites of the Antebellum South: Tenants and Laborers in Central North Carolina and Northeast Mississippi* (Durham, 1994); on security see James A. Henretta, "Families and Farms: *Mentalité* in Pre-Industrial America," *William and Mary Quarterly*, 35 (1978): 1–32; and Richard L. Bushman, "Family Security in the Transition from Farm to City, 1750–1850," *Journal of Family History*, 6 (1981): 238–56.

22. Susan E. Gray, *The Yankee West: Community Life on the Michigan Frontier* (Chapel Hill, 1996); see also Susan Sessions Rugh, *Our Common Country: Family Farming, Culture, and Community in the Nineteenth-Century Midwest* (Bloomington, 2001); see also Lori Merish, *Sentimental Materialism: Gender, Commodity Culture and Nineteenth-Century American Literature* (Durham, 1999).

important to evaluate how inequalities shaped farm families' adaptations to the processes of change in the countryside. Some important studies have noted the extent to which rural communities were the progenitors, not merely the receivers, of educational and other innovations that influenced individuals' life chances. How did patterns of wealth and poverty influence the transmission of social and cultural capital, the availability of rural labor for activities such as factory work, and the tendency for members of rural families to circulate through a variety of types of employment in the middle of the nineteenth century?[23] Debates continue over the character of class in American history. Rural societies had important parts to play in its development. In taking account of this we should also note the growing evidence that rural lives—from migration and farm making, to crop production and sociability—were shaped by patterns of cooperation as well as individualism.[24]

"History from below" concerns the agency of those without much power. Taking the view from the farmhouse encourages us to emphasize the agency of rural people in the patterns of change that touched their lives. Studies of slaves, the poor, and women, have all addressed the degrees to which they could negotiate and influence the circumstances around them.[25] If we are not to romanticize or misinterpret their situations, we shall need to contemplate their activities within the systems of

---

23. On education, reading, and institutions that fostered the creation of cultural capital, see Robert A. Gross, "Much Instruction from Little Reading: Books and Libraries in Thoreau's Concord," *Proceedings of the American Antiquarian Society*, 97 (1987): 129–88; Joyce O. Appleby, *Inheriting the Revolution: The First Generation of Americans* (Cambridge, MA, 2000), 90–128. William J. Gilmore, *Reading Becomes a Necessity of Life: Material and Cultural Life in Rural New England, 1780–1835* (Knoxville, 1989); and David P. Jaffee, "The Village Enlightenment in New England, 1760–1820," *William and Mary Quarterly*, 47 (1990): 327–46, both emphasize that rural settings were producers of cultural developments in the early nineteenth century, not simply receivers of urban culture.

24. On aspects of cooperation in rural culture, see Gray, *The Yankee West*; Alan L. Olmstead and Paul W. Rhode, "Beyond the Threshold: An Analysis of the Characteristics and Behavior of Early Reaper Adopters," *Journal of Economic History*, 55 (1995): 27–57; and David Blanke, *Sowing the American Dream: How Consumer Culture Took Root in the Rural Midwest* (Athens, OH, 2000).

25. Walter Johnson, *Soul by Soul: Life inside the Antebellum Slave Market* (Cambridge, MA, 1999).

power and authority that enfolded them, including the discursive patterns that assigned them passive roles or ignored them altogether. Yet a focus on agency can open up a wider array of understanding about the rationality and motivations of individuals and groups in the past. Uncovering the lives of individual rural men and women has provided the possibility of a non-stereotyped picture of early Americans and what made them tick. It also provides some materials for tasks that social historians were initially reluctant to undertake. How can we reconcile the assumption that government (or "the State") played a relatively minor role in nineteenth-century rural peoples' lives with the evidence that this was a period of considerable democratization?[26] A more rounded understanding of the array of views the farmhouses of early America afforded their myriad inhabitants may help us "put the politics back in" to an informed picture of rural societies in flux.

---

26. Among works that already do this, see John L. Brooke, *The Heart of the Commonwealth: Society and Political Culture in Worcester County, Massachusetts, 1713–1861* (Cambridge, UK, 1989); see also Catherine McNicol Stock and Robert D. Johnston, eds., *The Countryside in the Age of the Modern State: Political Histories of Rural America* (Ithaca, 2001).

The Limits of *Homo Economicus*

An Appraisal of Early American Entrepreneurship

BARBARA M. TUCKER AND
KENNETH H. TUCKER, JR.

Early American entrepreneurial history encompasses a broad range of individuals, activities, and institutions disseminated throughout the United States. Bankers, plantation owners, workshop proprietors, and manufacturers among others all exercised their considerable entrepreneurial skills and innovative capabilities during the early republic. The factory system, and more particularly the northern textile mills and the men who owned and operated them, continues to fascinate historians; they had an inordinate impact on American economic and social development.[1] In this essay, we will address substantive and methodological issues regarding the history of entrepreneurial activity in the United States. Drawing primarily from the experiences of early New England textile manufacturers such as Samuel Slater and Amos Lawrence, we argue that cultural beliefs and mores dramatically influenced the attitudes and behaviors of these men. We also suggest that entrepreneurial

Barbara M. Tucker, Professor of History and Director, Center for Connecticut Studies, Eastern Connecticut State University. She is the author of *Samuel Slater and the Origins of the American Textile Industry* (1984) and has published articles in *Labor History, Business History Review* and *Agricultural History*.

Kenneth H. Tucker, Jr., Professor of Sociology, Mt. Holyoke College is the author of *French Revolutionary Syndicalism and the Public Sphere, Anthony Giddens and Modern Social Theory,* and *Classical Social Theory: A Contemporary Approach* (2002).

1. Alfred D. Chandler Jr., *The Visible Hand: The Managerial Revolution in American Business* (Cambridge, MA, 1977), 60. According to Chandler, between 83 and 86 percent of all manufacturing companies listed in the 1832 *McLane Report* were textile firms.

history can be enriched by exploring the family and intergenerational dynamics of early entrepreneurs, their surprising philanthropic gestures, and their complex interactions with other groups from women to male wage workers.[2]

Historians continue to study early American entrepreneurship using the categories borrowed from economics that emphasize market growth, competition, and management strategies among other issues. Such a model has severe limitations for a number of reasons. During the early nineteenth century, the market was only emerging and an agrarian republic rather than a capitalist society prevailed.[3] At this time, entrepreneurial practices varied remarkably. Family firms often predominated, mercantile practices continued to be employed, and efficiency and profit frequently were subordinated to other concerns. Methodologically, the history of entrepreneurs has not fully absorbed the cultural turn that has characterized much recent scholarship. Many historians argue that language, beliefs, or more commonly culture, are not the passive reflection of material and social circumstances or simply a set of shared beliefs and customs automatically passed on from generation to generation. Rather culture is contested, plural, and represents a porous set of concepts and practices. Its shape depended on the contingent, constantly shifting outcome of the struggles of different groups.[4]

The beliefs and practices of early entrepreneurs cannot be appreciated fully without an understanding of the complex culture of early-nineteenth-century America. In the textile industry, for example, Samuel

---

2. Although this essay emphasizes the New England textile industry, do the conclusions suggested here apply to other economic ventures and to other regions? Entrepreneurship in the mid-Atlantic region, for example, requires further examination. How significant were family firms? Did the second generation continue in the business or pursue other endeavors? If so, what were they? What was the attitude of the founding generation to work and family? Did they feel obligated to their communities or were they more concerned with accumulating wealth and enjoying it? Also did entrepreneurs employ testamentary trusts and charitable foundations, legal instruments designed to conserve patrimonial capital and to transmit wealth from one generation to another, in the mid-Atlantic states?

3. Naomi R. Lamoreaux, Daniel M.G. Raff, and Peter Temin, "Beyond Markets and Hierarchies: Toward a New Synthesis of American Business History," *American Historical Review*, 108 (2003): 412–13.

4. *Ibid.*, and Paula Fass, "Cultural History/Social History: Some Reflections on a Continuing Dialogue," *Journal of Social History*, 37 (2003): 39–54.

Slater's mills were among the earliest and most successful enterprises of the era. His factories represented a compromise between an agricultural and traditional way of life and the needs and demands of the new production system. Paternalism prevailed both in his communities and on the factory floor. Slater employed entire families to work in his factories, contracted with the head of the household for the labor of his or her family, provided jobs based on the age and gender of the workers, and followed traditional methods of discipline. The values of internal self-control taught in the family and the church helped to discipline workers. The continued use of family labor well into the 1830s certainly was not cost effective; Slater found that labor costs accounted for about one half of all expenses involved in the production of cloth.

As demonstrated by Samuel Slater, the economic assumption of the rational actor, *homo economicus*, was conditioned by the moral and cultural context of the time. However, as competition increased and the market for goods expanded, entrepreneurs were forced to adjust to new economic circumstances. For Slater, the downturn of 1829 caused him to reevaluate his business practices and assumptions. Earlier that decade, Slater had endorsed about $300,000 in notes for family and friends, and when their firms went under in 1829, he fell liable for the debts. Although he remained optimistic that he could recover, the situation worsened. Slater had to sell several of his factories including his interest in the Slatersville and Pawtucket mills. While he later bought back the Slatersville property, Pawtucket was lost. Unaccustomed to failure, he came to believe that his business practices were outdated: competition, efficiency, profit maximization, and a different business morality now governed the market place. By the early 1830s he began to take steps to separate entrepreneurial functions from operating duties. He formed a corporation, Samuel Slater and Sons, made Providence his headquarters, and relinquished partial control of the business to his three sons. The Slater sons continued reorganizing the business. To retain and enlarge their share of the market, they cut costs. Every aspect of their business was reviewed, and in the 1830s they consolidated some properties, incorporated others, and separated ownership from management.

While these organizational forms were practiced throughout the industry, other changes introduced by the Slater family were more innovative. Samuel Slater and Sons introduced cost accounting around 1839, diversified their product line, and designed a stamp to be placed on their manufactured goods. Although Samuel Slater and Sons did not pioneer the use of brand names, it realized early the attraction its name held for the public. Capitalizing on the patriotism engendered by the Mexican War, the firm advertised its goods under the ticket, "Triumph of American Manufacturers." It became a success. During the 1830s and 1840s they also tried to limit the use of commission agents for purchasing cotton and marketing cloth. Concerned with long-term growth and stability, knowing that labor costs were higher than most of their competitors, they also began to dismantle the family system of labor and hire workers individually. Many of these new workers were French Canadians. Under these circumstances, ideas about the meaning of work, wealth, and family were transformed. The impact these ideas and innovations had on the economy and society represents a rich area of investigation for business and labor historians.[5]

Paternalism also should be reexamined. Under the new economic and social conditions of the 1830s, existing ideas about paternalism were challenged. Paternalism uneasily coexisted with republican beliefs stressing individual responsibility, simplicity, frugality, and devotion to duty and the public good. The republican vocabulary of virtue and corruption provided a tool for the moral evaluation of business practices and the distribution of wealth. For example, the rough equality believed to have existed in the early republic questioned the assumption that property should be passed to children who did not necessarily deserve it. Writing in 1838, Henry C. Carey argued it this way:

property can be perpetuated in no family, except by enterprise and virtue. . . . Through improvidence and vice, the children of the opulent are perpetually descending from their elevation, to learn, in the school of poverty, the necessity of diligence and prudence. . . . In such a state of things, industry and thrift cease to be derogatory; they become associated in the minds of the people with merit; and strangely as it may sound in foreign ears, there are parts of this country where an idler, however affluent, could with difficulty maintain his place in society.[6]

---

5. For a discussion of the Slater system, see Barbara M. Tucker, *Samuel Slater and the Origins of the American Textile Industry, 1790–1860* (Ithaca, 1984).

6. H. C. Carey, "Essay on the Rate of Wages," *New York Review*, 2 (1838), 9–10; Calvin Colton, *Public Economy for the United States* (New York, 1848), 320.

Thus the fear of the corrupting influence of dissolute behavior and ill-gotten wealth had to be addressed. Entrepreneurs took these ideas seriously and applied them to their own situations and families.

Cultural ideals intersected in complex ways with family and generational changes concerning work and responsibility. This requires further examination. A host of important families who dominated the economic scene in the early years of the republic have not been examined beyond the first generation; and new questions should be asked of those who have been studied.[7] Even among the Boston Associates much can be learned. Amos Lawrence is a case in point. Believed to be one of the most successful entrepreneurs of his time, he joined forces with his brother Abbott to operate a flourishing mercantile business. Despite his financial accomplishments, he nevertheless cannot be defined simply as *homo economicus.* During the depression of the 1830s he confided to his son William:

my nerves are in such a shattered state, that I am quite unfit to encounter the responsibilities incident to my station and I am ashamed of myself to thus expose my weakness. . . . The property I possess is more than I need and if those who come after me make good use of it there will be as much as will be good for them, if bad use, more than will be good for them, as it will prove a means of condemnation.

He repeatedly chided his son William for his irresponsible behavior:

You ought to have some *steady pursuit* is quite certain. *No* young man can have any standing in this community without it, only you had better be engaged in printing *little stories* than doing nothing: persons having no duties become a small consequence, however large their property. Whatever you undertake ought to be pursued

---

7. There are a number of biographies on merchants and early manufacturers; among the best are those on Nathan Appleton, Nathan Trotter, Robert Oliver, John Hancock, and the Brown family. However, rarely do the authors of these studies move beyond the founding generation. We learn little of what happened to the considerable fortune left to their families or the professional activities, life styles, and investment patterns of subsequent generations. Also, were their lives totally consumed by their business activities? Samuel Slater retired from business about six years before his death, and Amos Lawrence, because of ill health, retired early. Was this a pattern?

with a determination to make yourself to be respected and respectable: —whether it is *trafficking* or *tinkering*, is of much less consequence than to have no pursuit.

If William planned to remain in Boston, he needed to change his behavior for "men having no pursuit here occupy a very small space in the public estimation." Apparently the warning failed in its desired effect and Amos Lawrence once again had to admonish his son. "As I have before said, I had rather you would engage in the most common business than not to be in any business. An idle man here can have no standing in society. No matter how much money he has, he must work with his head or his hands, else he may as well at once be content to be set down as a useless encumbrance."[8] At this time, William Lawrence was twenty-four.

The Slater family also should be studied in greater depth. While Samuel Slater has been examined in considerable detail, little is written about

---

8. Amos Lawrence to William Lawrence, Boston, Mar. 29, 1836; *ibid.*, Feb. 28, 1836, Amos Lawrence Papers (Massachusetts Historical Society, Boston). Is this an era in which attitudes toward wealth and work changed? Did the number of bankruptcies increase and the attitude toward failure change? While many entrepreneurs viewed failure as a blemish on their characters and as a judgment against them as men as well as businessmen, was this the prevailing view? While Samuel Slater and Amos Lawrence feared bankruptcy, other entrepreneurs frequently defaulted on their loans. During the early republic, speculation soared. Roswell L. Colt, entrepreneur and speculator, and Charles Ogden, land speculator and businessman, were merely two of the more prominent men whose character and actions were questionable. Roswell Colt of Paterson, New Jersey, engaged in a variety of schemes to enrich himself. He was known for his willingness to take a chance and not for his prudence in business. Charles Ogden, son-in-law of Philadelphia merchant and businessman, Jonathan Meredith, speculated in western New York land, territory then occupied by the Oneida, Brothertown, and other New York Native-American tribes. Through bribery, corruption, and trickery, his company tried to remove the Indians from their land. The property involved in this speculation scheme is still being litigated today. Are Colt and Ogden more representative of the entrepreneurs who emerged in the 1830s? Was the moral and business climate of New England different from the rest of the country? For more information, see Barbara M. Tucker, "Kinship and Investment Patterns in the Middle Atlantic Region, 1780–1840," unpublished paper presented at the Philadelphia Center for Early American Studies, University of Pennsylvania, Philadelphia, Pennsylvania. See also "Claim of the Ogden Land Company" (Rochester, NY, n.d.), 1–11.

his brother John Slater who came to the United States around 1804. John acquired an interest in several factories including those at Slatersville, Rhode Island, Hopeville, Connecticut, and Jewett City, Connecticut. He expected his children, William and John, to follow him into the factory, and unlike Amos Lawrence, there does not appear to be any question about their involvement in the family business. At the age of seventeen, his son John Fox Slater was put to work in the Hopeville mill, and by the age of twenty-one he managed it. After the death of John Slater, his sons continued in the textile business.[9]

Unlike his father and uncle who devoted their working lives to the growth of their mills, John Fox Slater believed he owed something to his community and country. He actively supported various educational and religious institutions. He provided part of the funds for educational and religious projects in eastern Connecticut such as the Jewett City Public Library and the Park Congregational Church. All of this paled, however, with his million dollar endowment of the John F. Slater Fund for the Education of Freedmen. Why did he choose these projects? Did he want personal recognition or to secure his place in history? Not according to a friend, Daniel C. Gilman, who claimed, "He was a frequent, unostentatious contributor to benevolent undertakings, especially such as were brought to his attention in the town where he resided [Norwich, Connecticut] and in the church which he attended. From all positions which made him conspicuous he was inclined to withdraw himself."[10]

Contrast Slater's activities with those of Amos Lawrence, who donated money to a variety of individuals and institutions including prison discipline, female workers, and the Catholic poor, or his son, Amos Adams Lawrence, who took a much more public stand on charitable giving and national issues. Then there were those entrepreneurs like Horatio Nelson Slater, son of Samuel Slater, who avoided public giving altogether and continued to run their family firms and company farms. Business philanthropy is commonly associated with the late nineteenth century; Andrew Carnegie and others developed a gospel of wealth stewardship and philanthropic responsibility as they gained their enormous fortunes. Yet phil-

---

9. *Memorial of John F. Slater of Norwich, Connecticut, 1815–1884* (Norwich, 1885), 5–32.

10. *Ibid.*, 5. John Fox Slater operated his business and conducted his philanthropic enterprises from his home in Norwich, Connecticut. It was said that he spent limited time at his factories, visiting them about once a week.

anthropic endeavors existed among early entrepreneurs, who were clearly influenced by moral and cultural beliefs beyond profit maximization.[11] There is no study of the Slater cousins or information on the scores of other entrepreneurs who contributed to philanthropic enterprises, expanded their family firms, introduced novel business strategies, and influenced the society in which they lived.

No discussion of entrepreneurs would be complete without reference to working men and women. How did entrepreneurs' notions of work, family, and philanthropy affect their employees? Were they willing to reward those who met or exceeded their expectations? Did they criticize those who, like some of their self-indulgent sons, preferred ostentatious display and dissolute behavior? How did their attitudes toward female employees influence the interpersonal dynamics within working-class families? As Christine Stansell noted: "When we know more about the history of gender among laboring people, we may discover that America as a whole in the 1830s was as volatile, as laden with possibilities for change between the sexes as was working-class England."[12]

Many men and women struggled with each other as well as with manufacturers during the early years of the Republic to dominate the factory floor. The struggle between working-class men and women was not static, not confined to merely one period, but preceded in waves. During various periods, public figures both favored and condemned the entry of women into the industrial labor force. While the role of women in the early industrial revolution has received considerable historical attention, gaps remain in our knowledge. Early textile workers were not always machine tenders. They could be found in skilled and supervisory posi-

---

11. Peter Dobkin Hall, *The Organization of American Culture, 1700–1900: Private Institutions, Elites, and the Origins of American Nationality* (New York, 1984), 60–75, 114–24; Naomi R. Lamoreaux and Christopher Glaisek, "Vehicles of Privilege or Mobility? Banks in Providence, Rhode Island, during the Age of Jackson," *Business History Review*, 65 (Autumn 1991): 521–27; William R. Lawrence, ed., *Extracts from the Diary and Correspondence of the Late Amos Lawrence; with a Brief Account of Some Incidents in his Life* (Boston, 1855), 92–95, 200–01. Why were both John Fox Slater and Amos Adams Lawrence, son of Amos Lawrence, keenly interested in slavery and its aftermath? See Samuel A. Johnson, "The Genesis of the New England Emigrant Aid Company," *New England Quarterly*, 3 (1930): 95–121.

12. Christine Stansell, *City of Women: Sex and Class in New York, 1789–1860* (New York, 1986), 143.

tions such as mule spinners and engaged in apprenticeship programs. Many manufacturers believed that "females are the most productive class of laborers," a fact "no one who is at all acquainted with the subject, will pretend to deny."[13] Pleas for additional jobs, expanded opportunities, and higher wages for women found a public hearing. This support often came from businessmen and philanthropists with little support from working-class men or fashionable ladies. In his report "Wages of Female Labour," Matthew Carey noted: "Let the employments of females be multiplied as much as possible. They are admirably calculated for various occupations from which they are at present in a great degree excluded."[14] The *Niles' Weekly Register* argued in 1834 that there were many "branches of business suited to them—and we earnestly hope that public spirited individuals will every where endeavor to ameliorate [their] condition . . . by furnishing them with proper employments."[15] Others supported increased wages for women. One author lamented that "Woman is, by the law of her being, excluded from paths in which coarser man may make a livelihood; and by the custom of society is obliged to accept LESS THAN HALF OF WHAT THE MOST STUPID OF THE OTHER SEX CAN OBTAIN!!"[16] Why should women work for less than a man?

---

13. [Samuel] Stanley, *An Essay on the Manufacture of Straw Bonnets containing an historical account of the introduction of the manufacture, its effects upon the Employments, Dress, Food, Health, Morals, Social Intercourse &c. of the inhabitants of the several Towns in which it has been carried on; with moral, political and miscellaneous remarks* (Providence, 1825), 3.

14. Matthew Carey, "Wages of Female Labour" (Philadelphia, 1829), 1–2.

15. *Niles' Weekly Register,* Oct. 25, 1834.

16. *Solemn Address to the Mothers, Wives, Sisters and Daughters of Citizens of Philadelphia* (Philadelphia, 1837). During the earliest years of the Industrial Revolution, the timing, the form (cash or kind), and the amount of wages to be paid to workers represented a major problem. Some of the early factory masters came from mercantile houses which were accustomed to extending long term credit to customers. They tried to transfer such notions to the factories they operated. Samuel Slater's first partners, William Almy and Smith Brown, were merchants, and they transferred their ideas concerning wages and credit to the new firm. The credit system with which they were familiar as merchants was haphazard at best and explained part of their difficulty in promptly honoring their commitments to their workers. Sometimes they supplied Slater with cash or goods for the hands each month while other times workers had to wait six or even eight months for a settlement. Slater once even threatened to shut down the mill and sell off the

But these pleas for higher wages coincided with demographic changes. French Canadian and Irish immigrants flooded into the northern industrial towns and villages looking for work. Men, women and children entered the factories, moved into company housing, and accepted the prevailing rates of pay.

Paternalism in employment was transformed in the context of these tensions between and among men and women. These conflicts and debates demonstrate that the gendering of manufacturing work as male was a contested social and cultural accomplishment. Industrialization turned out to be a contingent process, for the very shape of the workplace depended on the outcome of social struggles among various groups. There is no inevitable industrialization process that necessarily occurred in early America. Entrepreneurs did not act in a cultural vacuum; they had no choice but to interact and sometimes struggle with other groups. This was not always simply a clash between working-class and entrepreneurial interests. Depending on circumstances, manufacturers might align with women workers, while working-class men might align with middle-class women. Sometimes material interest informed these choices; at other times shared cultural beliefs did so. Entrepreneurs had to take into account the interests and behaviors of different groups. Thus, historians should remain cautious about generalizing about cultural beliefs that remain constant over time, as well as class interests that seemingly do not change.

Do these considerations leave *homo economicus* in tatters? Hardly. The study of entrepreneurial history must always have as a focal point the examination of markets and profit maximization. The emergence of the market in the early nineteenth century often encouraged entrepreneurs to adopt more bureaucratic and economically efficient forms of organization. But the history of entrepreneurship cannot be understood without the incorporation of many other areas of inquiry from family dynamics to intergenerational change. Entrepreneurial history allows social inequalities of all sorts from gender to class to be studied as part of economic activity. And business history reminds us that *homo economicus* is bounded by cultural and moral norms that should be taken into

---

machinery if his partners were not forthcoming in a timely fashion with workers' wages. Wage payment represents another important area for additional research. See Tucker, *Samuel Slater*, 53–57.

account in an analysis of economic interests and pursuits. The quest for profits and economic efficiency in the early nineteenth century had to be legitimated in the context of a cultural context informed by republican and paternalistic traditions that remained suspicious of, if not fully hostile to, market calculations divorced from moral and familial concerns. Entrepreneurs attempted to fuse economic considerations with the disparate values of paternalism and republicanism, constantly revising these cultural traditions in the process. Any dynamic understanding of early entrepreneurial history should account for this constant interchange of business and culture, as businessmen both molded and reflected the values of their communities.

Economic Landscapes Yet to be Discovered

The Early American Republic and Historians' Unsubtle Adoption of Political Economy

JAMES L. HUSTON

Economic history and the accounts of the early republic enjoy a somewhat strange but interesting relationship. Economic history, as presented either by cliometricians or by business historians, has been on the wane for some years; yet the need for accurate studies of the nation's early economy has never been greater. The reason lies in the popularity of the "new social history" and the profession's massive switch to that mode of investigation. The strangeness lies in the ironic fact that most social history relies upon a careful depiction of society's economic base, the study of which has continued to stagnate. However, it may be that economic history (and political history too) may be making a resurgence in the guise of "political economy."[1]

Certain research areas in economic history have anticipated current interpretive trends and some others have perhaps been overdone. At the moment, the profession is preoccupied with the idea of "transnationalism." Economic historians, especially of the colonial and early republican periods, long have held a transnational perspective because the enter-

James L. Huston, Professor of History, Oklahoma State University, recently published *Calculating the Value of the Union: Slavery, Property Rights, and the Economic Origins of the Civil War* (2003).

1. Just to underscore the point, all one needs to do is to plow through the pages of the *Directory of Departments of History* and note how few scholars label themselves economic historians. Moreover, they do not seem to overwhelm the Departments of Economics either.

prise and growth of the American economy always was tied to exports. For many years export and import statistics provided virtually the only reliable numbers that historians could find before the census of 1850 (for proof witness the appendices of Douglass C. North's and George Rogers Taylor's great works).[2] Numbers for the domestic economy, except on a small local scale, have been much harder to come by, giving rise to the depiction of the years 1790–1820 as the statistical dark ages of American economic history. Some of that darkness has lifted, but forceful, detailed depictions of the national economy from 1790–1825 remain surprisingly elusive.[3] Other topics have been the core of intensive research and controversy for decades: the transition from semi-self-sufficiency in agriculture to commercial agriculture (or the rise of capitalism), the creation of plantation society, the establishment of southern yeoman communities, the origin and then expansion of industrialization.[4] Undoubtedly these topics will continue to entice researchers and yield new studies.

In the 1990s, both the fields of economic history and political history found new life in the area that has come to be known as "political econ-

2. Douglass C. North, *The Economic Growth of the United States, 1790–1860* (New York, 1961); George Rogers Taylor, *The Transportation Revolution, 1815–1860* (New York, 1951); see also Gary M. Walton and James F. Sheperd, *The Economic Rise of Early America* (Cambridge, UK, 1979).

3. On the other hand, see the recent work of Howard Bodenhorn and his discussion of investigations into the economic history of the early republic: *A History of Banking in Antebellum America: Financial Markets and Economic Development in an Era of Nation-Building* (Cambridge, UK, 2000).

4. Just to name a few, Peter Temin, ed., *Engines of Enterprise: An Economic History of New England* (Cambridge, MA, 2000); Rachel N. Klein, *Unification of a Slave State: The Rise of the Planter Class in the South Carolina Backcountry, 1760–1808* (Chapel Hill, 1990); Lacy K. Ford Jr., *Origins of Southern Radicalism: The South Carolina Upcountry, 1800–1860* (New York, 1988); Stephen Aron, *How the West Was Lost: The Transformation of Kentucky from Daniel Boone to Henry Clay* (Baltimore, 1996); Winifred B. Rothenberg, *From Market-Places to a Market Economy: The Transformation of Rural Massachusetts, 1750–1850* (Chicago, 1992); James A. Henretta, *The Origins of American Capitalism: Collected Essays* (Boston, 1991); Allan Kulikoff, *The Agrarian Origins of American Capitalism* (Charlottesville, 1992); Peter A. Coclanis, *The Shadow of a Dream: Economic Life and Death in the South Carolina Low Country, 1670–1920* (New York, 1989); Bill Cecil-Fronsman, *Common Whites: Class and Culture in Antebellum North Carolina* (Lexington, KY, 1992); Charles G. Sellers, *The Market Revolution: Jacksonian America, 1815–1846* (New York, 1991).

omy," and it is works connected with this subject that will probably inform and attract innovative scholarship. This development arose from a change in the mood of the profession in the 1960s. At that time, political history lost its attractiveness as numerous scholars rejected its agenda of quantitative assessment of the electorate and elections. Coincidentally, economic history became the province of economists who demanded the use of econometric models to probe the past, thereby sending historians scurrying into the arms of business history. Within the profession, the victor was social history. But what was missing from the history generally was an appreciation of governance and attention to the actual functioning of the marketplace. In response to these deficiencies was born an interest in "political economy."

Political economy turns out to be a most elastic term. From the seventeenth century to the end of the nineteenth, the phrase had a fairly precise meaning: the study of economic theory, the forerunner of today's microeconomics. The "political" part of the phrase came from writers' convictions that to obtain good economics, an appropriate political framework was required. In the late eighteenth century—the age of Adam Smith—that meant attacking aristocratic systems of monopoly and special privilege. By the last decade of the nineteenth century, it meant comparison of capitalism with socialism, a mode of investigation that continues to define the term in many contexts.[5] As the phrase has come to be used, however, political economy now encompasses two basic areas: the realm of economic thought and the interaction of politics and economics with each other.[6] Thus modern studies of political economy cover a vast intellectual territory.

Interestingly enough, the new interest in political economy marks a return to the older style of political history, albeit with more sophisti-

---

5. For example, Barry Clark, *Political Economy: A Comparative Approach* (New York, 1991); Howard Sherman, *Radical Political Economy: Capitalism and Socialism from a Marxist-Humanist Perspective* (New York, 1972); James F. Becker, *Marxian Political Economy: An Outline* (Cambridge, UK, 1977); Paul M. Sweezy, *The Theory of Capitalist Development: Principles of Marxian Political Economy* (1942; rep., New York, 1956).

6. The case can be made that the entanglement between economics and politics is fundamental and that there exists no such thing as a separate politics and a separate economics. Without politics, economics could not exist; and there can be no such thing as politics without a corresponding effect upon economics.

cated tools and concepts. The political history that dominated the profession between 1900 and 1960 was absorbed with fleshing out the economic consequences of governmental policies, a reflection of progressivism's lingering power in the profession. Many, if not most, of the political monographs at that time really studied political economy, as evidenced by investigations of the banking system, state involvement in internal improvements, soil exhaustion in the South, public land policies, and intellectual thought of the Gilded Age. So entangled were political history and economic history that scholars of the latter persuasion charged the former with stealing their clothing.[7]

Historians' interest in politics and economics never ceased during the decades when the "new histories" held sway. Numerous monographs included "political economy" in their titles, and most ideological studies included a section on economic principles (or values).[8] By the middle of the 1980s, however, more studies appeared that explicitly embraced the

---

7. Just for some prominent examples, Paul W. Gates and Robert W. Swenson, *History of Public Land Law Development* (Washington, DC, 1968); Louis M. Hacker, *The Triumph of American Capitalism: The Development of Forces in American History to the End of the Nineteenth Century* (New York, 1940); Oscar Handlin and Mary Flug Handlin, *Commonwealth: A Study of the Role of Government in the American Economy: Massachusetts, 1774–1861* (1947; 2nd ed.; Cambridge, MA, 1969); Louis Hartz, *Economic Policy and Democratic Thought: Pennsylvania, 1776–1860* (Cambridge, MA, 1948); Milton Sidney Heath, *Constructive Liberalism; The Role of the State in Economic Development in Georgia to 1860* (Cambridge, MA, 1954); Roy M. Robbins, *Our Landed Heritage: The Public Domain, 1776–1936* (1942; rep., New York, 1950).

8. Eugene D. Genovese, *The Political Economy of Slavery: Studies in the Economy and Society of the Slave South* (New York, 1965); Robert F. Dalzell Jr., "The Rise of the Waltham-Lowell System and Some Thoughts on the Political Economy of Modernization in Ante-Bellum Massachusetts," *Perspectives in American History*, 9 (1975), 227–68; Gerald N. Grob, "The Political System and Social Policy in the Nineteenth Century: Legacy of the Revolution," *Mid-America*, 58 (1976), 5–19; Daniel Walker Howe, *The Political Culture of American Whigs* (Chicago, 1979); John Ashworth, *"Agrarians" and "Aristocrats": Party Political Ideology in the United States, 1837–1846* (Cambridge, UK, 1983); Rush Welter, *The Mind of America, 1820–1860* (New York, 1975); Edward K. Spann, *Ideals and Politics: New York Intellectuals and Liberal Democracy, 1820–1880* (Albany, 1972); Gabor S. Boritt, *Lincoln and the Economics of the American Dream* (Memphis, 1978); Gavin Wright, *The Political Economy of the Cotton South: Households, Markets and Wealth in the Nineteenth Century* (New York, 1978); Paul Conkin, *Prophets of Prosperity: America's First Political Economists* (Bloomington, 1980).

concept of political economy, and by the 1990s political economy had nearly emerged as a distinct subfield under a rubric that sought to foster it: American Policy Studies.[9]

Today investigations about the connections between economics and politics follow several paths. Because studies of slavery, abolitionists, and reform ideology are eternally mired in a modern (capitalist) versus

---

9. See Richard R. John, "Farewell to the 'Party Period': Political Economy in Nineteenth-Century America," paper given at a session on the future of political history at the Organization of American Historians conference in Memphis, 2003; for books, consult Roger L. Ransom, *Conflict and Compromise: The Political Economy of Slavery, Emancipation, and the American Civil War* (Cambridge, UK, 1989); Leonard H. Neufeldt, *The Economists: Henry Thoreau and Enterprise* (New York, 1989); John R. Nelson Jr., *Liberty and Property: Political Economy and Policymaking in the New Nation, 1789-1812* (Baltimore, 1987); Richard H. Abbott, *Cotton and Capital: Boston Businessmen and Antislavery Reform, 1854-1868* (Amherst, MA, 1991); Edward J. Balleisen, "Vulture Capitalism in Antebellum America: The 1841 Federal Bankruptcy Act and the Exploitation of Financial Distress," *Business History Review*, 70 (1996): 473-516; Maurice G. Baxter, *Henry Clay and the American System* (Lexington, 1995); Thomas C. Cochran, *Challenges to American Values: Society, Business and Religion* (New York, 1985); Coclanis, *Shadow of a Dream*; Daniel Feller, *The Public Lands in Jacksonian Politics* (Madison, 1984); L. Ray Gunn, *The Decline of Authority: Public Economic Policy and Political Development in New York State, 1800-1860* (Ithaca, 1988); John L. Larson, *Internal Improvement; National Public Works and the Promise of Popular Government in the Early United States* (Chapel Hill, 2001); James L. Huston, *Securing the Fruits of Labor: The American Concept of Wealth Distribution, 1765-1900* (Baton Rouge, 1998); Huston, *Calculating the Value of the Union: Slavery, Property Rights, and the Economic Origins of the Civil War* (Chapel Hill, 2003); Robin L. Einhorn, *Property Rules: Political Economy in Chicago, 1833-1872* (Chicago, 2001); Richard R. John, *Spreading the News: The American Postal System from Franklin to Morse* (Cambridge, MA, 1995); Bruce H. Mann, *Republic of Debtors: Bankruptcy in the Age of American Independence* (Cambridge, MA, 2002); Olivier Frayssé, *Lincoln, Land, and Labor, 1809-60*, trans. Sylvia Neely (Urbana, 1994); Roger G. Kennedy, *Mr. Jefferson's Lost Cause: Land, Farmers, Slavery, and the Louisiana Purchase* (New York, 2003); Herbert E. Sloan, *Principle and Interest: Thomas Jefferson and the Problem of Debt* (New York, 1995); Steven E. Siry, *De Witt Clinton and the American Political Economy: Sectionalism, Politics, and Republican Ideology, 1787-1828* (New York, 1990). The Policy Studies group is evidently not an association, but those interested scholars have a journal, *Journal of Policy Studies*; they also work closely with a group in political science, labeled American Political Development, a branch of the American Political Science Association.

premodern (anticapitalist) mudpit, such research continues to rely on political economy.[10] The field of legal research provides another prop for political economy, especially in the form of studies asking how government regulated the acquisition and disposition of property—a focus that, one hundred years ago, defined the core of political economy and comparative studies of economic systems.[11] Much of the recent interest

---

10. Such works have always been heavily invested with political economy; for example, see Jonathan A. Glickstein, " 'Poverty is Not Slavery': Abolitionists and the Competitive Labor Market," in Lewis Perry and Michael Fellman, eds., *Antislavery Reconsidered: New Perspectives on the Abolitionists* (Baton Rouge, 1979), 195–218; Jonathan A. Glickstein, *American Exceptionalism, American Anxiety: Wages, Competition, and Degraded Labor in the Antebellum United States* (Charlottesville, 2002); Hugh Davis, *Joshua Leavitt: Evangelical Abolitionist* (Baton Rouge, 1990); Lawrence B. Goodheart, *Abolitionist, Actuary, Atheist: Elizur Wright and the Reform Impulse* (Kent, OH, 1990); Amy Dru Stanley, *From Bondage to Contract: Wage Labor, Marriage, and the Market in the Age of Slave Emancipation* (Cambridge, UK, 1998); Jamie L. Bronstein, *Land Reform and Working-Class Experience in Britain and the United States, 1800–1862* (Stanford, 1999); Mark Voss-Hubbard, "The Political Culture of Emancipation: Morality, Politics, and the State in Garrisonian Abolitionism, 1854–1863," *Journal of American Studies*, 29 (1995): 159–84; Jeffrey Rogers Hummel, *Emancipating Slaves, Enslaving Free Men: A History of the American Civil War* (Chicago, 1996); Laurence Shore, *Southern Capitalists: The Ideological Leadership of an Elite, 1832–1885* (Chapel Hill, 1986); Stanley Harrold, *Gamaliel Bailey and Antislavery Union* (Kent, 1986); John Ashworth, *Slavery, Capitalism, and Politics in the Antebellum Republic: Vol. I: Commerce and Compromise, 1820–1850* (Cambridge, UK, 1995); Daniel J. McInerney, *The Fortunate Heirs of Freedom: Abolition and Republican Thought* (Lincoln, 1994); Louis S. Gerteis, *Morality and Utility in American Antislavery Reform* (Chapel Hill, 1987).

11. Legal research has been knee-deep in political economy. James W. Ely Jr., *The Guardian of Every Other Right: A Constitutional History of Property Rights* (1992; 2nd ed., New York, 1998); Toby L. Ditz, *Property and Kinship: Inheritance in Early Connecticut, 1750–1820* (Princeton, 1986); Carole Shammas, Marylynn Salmon, and Michel Dahlin, *Inheritance in America from Colonial Times to the Present* (New Brunswick, NJ, 1987); Norma Basch, *In the Eyes of the Law: Women, Marriage, and Property in Nineteenth-Century New York* (Ithaca, 1982); Tom Downey, "Riparian Rights and Manufacturing in Antebellum South Carolina: William Gregg and the Origins of the 'Industrial Mind,' " *Journal of Southern History*, 65 (1999): 77–108; Tony Allen Freyer, *Producers Versus Capitalists: Constitutional Conflict in Antebellum America* (Charlottesville, 1994); Lawrence M. Friedman, *Contract Law in America: A Social and Economic Case Study* (Madison, 1965); Hendrik Hartog, *Public Property and Private Power: The Corporation of*

in political economy has been how laws (but not strictly legal history) shaped the market economy. In no area has that interest been more evident than in banking, a subject that will undoubtedly continue to attract attention.[12] Other subjects, however, beckon: the tariff has been ignored for decades now, the land laws could stand re-examination, the

---

the City of New York in American Law, 1730–1870 (Chapel Hill, 1983); James Willard Hurst, Law and the Conditions of Freedom in the Nineteenth-Century United States (Madison, 1956); Stanley N. Katz, "Republicanism and the Law of Inheritance in the American Revolutionary Era," Michigan Law Review, 76 (Nov. 1977): 1–29; Stanley I. Kutler, Privilege and Creative Destruction: The Charles River Bridge Case (Philadelphia, 1971); Jenny Bourne Wahl, The Bondsman's Burden: An Economic Analysis of the Common Law of Southern Slavery (Cambridge, UK, 1998); Gregory S. Alexander, Commodity and Propriety: Competing Visions of Property in American Legal Thought, 1776–1970 (Chicago, 1997); Herbert Hovenkamp, Enterprise and American Law, 1836–1937 (Cambridge, MA, 1991); Jennifer Nedelsky, Private Property and the Limits of American Constitutionalism: The Madisonian Framework and Its Legacy (Chicago, 1990); William E. Nelson, Americanization of the Common Law: The Impact of Legal Change on Massachusetts Society, 1760–1830 (Cambridge, MA, 1975); Donald J. Pisani, "Promotion and Regulation: Constitutionalism and the American Economy," Journal of American History, 74 (1987), 740–68; Ronald E. Seavoy, The Origins of the American Business Corporation, 1784–1855: Broadening the Concept of Public Service During Industrialization (Westport, 1982); Christopher L. Tomlins, Law, Labor, and Ideology in the Early American Republic (Cambridge, UK, 1993); Morton J. Horwitz, Transformation of American Law, 1780–1860 (Cambridge, MA, 1977); William J. Novak, The People's Welfare: Law and Regulation in Nineteenth-Century America (Chapel Hill, 1996). One can see the influence of the definition of property throughout a number of works that do not fit the category of political economy: Stephanie McCurry, Masters of Small Worlds: Yeoman Households, Gender Relations, and the Political Culture of the Antebellum South Carolina Low Country (New York, 1995); Walter Johnson, Soul by Soul: Life Inside the Antebellum Slave Market (Cambridge, MA, 1999); John Hope Franklin and Loren Schweninger, Runaway Slaves: Rebels on the Plantation (New York, 1999); Susan E. Gray, The Yankee West: Community Life on the Michigan Frontier (Chapel Hill, 1996). Moreover, it is through law and its governance of domestic relations that political history can incorporate women and the family in its investigations. Although social historians are using legal records to chart class and ethnic conflicts, the same records can be looked at from a political economy perspective.

12. Among the more discerning and informative historians working in this area are Edwin J. Perkins, American Public Finance and Financial Services, 1700–1815 (Columbus, 1994); and Bodenhorn, History of Banking in Antebellum America.

popular hostility to corporations remains mysterious, and the realm of state legislation—indeed, state financing and the development of state bureaucracies—is virtually *terra incognito*.[13]

One area that might almost be labeled a cliometric enterprise is to estimate the amount of public wealth in the United States and the impact that that wealth had over time. This subject obviously includes the way governments promoted the formation of human capital (schooling) and scientific discovery (for example, arms manufacturing).[14] But just as important is the public wealth that was invested in roads, churches, and public buildings. Most wealth studies have depended on probate records, records that by their nature exclude public investment. Surely public wealth eventually pays for increased economic activity as does private investment, and if one included public wealth in estimates along with private wealth, it may turn out that the New England states compared not so unfavorably to the slave states as Alice Hanson Jones thought—and in

---

13. For land laws, see Feller, *Public Lands in Jacksonian Politics*. Notice the interesting comment by Peter Temin that the Massachusetts "miracle" in antebellum manufacturing was made possible by the protective tariff, a claim that has not been heard in historical circles since the early protectionist works of Edward Stanwood. Peter Temin, "The Industrialization of New England, 1830–1880," in Temin, ed., *Engines of Enterprise: An Economic History of New England* (Cambridge, MA, 2000), 113–15; Edward Stanwood, *American Tariff Controversies in the Nineteenth Century* (New York, 1903). One wonders how long it will take for historians to give protectionism its due weight given today's criticism of the World Trade Organization and NAFTA; the arguments one presently hears are but pale shadows of the theories of Henry C. Carey and other protectionists.

14. For example, on education, Carl F. Kaestle, *Pillars of the Republic: Common Schools and American Society, 1780–1860* (New York, 1983); Lee Soltow and Edward Stevens, *The Rise of Literacy and the Common School in the United States: A Socioeconomic Analysis to 1870* (Chicago, 1981); and Ronald J. Zboray, *A Fictive People: Antebellum Economic Development and the American Reading Public* (New York, 1993). On human capital, see Ronald A. Wykstra, *Education and the Economics of Human Capital* (New York, 1971). The importance of government funding for advances in knowledge has not received the appreciation it merits, as the armories discovered means of manufacturing that has profoundly shaped American economic and social development: Nathan Rosenberg, *Technology and American Economic Growth* (New York, 1972); Merritt Roe Smith, *Harpers Ferry Armory and the New Technology: The Challenge of Change* (Ithaca, 1977); David A. Hounshell, *From the American System to Mass Production: The Development of Manufacturing Technology in the United States* (Baltimore, 1984).

the long run, the public wealth of New England perhaps laid the foundation for that region's rise in prosperity by the middle of the nineteenth century.[15]

But in terms of pressing research areas for the history of the early republic, the most important is the nature of the country's agricultural economy because it influenced every other facet of life. It is truly unfortunate, given the importance of understanding economic relations and the material base of society, that histories of the agricultural economy in the founding period have been so scarce. Most studies have focused on either the southern plantation or New England's march into industrialization. Clearly a key to understanding the early republic lies in understanding the agricultural nature of early American society, especially in neglected areas like the border South. And while the historians have been obsessed with the "market revolution" and the coming of capitalism, scholars need still to recognize that rural capitalism was considerably different from urban capitalism and industrialization.[16]

Therefore, Chris Clark, in his essay, raises questions that desperately need to be addressed.[17] Despite industrialization and urbanization, most Americans dwelt in rural villages or towns and lived according to a rural cadence. The economic quality of those lives needs to be assessed for precisely the reasons Clark points out: expectations about future activity, the connections between farm life and politics (such as the free labor ideology and public policy), the general view of economic change, and the standard of living. Likewise, a realistic assessment needs to be made of the tensions and divisions within the farm community. The suggestion made that the unit of analysis should be the farm household and not

---

15. Alice Hanson Jones, *Wealth of a Nation to Be: the American Colonies on the Eve of the Revolution* (New York, 1980).

16. Any brief familiarity with the literature between 1900 and 1945 should convince a reader that the older historians of the farm (John Hicks and Gilbert Fite for examples) found profound differences between agrarian economics and urban economics; Gilbert C. Fite and Jim E. Reese, *An Economic History of the United States* (1959; 3rd ed., Boston, 1973); John D. Hicks, *The Populist Revolt: A History of the Farmers' Alliance and the People's Party* (Minneapolis, 1931); also, Hal S. Barron, *Those Who Stayed Behind: Rural Society in Nineteenth-Century New England* (Cambridge, UK, 1984).

17. Christopher Clark is the author of *The Roots of Rural Capitalism: Western Massachusetts, 1780–1860* (Ithaca, 1990).

merely the male head of household is surely correct. And most vitally, other portions of the early republic need to be drawn into the discussion. Save for a few magnificent exceptions, histories of the middle states— Tennessee, Kentucky, Missouri, Indiana, Illinois, Ohio, Pennsylvania, and Virginia—are shockingly inadequate. Eventually historians have to break free of the stranglehold South Carolina and Massachusetts have had on their imaginations.

A second area that undoubtedly will see a reassessment is the quality of entrepreneurs and entrepreneurship in the formative years of the Republic. Too often commentary on entrepreneurs is limited to theoretical standards—*homo economicus*—and not behavioral patterns that deviated from the standard model. The entrepreneurs of the founding period were not like the Robber Barons a century later; who could possibly be offered as the early-nineteenth-century counterpart of Diamond Jim Fiske and Jay Gould? Barbara Tucker and Kenneth Tucker display some of the paths that entrepreneurial and business history might profitably take (no pun intended). Historians need to delineate the cultural norms that probably blunted the raw pursuit of self-interest and, indeed, to determine to what extent early American culture demanded altruistic behavior. (The last point is a vital finding because in economics, sociology, and psychology, the battle over the reality of self-interest and altruism waxes hot.) Paternalism may have been less a reflex to control subordinates than a cultural demand placed on the elite. Moreover, as the Tuckers point out, historians need to map out the timing and pressures it took to produce *homo economicus* as an actual presence.[18]

---

18. Barbara Tucker is author of *Samuel Slater and the Origins of the American Textile Industry, 1790–1860* (Ithaca, 1984). On the question of entrepreneurship, see the recent article of Naomi R. Lamoreaux, "Rethinking the Transition to Capitalism in the Early American Northeast," *Journal of American History*, 90 (2003): 437–61. The differences in portrayal of entrepreneurs could sometimes hardly be more stark. Winifred Rothenberg called the Boston Associates "a remarkable group of honorable men, concerned above all for their reputations among honorable men." Put that against the descriptions of the early manufacturers supplied by Jonathan Prude, Hannah Josephson, and Thomas Dublin; Winifred Barr Rothenberg, "The Invention of American Capitalism: The Economy of New England in the Federal Period," in Temin, ed., *Engines of Enterprise*, 100; Jonathan Prude, *The Coming of Industrial Order: Town and Factory Life in Rural Massachusetts, 1810–1860* (Cambridge, UK, 1983); Thomas C. Cochran and William Miller, *The Age of Enterprise: A Social History of Industrial America* (New York,

The Tuckers stress that relationships between workers and owners were not governed by a simple model of economic efficiency but that it was mediated by cultural values, values that were at once inherited but still evolving in strange ways due to continuous battles over what those values should be. They make a most valuable suggestion by arguing for the exploration of the transference of attitudes and management techniques from one generation to another—here lies an area of research begging for authors. Another topic they believe requires elaboration is cost accounting, a subject that indeed separates modern business practices from premodern ones. The Tuckers find Samuel Slater and his sons using cost accounting by 1840; Judith McGaw also found cost accounting among paper manufacturers by the 1850s.[19] When accounting became widespread, and indeed, useful, remains a potent question about the state of modernization in the American economy and indeed in the entire society.[20]

Finally, the area of economic thought deserves consideration. All kinds of potential topics arise here—not least the bizarre fascination Americans had for population theory—and much solid work has been done on looking carefully at the economic doctrines being espoused at the start of the nineteenth century.[21] Religious thought and economic

---

1942); Hannah Josephson, *Golden Threads; New England's Mill Girls and Magnates* (New York, 1941); Thomas Dublin, *Women at Work: The Transformation of Work and Community in Lowell, Massachusetts, 1826–1860* (New York, 1979).

19. Judith A. McGaw, *Most Wonderful Machine: Mechanization and Social Change in Berkshire Paper Making, 1801–1885* (Princeton, 1987), 155–56.

20. Another subject of significance arises in one of the quotes that the Tuckers use. Amos Lawrence wrote to his son that no matter the amount of money a person had, "he must work with his head or his hands" or be considered a community disgrace. The question of head labor versus manual labor deserves investigation because it reveals the differentiation of American society as well as its potential shift in core values. See Jonathan Glickstein, *Concepts of Free Labor in Antebellum America* (New Haven, 1991), chap. 2 and *passim*.

21. The standard work is Joseph Dorfman, *The Economic Mind in American Civilization* (5 vols., New York, 1946–59); among the other prominent studies are Paul Conkin, *Prophets of Prosperity; America's First Political Economists* (Bloomington, 1980); Jacob E. Cooke, *Tench Coxe and the Early Republic* (Chapel Hill, 1978); William D. Grampp, *Economic Liberalism* (2 vols., New York, 1965); E. A. J. Johnson, *The Foundations of American Economic Freedom: Government and Enterprise in the Age of Washington* (Minneapolis, 1973); Michael Hudson, *Economics and Technology in 19th Century American Thought: The Neglected*

thought surprisingly have not been paired together often, historians preferring to ignore the subject or rely on the older ideas of R. H. Tawney, Max Weber, and Henry F. May.[22] In the most recent twenty years no subfield of history has been more active than religious history, but those scholars seldom venture into economic doctrines or even broad religious values and the economy. Rather, most have looked at the "democratization" of Calvinist faiths, the effects of postmillennial versus premillennial thought, and the slavery issue.[23] Yet it turns out that Adam Smith was

---

American Economists (New York, 1975); Allen Kaufman, *Capitalism, Slavery, and Republican Values: Antebellum Political Economists, 1819–1848* (Austin, 1982); and Huston, *Securing the Fruits of Labor.*

22. Max Weber, *The Protestant Ethic and the Spirit of Capitalism*, trans. Talcott Parsons (New York, 1958); R. H. Tawney, *Religion and the Rise of Capitalism: A Historical Study* (New York, 1926); Henry F. May, *Protestant Churches and Industrial America* (1949; rep., New York, 1967).

23. Without going into any depth on this literature, the absence of economic themes in the following works is striking: Richard J. Carwardine, *Evangelicals and Politics in Antebellum America* (New Haven, 1993); Robert H. Abzug, *Cosmos Crumbling: American Reform and the Religious Imagination* (New York, 1994); Anne C. Loveland, *Southern Evangelicals and the Social Order, 1800–1860* (Baton Rouge, 1980); Donald G. Mathews, *Religion in the Old South* (Chicago, 1977); Paul K. Conkin, *The Uneasy Center: Reformed Christianity in Antebellum America* (Chapel Hill, 1995); Nathan O. Hatch, *The Democratization of American Christianity* (New Haven, 1989); Leo P. Hirrel, *Children of Wrath: New School Calvinism and Antebellum Reform* (Lexington, 1998); Mitchell Snay and John R. McKivigan, eds., *Religion and the Antebellum Debate over Slavery* (Athens, GA, 1998); Mark Y. Hanley, *Beyond a Christian Commonwealth: The Protestant Quarrel with the American Republic, 1830–1860* (Chapel Hill, 1994); Randall M. Miller, Harry S. Stout, and Charles Reagan Wilson, eds., *Religion and the American Civil War* (New York, 1998); Curtis D. Johnson, *Redeeming America: Evangelicals and the Road to Civil War* (Chicago, 1993); John H. Wigger, *Taking Heaven By Storm: Methodism and the Rise of Popular Christianity in America* (New York, 1998); Mitchell Snay, *Gospel of Disunion: Religion and Separatism in the Antebellum South* (Cambridge, UK, 1993). The major exception to the above generalization was the attempt of Charles G. Sellers to find an antinomian-arminian split in reaction to the Market Revolution, but that has been strongly criticized by others. Charles Sellers, *The Market Revolution: Jacksonian America, 1815–1846* (New York, 1991); Richard Carwardine, " 'Antinominans' and 'Arminians': Methodists and the Market Revolution," in Melvyn Stokes and Stephen Conway, eds., *The Market Revolution in America: Social, Political, and Religious Expressions, 1800–1880* (Charlottesville, 1996), 282–307. A recent exploration of some connections between economics and religion is John Patrick Daly, *When Slavery*

considered profoundly anti-Christian in his day and in England was pilloried by the clergy. It then becomes something of a mystery why religion in North America had so little to say about the market revolution, industrialization, and other economic changes.[24]

Stewart Davenport picks up this question and outlines an approach to an answer. He couches the question in terms of liberal America versus Protestant America, and suggests that within Americans a constant tension or battle ensued trying to balance successfully the demands of self-interest with the requirements of the golden rule of selflessness. He argues, correctly, that political and economic historians' use of the findings of religious historians has not been as fruitful as it could be. He suggests that historians should seek the equipoise early Americans achieved in order to reconcile conflicting impulses and ideals, and he intimates that out of this battle came the early embrace of pragmatism. Instead of focusing entirely on group conflict, scholars might look at the internal conflict individuals had with these dissonant ideals (Lockean liberalism *v.* Christianity) and how different actors resolved them; Davenport specifically points to various economic publicists and theologians. Of course one important possibility should be mentioned: despite our infatuation with the market revolution, maybe the rise of a market economy was not strong enough yet to shake basic Christian tenets, and that was why the real reaction to a market society came at the end of the nineteenth century, not at its middle.

However one looks upon wealth in the economic sense, the future studies of political economy of the early republic should provide more than its share of intellectual treasures.

Was Called Freedom: Evangelicalism, Proslavery, and the Causes of the Civil War (Lexington, 2002).

24. According to Athol Fitzgibbons, British theologians criticized Adam Smith well into the nineteenth century for proposing the wrong type of morality. If that be so, it would seem that there should be more friction between the American clergy and the rise of the market than American historians have found. See the intriguing account of Adam Smith's economics and ethics in Athol Fitzgibbons, *Adam Smith's System of Liberty, Wealth, and Virtue: The Moral and Political Foundations of the Wealth of Nations* (Oxford, UK, 1995), 150–51.

PART III

Interactive Landscapes

... embracing those aspects of environmental history that expose the interactions of human beings with climate, plants, animals, and germs.

TED STEINBERG, CHAIR

Environmental history is surging in both interest and importance, driven by the twin forces of extraordinary work by a generation of western historians and also the rising interest of colonial and early republic scholars in the wake of William Cronon's enormously successful Changes in the Land *(1983). Theodore Steinberg stands as one of the leading voices in the environmental history community, and one of the leading scholars whose work is NOT primarily anchored in the western United States. With powerful studies of New England water, natural disasters, and a new survey textbook notched on his word processor, Ted seemed like the ideal person to gather for our benefit a team of specialists whose work focuses on the environment and its place in the early United States. Environmental history being unavoidable place-specific, he chose to recruit contributors according to a regional template: Brian Donahue for New England, Mart Stewart for the antebellum South, Conevery Valenčius for the early West (that is, the humid antebellum frontiers before John Muir became famous or Walter Webb introduced the six-gun, barbed-wire, and windmill formula for understanding frontier history). What follows are three provocative essays and Steinberg's summary reflections on what may prove to be one of the more open and promising areas of study in the decade or two ahead.*

Environmental Stewardship and Decline in Old New England

BRIAN DONAHUE

In March of 1845, Henry Thoreau went up to the woods and cut down six pine trees, framing the house where he would write the first draft of *Walden*, published in 1854. Thoreau's sojourn at the pond marks the symbolic turning point in American environmental history. The frontier had long passed Concord. Commercial agriculture had driven the forest to its low ebb, a mere 11 percent of the landscape. The railroad, which beat Thoreau to the pond by a few months, embodied the industrial revolution that was transforming New England and opening the entire continent to the rapid extraction of natural resources. Northern farmers had burst out of the forest onto the fertile prairies, the cotton empire was sweeping across the South, and the Mexican War was setting the stage for a full assault on the riches of the West. *Walden* appeared just as American industrial capitalism was emerging from its agrarian birthplace in the Northeast and hitting its continental stride.

At this moment, Thoreau launched an environmental counter-movement by "speaking a word for nature," as he put it in "Walking." He was not alone. Also raising the alarm was George Perkins Marsh, who in his 1847 Address to the Rutland County Agricultural Society warned that agricultural civilization was fully capable of degrading forests, soils, waterways, and climate, and that even young Vermont was already witnessing such improvident waste. And so Marsh and Thoreau, utilitarian

Brian Donahue is Associate Professor of American Environmental Studies on the Jack Meyerhoff Foundation at Brandeis University. He is the author of *Reclaiming the Commons: Community Farms and Forests in A New England Town* (1999), and *The Great Meadow: Farmers and the Land in Colonial Concord* (2004).

and Romantic, led on to Pinchot and Muir and the modern conservation movement that has labored to restrain industrial capitalism's exploitation of nature.

That is the grand narrative of environmental history: pristine (or Native) natural harmony, overturned by frontier exploitation and impoverishment of nature, engendering an ongoing struggle (and symbiosis) between mature capitalism and rising conservation consciousness. Richard Judd has called this the western synthesis because it looks back from the monumental twentieth-century battles over the landscape of the West.[1] New England provides the prelude for this larger national drama. William Cronon began his seminal *Changes in the Land* at Walden Pond with Thoreau, surveying the diminished landscape that had resulted from the encounter between Europeans and the first American frontier, the East. Environmental decline to this point was not so dramatic as what would shortly follow, given the initially small European population and the lack of industrial tools, but there was little doubt about the outcome—from the beginning, the changes were for the worse. For Cronon, the essential change was from the Native system of usufruct land rights to the newcomers' system of private property embedded in a market economy. Commodification of the land and its wildlife, vegetation, soil, and water, led decisively to degradation.[2]

Carolyn Merchant offered an important complication to Cronon's narrative, introducing the idea of not one but two "ecological revolutions," colonial and capitalist, in the two centuries leading up to Marsh and Thoreau. She thus aligned New England environmental history with the prevailing theory of a market revolution in the early republic. A patriarchal ecological regime expanded until it encountered a demographic contradiction between its requirement for large families and the requirement of its extensive, exhausting agriculture for fresh land. In response to this crisis and with the full emergence of a market economy, farming intensified and became more specialized and productive, but even more alienated from nature and destructive of the environment. Theodore Steinberg and John Cumbler carried the story further into nineteenth-

---

1. Richard W. Judd, "Writing Environmental History from East to West," in Ben A. Minteer and Robert E. Manning, eds., *Reconstructing Conservation: Finding Common Ground* (Washington, DC, 2003).

2. William Cronon, *Changes in the Land: Indians, Colonists, and the Ecology of New England* (New York, 1983).

century industrialization and urbanization, charting the control of New England waterways by an emerging capitalist elite. With the market revolution came the legal and political power to undermine the older agrarian order, impose new depths of degradation, and frustrate early efforts for environmental reform. All these works essentially agree: the development of a market economy in America led to environmental decline, which led to the difficult birth of conservation.[3]

I am a confirmed declensionist. The fundamental questions posed by this body of work still animate me: what impact did the arrival of Europeans with their expanding market economy have on America, did economic growth cause environmental degradation, what has been done about it, what can be done about it? I remain convinced that on the whole, the rise of capitalism has been the driving force behind environmental decline in America. But what is environmental decline, and when and why did it begin? There are problems with the New England chapter in this grand narrative that have to do with depth of time and definition of terms. My own work on Concord suggests some new ways of getting at these problems, but because it is only one study of one small place, it opens many more questions than it alone can answer.

First, time: from when William Bradford confronted the howling wilderness in Plymouth until Henry Thoreau finally spoke up for wildness in Concord, over two centuries had passed—considerably more time than has elapsed since. Many of the same families had inhabited Concord throughout that entire period, quite a few of them working the same pieces of land. Seven generations is a long time to go on ravaging a farm—or to degrade it twice, first as extensive patriarchs and then again as intensive entrepreneurs. Perhaps there is more to this story than a long, uninterrupted slide from wilderness to wasted land.

Second, terms: when we say that the land was degraded, what do we mean? Thoreau and Marsh accused their farming neighbors of being improvident and wasteful: were they? How do we know? Removal of the forest may be degradation of one kind, but how are we to evaluate the ecological health of the agrarian landscape that replaced it? These are

---

3. Carolyn Merchant, *Ecological Revolutions: Nature, Gender and Science in New England* (Chapel Hill, 1989); Theodore Steinberg, *Nature Incorporated: Industrialization and the Waters of New England* (New York, 1991); John T. Cumbler, *Reasonable Use: The People, the Environment, and the State, New England, 1790–1930* (New York, 2001).

two separate (though perhaps overlapping) problems, but environmental historians using a simple wilderness or native standard of ecological fitness frequently conflate them. If by environmental degradation we simply mean that the forest of New England was cut down and converted to farmland, and by ecological recovery we simply mean that farmland was then abandoned and the forest grew back, we don't have much of a story—especially since that "recovery" came at the expense of new regions supplying the same resources—places like the Dust Bowl. Can we demonstrate more precisely when and how New Englanders overstepped the sustainable limits of their land, and can we explicate the tension between the forces that drove them to exploit and those that constrained them to conserve?

In recent years provocative work has begun to appear suggesting that the ideal of stewardship did not begin with Thoreau and Marsh, but had deeper roots. In *Larding the Lean Earth*, Steven Stoll locates the ground that nourished Marsh. Between 1820 and 1850, in the historical moment between the market revolution and the industrial revolution, "improvers" promoted an agriculture of permanence in the East. They decried profligacy, waste, and headlong removal to the West, and attacked farming that cleared too much forest and exhausted the soil. As Stoll explains, this oddly conservative progressive movement could not overcome the lure of cheap, fertile land on the frontier, nor could its labor-intensive methods compete with new, more efficient scientific and industrial tools ranging from guano to the reaper. Its moment passed, but not before preparing the way for the conservation movement to follow.[4]

Stoll's treatment of the literature of agricultural improvement cries out for investigation into what was happening on the ground. Were there any farmers in the Northeast who practiced anything like what the improvers recommended, and what did it mean to the land? Agricultural and economic historians have explored this to some extent, but not from a detailed, ecological point of view. Stoll depicts the "agricultural revolution" (which featured clover rotations, manure recycling, and drainage) as a novel philosophy imported from England by intellectuals and gentleman farmers, who then faced the difficulty of imposing it upon a recalcitrant agrarian populace. Historians have largely accepted the improvers' claim

---

4. Steven Stoll, *Larding the Lean Earth: Soil and Society in Nineteenth-Century America* (New York, 2002).

that nothing like this had ever been tried in America—that husbandry during the colonial era was always the crude, extensive, slash-and-burn soil scratching of the frontier. Was it? How can we find out what ordinary farmers were really doing, beyond taking the word of those who denigrated them?

Richard Judd's work on northern New England points toward deeper agrarian roots for stewardship than the improvers. According to Judd, the culture of common farmers included a moral imperative to create a harmonious rural world—nature surely was given by the Creator for human use and domination, but it also required care. As their own aggressive drive to clear and improve the land clashed with larger-scale industrial exploitation of forests and fisheries, rural people helped shape the conservation movement of the late-nineteenth century to match their vision of an ordained, balanced landscape. Conservation was not simply an invention of an urban elite, imposed on a crudely materialistic countryside. Although Judd does not much address the colonial period, his work implies that agrarian culture arrived in America with embedded principles of stewardship, and that those principles survived.[5]

I think they did. The grand environmental history narrative works better if we begin with the more nuanced hypothesis that a system of resource conservation at the community level was built into traditional agrarian society, which then had to adapt itself to the rise of a market economy. A reasonably balanced integration of cropland, pasture, livestock, woodland, and water had been necessary to the long survival of this society in Europe. Such a complex system required a high degree of understanding and skill, at both the farmstead and the community, landscape level. Its European record was far from perfect—it was not terribly productive by later standards, and it had difficulty conserving woodland in the face of expanding cropland and pasture. It suffered from an intractable, occasionally disastrous contradiction between the advantages of rearing a large supply of family labor and the limited supply of land. This European agrarian system was brought to America wherever people settled in communities—it was not immediately replaced with an atomized, individualistic rush to the frontier. It had to be modified to work on this side of the Atlantic but not very much, because northeastern

---

5. Richard W. Judd, *Common Lands, Common People: The Origins of Conservation in Northern New England* (Cambridge, MA, 1997).

America is more similar to Western Europe than it is different. In Concord, which I have investigated in some detail, a successful adaptation was accomplished within two or three generations. The people who practiced it had a term for this diverse system of land use: they called it husbandry.

The tradition of husbandry and the revolutionary force of nascent market capitalism arrived in America together. From that day to this they have co-existed in complex tension within American agrarian society, with varying results in different places and times. In colonial New England, the social and ecological realities of small rural communities with only tenuous links to outside markets greatly constrained pure market calculus. In Concord, families occupied the same farms for generations, even as surplus children were dispatched to frontier towns. The land was not exhausted. Carefully conserved manure, derived from hay grown on low-lying meadows with intricate water-management systems, maintained the fertility of the tilled land. Adequate woodland was necessary not only to building and heating homes but also to the local artisan economy—the coopers, wheelwrights, blacksmiths, and tanners—and so woodland appears to have held steady between 25 and 40 percent of the landscape from about 1750 to 1825, in a town that was straining at the demographic seams. The slow but steady economic growth that marked colonial New England would not have been possible had husbandmen simply run out the land and moved on. Population growth brought Concord to fullness and stress by 1750, but not to exhaustion and decline.[6]

The ecological limits that bounded such local economies were demolished by the market revolution. This transformation was not exogenous to American agrarian society but followed the release of commercial drives bound up within it, which finally gained commanding economic and political power. One result of the shift to more commercial, specialized farming was a rise in agricultural productivity, but this was often underwritten—and soon undermined—by environmental degradation. Any northeastern farmer who sought to improve upon the tradition of manure-based mixed husbandry by adopting legume-based convertible husbandry had to do so in an environment of rapidly expanding national agricultural production. The time-honored observation that land in

6. Brian Donahue, *The Great Meadow: Farmers and the Land in Colonial Concord* (New Haven, 2004).

America was abundant while labor was scarce may have had *some* significance when agrarian life revolved around local subsistence, but took on *overwhelming* significance when it was organized to supply larger markets.

Market connections drove a more extensive, exploitative approach to farming not only on the frontier, but also in many adjusting settled regions. New England, for example, saw a spectacular burst of land clearing—famously for sheep and wool upcountry, but also for beef and dairy cattle in the older districts. Concord, which had been fully settled for generations, suddenly cut down most of its remaining forest in the second quarter of the nineteenth century. Deforestation reached a point where streamflow was seriously affected, and the upland pastures and hayfields that replaced the forest were quickly depleted of nutrients and then overgrown with brush.[7] This was the environmental crisis that Thoreau and Marsh confronted, and it had little to do with the survival of old-fashioned, slovenly farming habits. It had much to do with liberation from the chafing limits built into traditional husbandry, and with the great difficulty of fully enacting an improved, sustainable convertible husbandry given the economic reality of the new commercial environment. It was the direct result of the market revolution.

The agrarian tradition of stewardship did not die. American farmers have always struggled to reconcile the allure of commercial farming with a compelling desire (and community expectations) to husband both their own land and the wider countryside. But the notion promoted by the early nineteenth-century improvers and by virtually all American agricultural institutions ever since—that ecological health and profitability would go hand in hand—has proven to be cruelly deceptive at most times and places. During the early republic this was not a simple story of exogenous capitalism transforming traditional agrarian society, or of the failed attempt of an elite to impose novel improvements (and later, a conservation ethic) on a mass of backwards farmers. It was the decisive moment in an internal conflict between habits of stewardship embedded in agrarian mixed husbandry, and a drive for material success that has been firmly rooted in most Americans from Jamestown and Plymouth on.

---

7. Brian Donahue, "'Dammed at Both Ends and Cursed in the Middle': The 'Flowage' of the Concord River Meadows, 1798–1862," *Environmental Review*, 13 (1989).

How did this tension play out at various places and times? Were there normative patterns of husbandry, forest use, and water management within distinct regions, and were they exploitative or sustainable? How did they change as farmers and artisans became more engaged with commodity production for outside markets? Was land being worn out, or husbanded for generations? One way to get at these patterns of land use is to take the information contained in account books, tax valuations, census returns, deeds, and probated estates, and map it across representative chunks of countryside. In doing this historians can work closely with historical ecologists capable of conducting field studies of changes in geomorphology, soil, and vegetation within the same landscape. This will give a harder edge to our estimations of environmental degradation and sustainability—though these terms will always remain somewhat soft. Wherever possible, those whose business is to understand changes should work alongside those whose business is to understand the land.

The first agenda of environmental history, which was to explain the impact of the market economy on the American landscape, is not yet finished. The habit of degrading land runs very deep in American economic culture, and it still needs to be acknowledged, confronted, and restrained. That is what gives the existing body of New England environmental history its compelling moral force. But the habit of stewardship runs deep, too. To the extent that there was an agrarian sense of stewardship that preceded and survived the market revolution, that is a source of hope. To the extent that such stewardship was flawed or inadequate, that is a source of instruction. Conservation was not simply an invention of an affluent, post-industrial elite, or part of a pristine native world now irretrievably lost. It has been a vital, though beleaguered presence throughout the development of American culture. As Henry Thoreau reminds us, "husbandry was once a sacred art."

Re-Greening the South and Southernizing the Rest

MART A. STEWART

In 1759, not long after he was appointed the first governor of the relatively new colony of Georgia, Henry Ellis, who went about the streets of the capital under an umbrella with a thermometer suspended from it, wrote to the folks back home in London that the inhabitants of Savannah "breathe a hotter air than any other people on the face of the earth."[1] His calculation of temperature was a dialogue between instrument and body, which factored in prominently his own discomfort and engaged in a hyperbole that participated in a larger projection about the climate of Savannah's latitude. Ellis returned to England soon after, but for English settlers in Virginia, the Carolinas, Georgia, and later, Florida, the South was, for part of the year anyway, a distinctively near-tropical land. Historians have long acknowledged that the southern environment was different—that Native Americans lived differently on the land in the southern regions than elsewhere in North America, and that the process of adaptation, or "seasoning," as it was called by early setters—was more complicated for Europeans in southeastern North America than in New

---

Mart Stewart is Professor of History and Affiliate Professor at Huxley College of the Environment at Western Washington University and author of *"What Nature Suffers to Groe": Life, Labor, and Landscape on the Georgia Coast, 1680–1920* (1996). He is currently working on a cultural history of climate in America.

1. Henry Ellis, "An Account of the Heat of the Weather in Georgia," *London Magazine*, Mar. 1759, 371. Conevery Bolton Valenčius, *The Health of the Country: How American Settlers Understood Themselves and Their Land* (New York, 2002), convincingly demonstrates that physical environments were more significantly measured by intimate exchanges between bodies and airs, waters, and soils than by observations with instruments by early Americans. Ellis took measurements, but was ultimately driven to return to England by what he breathed.

England. Part of this region, along the Atlantic and Gulf coasts especially, in environmental terms resembled the Caribbean or West Africa
more than Europe. For many European organisms, including human beings (whether with thermometer or not), the South was not a neo-
Europe. Even those that thrived in southern environments did so in a
different way than in other parts of North America.[2]

It was not quite a neo-Africa, either. Organisms from Africa and Europe met in the environmental circumstances of the South to create much
of what was distinctive about the South: open-range cattle raising, a fear
of fevers, wet-culture rice production, and the other long-season crops
such as sugar, tobacco, and "king cotton." The literature on southern
agriculture and labor systems, on diseases and on southern medicine,
and on cattle herding practices in the South, is vast, but much of it still
does not take into account the intimate—breathing—relationship human
and other organisms had with the climate, soils, and waters that they
sought to inhabit. Nor does existing scholarship accomplish a ground-
level analysis of the environments that produced the South. Much of the
literature about agriculture, disease, and other subjects related to the
South in fact has extracted its subject from that which is most crucial to
understanding it: the contextual relationship of organisms to the physical
environments. Recovering how humans *understood* these relationships is
also important. As Robert Weir advised twenty years ago in his fine
history of colonial South Carolina, early settlers paid remarkable attention "to details which only a few individuals would now notice, such as
the direction of the prevailing winds, the height of the tides, and the
consistency of the soil. These observations suggest something which
should be obvious but is frequently overlooked in a period of technological and scientific hubris. During the seventeenth and eighteenth centu-

---

2. On "Neo-Europes," see Alfred W. Crosby, *Ecological Imperialism and the
Biological Expansion of Europe, 900–1900* (Cambridge, UK, 1986), *passim*. On
the relationship between the physical environments of the southern low country
and West Indies (such as Barbados) and West Africa, see Peter Wood, *Black
Majority: Negroes in Colonial South Carolina from 1670 through the Stono Rebellion* (New York, 1974), 13–94; Daniel Littlefield, *Rice and Slaves: Ethnicity and
the Slave Trade in Colonial South Carolina* (Baton Rouge, 1981), 84–92; Mart A.
Stewart, *"What Nature Suffers to Groe": Life, Labor, and Landscape on the Georgia Coast, 1680–1920* (Athens, GA, 1996), 138–50; and Judith Carney, *Black
Rice: The African Origins of Rice Cultivation in the Americas* (Cambridge, MA,
2001).

ries, everyone, even the most wealthy and sophisticated, lived relatively close to nature." Simply, he noted, "physical geography made a difference."[3] How the physical environment, and the organisms that were a part of it, were perceived, experienced, and manipulated was crucial to how the South came to define itself.

Take the cattle raising industry that was so important to southern economies in the colonial period and well into the early republic. Historians have examined in almost excruciating detail the herding and branding practices of southern open-range cattle raising, the possible cultural antecedents (sources of "pre-adaptation") of herding practices, the evolution of "fence" and then "stock" laws for regulating the relationship between crops and stock, and (to a lesser extent) the economics of cattle raising. A few accounts of cattle raising have paid some attention to the ecological relationship between cattle, human settlements, and local environments; but most analyses of cattle raising focus on larger patterns and cultural practices. They have not looked at what colonial herders themselves had to take most seriously: the relationship between seasonal availability of feed and water on a scale large enough to support the large herds of cattle that were fundamental to the success of open-range cattle raising. Herders also had to consider the behavior of cattle themselves, who went feral when given the opportunity at an early age. The practices and conceptions of cattle that colonists brought with them shaped their understanding of their animals' behavior; but the impact of local ecosystems—what cattle could eat and where—was much more crucial to the development of the industry in each locale. And as controversial as the point may appear to be to historians, who after all are specialists in the study of humans, cattle too had agency.[4]

---

3. Robert M. Weir, *Colonial South Carolina: A History* (Millwood, NY, 1983), 35.

4. Several scholars, as part of a lively sometimes tumultuous debate that has important implications for environmental history, have argued that cattle-herding in South Carolina was merely the first application in North America of "pre-adapted" cultural baggage carried by certain ethnic groups, mainly West African and Celtic: Wood, *Black Majority,* 28–33; John Solomon Otto, "The Origins of Cattle-Ranching in Colonial South Carolina, 1670–1715," *South Carolina Historical Magazine,* 87 (1986): 117–24; Grady McWhiney and Forrest McDonald, "Celtic Origins of Southern Herding Practices," *Journal of Southern History,* 51 (1985): 165–82. Earlier studies that suggest Spanish (by way of the West Indies and Spanish Florida) origins for herds and herding practices include Lewis Cecil

How cattle herding was absorbed into deeply rooted ways of living on the land proved almost as important as how colonists modified, borrowed, or re-invented "pre-adapted" herding practices to meet local conditions. At first cattle were interlopers in Creek country, for example, but by the end of the eighteenth century most Creeks owned cattle and hogs. Cattle herds became an important indicator of wealth for the *métis* elite among the Creeks, and many Creeks possessed large enough herds that they qualified as ranchers more than farmers. Women also traded in cattle, in roles that complemented their traditional activities as traders. Creek herds were free-ranging, but Creek herders also required an adequate amount of browse within the larger areas within which their herds grazed. The relatively mild winters of the Southeast made it possible to keep cattle out on the open range year-round in the first place, but winter

---

Gray, *History of Agriculture in the Southern United States* (2 vols., Washington, DC, 1933), 1:140, 151, see also 78–79; and Frank Lawrence Owsley, *Plain Folk of the Old South* (Baton Rouge, 1949), 26–29. Terry Jordan and Matti Kaups claim that the influence of Savo-Karelian culture provided crucial components of "American backwoods" culture in general: *The American Backwoods Frontier: An Ethnic and Ecological Interpretation* (Baltimore, 1989). Several other studies examine southern cattle-raising in general in Virginia, South Carolina, Georgia, or Alabama, but the most comprehensive examination of cattle raising practices in the early South, which also argues that characteristic herding practices traveled a trail from South Carolina to Texas is Terry G. Jordan, *North American Cattle-Ranching Frontiers: Origins, Diffusion and Differentiation* (Albuquerque, 1993). Interpretations of the struggle over the stock laws differ greatly. See, for example, Steven Hahn, "Hunting, Fishing, and Foraging: Common Rights and Class Relations in the Postbellum South," *Radical History Review,* 26 (1982): 37–64; and Shawn E. Kantor, *Politics and Property Rights: The Closing of the Open Range in the Postbellum South* (Chicago, 1998). Virginia DeJohn Anderson's "Animals into the Wilderness" steps around the debate about "pre-adaptation" by simply ignoring the literature and also by focusing on a colony more or less off the trail: Virginia. She adds to our understanding of cattle behavior in the southern colonies—how cattle had agency—as well as the perceptions and practices of the colonists who sought to manage and use them: Anderson, "Animals into the Wilderness: The Development of Livestock Husbandry in the Seventeenth-Century Chesapeake," *William and Mary Quarterly,* 59 (2002): 377–408. An earlier study that looks at a colony that *was* on the trail, Georgia, and that examines the behavior of cattle and local ecological conditions as well as the development of institutions and cultural structures for managing cattle raising within the colony, is: Mart Stewart, "Whether Wast, Deodand or Estray?": Cattle, Culture, and the Environment in Early Georgia, *Agricultural History,* 65 (Summer, 1991): 1–28.

feed was always a problem. Southern forests and savannah were rank with vegetation, and quite a bit of it was green in the winter, but little of this vegetation provided enough digestible protein to keep cattle alive in the winter. River reed cane, which remained succulent and green throughout the winter months and which provided both cover and feed for cattle and hogs, was essential to the Creek range, as it was to southern cattle herding everywhere. The fate of cattle herding in Creek country depended on the presence of large brakes of river cane in which cattle could keep themselves alive during the winter. Cane is a resilient plant and even thrives when brakes are disrupted or burned. But cattle tend to "patch graze"—they congregate and feed as a group. In canebrakes, this compacted the soil, which in turn inhibited new growth in the brakes, at the same time that the hungry stock stripped the cane of leaves. When hogs fed on the cane as well, they rooted out new cane shoots, which killed the plants. By the beginning of the nineteenth century, over-grazing had begun to destroy the canebrakes in Creek country. And though other factors affected the valuable cattle industry of the Creeks, overgrazing and the need to disperse to exploit better the range resources that were available in Creek country may have been important in changes in settlement patterns among the Creeks in the early nineteenth cen-tury—as they separated from central towns and scattered in smaller set-tlements and finally farmsteads throughout the countryside. Whether removal to farmsteads compromised matrilines, multi-family households, and communal farming practices and encouraged the development of patriarchal nuclear families requires more investigation. But in part be-cause of the changing relationship of cattle and cane in Creek country, Creek farming and ranching had by the early nineteenth century begun to look much like white frontier farming.[5]

---

5. Acknowledging that local conditions and adaptations were as least as impor-tant as "pre-adaptation" and "cultural hearths" to the history of southern cattle raising does not make an explanation that is "self-contradictory." Terry Jordan's *North American Cattle-Ranching Frontiers* (177) is unnecessarily combative on this point, as it appears in "Whether Wast, Deodand, or Estray?"; his study on the whole in any case attends to both "adaptation" and "pre-adaptation." For those who were actually doing the herding, what they found on the ground for their cattle and by way of their cattle was of more immediate importance than where their herding practices came from, and much more attention needs to be paid to discrete local ecological and cultural factors in the relationship between cattle and humans in the South—this is my point in "Whether Wast," and here.

Uncultivated parts of the South continued to provide both sustenance and social landscapes for antebellum southerners. Southerners of all kinds continued to raise cattle and hogs in the uncultivated spaces of the region until late in the nineteenth century when stock laws forced them to fence livestock in rather than out. In some locales open range herding continued to be an important economic activity until well into the twentieth century. Hunting and fishing supplemented livelihoods garnered from cultivation and raising livestock, and the open lands of the South remained important for these. Uncultivated "nature" also provided both highway and sanctuary to African Americans who were slaves on the farms and plantations of the South. Slaves who sought either to escape— even if just for a while—the harsh constraints of plantation life, or who traveled to other plantations to visit family, traveled or hid out off the roads. *Grand marronage*, as the French called it in Louisiana, was not common in the South, but also it was not unknown. More common was the *petit marronage* engaged in by slaves who sought temporary respite from a particularly repressive master or overseer or who wanted to visit with family on other plantations. Such periods of truancy to visit kinfolk dramatically improved the quality of family relations. The physical environment off the plantation, then, was an intricate part of the elaborate geography of kinship in the antebellum South.[6]

Uncultivated land—about 80 percent of the land on the eve of the Civil War—was never truly vacant, never really "out there" for southerners, in a way that fostered ideas about "wildness." The open places of the South were not as wild as open places elsewhere in the United States. No Puritan communities demonized the "wild" in the first place, and no Henry David Thoreau tried to make it sublime. In any case Thoreau's ideas would not likely have taken root in a region where environmental

---

For Creek herding practices, see Robbie Ethridge, *Creek Country: The Creek Indians and Their World* (Chapel Hill, 2003), 160–74.

6. Stewart, *"Whether Wast, Deodand or Stray,"* chaps. 3 and 4, *passim*; Gwendolyn Midlo Hall, *Africans in Colonial Louisiana: The Development of Afro-Creole Culture in the Eighteenth Century* (Baton Rouge, 1992), 201–36; Gilbert C. Din, *Spaniards, Planters, and Slaves: The Spanish Regulation of Slavery in Louisiana, 1763-1803* (College Station, TX, 1999), 19–34. Philip Morgan explains how recurrent patterns of running away by eighteenth-century slaves were connected to patterns of visiting, and even does the math: *Slave Counterpoint: Black Culture in the Eighteenth-Century Chesapeake and Lowcountry* (Chapel Hill, 1998), 524–30.

sensibilities have always been deeply agrarian—or at least, pastoral. "Wilderness," even where it was identified, was usually teeming with cattle and hogs, or hunters and fishermen. Or it was a place to run to, in efforts to escape extreme hardship or consolidate family connections. For African Americans who were slaves, the wilderness made quite a different impression than it made on Thoreau. Slaves plunged into the swamps not to find the world but to lose it. In the wilderness they found each other rather than themselves. Conservation and environmental thought consequently tapped different sources in the South than in other regions; southerners always assumed that environments conserved would also always be environments inhabited.

Conservation emerged not from an accommodation with wildness or wilderness and an eventual appreciation of it, nor out of fear of dwindling "natural resources," but out of concerns about the declining fertility of southern soils and the competitive advantage of the southern economy in a nation where the South had begun to feel embattled. In other words, in the antebellum South, conservation meant agricultural improvement. Planters especially were concerned about soil exhaustion in the older regions; the better educated in Virginia, South Carolina, and Georgia began to argue for changes in farming methods that would preserve or restore fertility, rather than mine it to death and then escape to fresh lands in the West. Such improvers "assumed that they had to be what one called, 'good stewards,' because the land was vulnerable and human beings had to work carefully within its limitations," explains Joan Cashin. Improving planters developed elaborate methods for manuring, rotating crops, resting arable land, and most famously, excavating and amending soils with marl. Their efforts did not really accomplish reform, and in the end the rhetoric of agricultural reform in the South produced a good deal more air than improvement. But at the heart of the efforts by improving planters to recover the fertility of the older agricultural regions of the South was an ecological sensibility. "Long before the science of ecology," Steven Stoll explains, "they came closer than anyone before them to a full (if sometimes inaccurate) sense of interdependence among organisms and interconnectedness in nature generally."[7]

---

7. Joan E. Cashin, "Landscape and Memory in Antebellum Virginia," *Virginia Magazine of History and Biography,* 102 (Oct. 1994): 483. See also Jack Temple Kirby, "Virginia's Environmental History: A Prospectus," *Virginia Magazine of*

The history of conservation in the South, or of the agricultural improvement movement in the United States in general, is the history of failure. Farmers and planters who sought to retard the flight to fresh westward lands and to inspire a more intricate and intimate relationship between husbandman and land were not successful, and ecological sensibilities were overcome by economic and demographic forces. But just because this kind of conservation failed does not mean that it was not deeply important to the South—a region that remained profoundly agrarian until at least World War II and that has been, after all, as much conditioned and defined by defeat and failure as by success.

Much of the history of these early conservation efforts in the South remains to be written, and it needs to be more fully connected to efforts to improve the productivity of slaves and make the institution of slavery more palatable to critics in both regions. The agricultural improvement movement in the South cannot be separated from the social context in which it took place, nor extracted from the political economy that shaped it. Paternalists all, improving planters sought to improve slave management techniques. While they advocated a more respectful attitude toward the land that gave them their livelihoods, they also argued for the humanity of slaves and a more humane treatment of the human property that also sustained them, modeling their role after that of the firm but understanding father toward his children.

Indeed, the shifting perceptions of slaves by their owners—who regarded them more as working pets than as humans—should also be studied more closely as part of a larger effort to discern the sources of conservation values in the South. Ideas about conserving nature were intricately connected to ideas about improving the management of slaves. They talked about modes of improvement with the same intensive detachment that they talked about labor in the fields, as if they themselves accomplished it. The enormous labors contributed by their slaves—in the work of marling and manuring as well as in the traditional tasks of southern agriculture—were simply invisible to them. Planters who sought

History and Biography, 99 (1991); Mart A. Stewart, *"What Nature Suffers to Groe,"* chap. 4; Jack Temple Kirby, *Poquosin: A Study of Rural Landscape and Society* (Chapel Hill, 1995), *passim*; and especially Steven Stoll, *Larding the Lean Earth: Soil and Society in Nineteenth-Century America* (New York, 2002), 120–68 (quotation at 167).

to improve the lots of both land and slaves were green paternalists, not husbandmen.[8]

Some historians have argued that this was the problem with the South: the relative value of labor to land prevented agricultural reform from accomplishing very much.[9] The development of conservation thought in nineteenth-century America and changing perceptions of African-American slaves were linked, no matter how perversely. Such conservative attitudes, bound up with a set of ideas about race that have been discredited entirely, may seem less interesting to historians who traditionally have favored more liberal shades of green. But that, of course, is judging the past by the standards of the present, and it also does not acknowledge the fact that environmental thought in the South may have important connections with the agrarian tradition.

Black southerners also created a conservation ethos, and this has only begun to be examined. African-American environmental values in the South have their roots in the history of slavery. A close attention to the land, cultivated and uncultivated, was also a form of resistance, and not just by running away. African Americans who knew where to find game or fish, who gathered wild foods to supplement their rations, or who planted patches of rice or corn in the woods, expressed an attention to the land that was discreet and nuanced, even while it derived from their status as slaves. How this ethos was further shaped by the experience of emancipation and the development of postbellum patterns of agriculture and segregation and later by contact with progressive ideas about agricultural improvement needs to be examined more fully, but it is a story that began in the early South.

Soil exhaustion and the political economy of the plantation are more important to an understanding of landscapes in the early South than questions about wilderness and sensibilities forged by an experience (or perception) of uninhabited nature. Southern life was intimately entwined with the environment with or without a thermometer to mediate it; but the peculiar American conceit about a "wilderness" or "pristine nature,"

---

8. For the history of the changing perceptions of slaves by masters, from a view that saw them as less savage and more "human," but that still likened them to domestic animals and to "pets," see Karl Jacoby, "Slaves by Nature? Domestic Animals and Human Slaves," *Slavery and Abolition,* 15 (1994): 89–99. For "green paternalism," see Stewart, *"What Nature Suffers to Groe,"* 186–88.

9. See Stoll, *Larding the Lean Earth,* 158.

that was unpeopled and even outside of history has never taken a strong hold in the South.

In this way the environmental history of the South looks a lot like the environmental history of just about everywhere else in the world outside of the United States. Recently a prominent American historian claimed that in regard to environmental history, the South was "again the backward region." As the environmental history of the South is exposed and recovered, and historians explain more fully the intimate relationship between agriculture, agrarian and pastoral sensibilities, the history of slavery, and the physical environment of the South, we may discover that the South is instead out in front, waiting for the rest of America to catch up. Environmental historians of other regions in the United States, or indeed environmentalists in general who are seeking a usable past, may once again find a great deal to learn from historians of the South.[10]

---

10. In a recent essay, Richard Judd argues from another region—New England—and observes that many of the basic questions that have driven discussions in environmental history really come out of the field's origins in the history of the West. See Richard W. Judd, "Writing Environmental History from East to West," in Ben A. Minteer and Robert E. Manning, eds., *Reconstructing Conservation: Finding Common Ground* (Washington, DC, 2003), 19–31. For the "backward region" characterization, see Otis Graham, "Again the Backward Region: Environmental History In and Of the American South," *Southern Cultures*, 6 (Summer 2000): 50–72. See also Mart Stewart, "Southern Environmental History," in John Boles, ed., *Blackwell Companion to the American South* (Malden, MA, 2002), 409–23.

Mudslides Make Good History

CONEVERY BOLTON VALENČIUS

Historians don't generally have much to do with the Big History Business of this country. Perhaps we should. Americans soak up documentaries, love to watch "historical" films, and have an authentic desire to understand more of our country's history. Sales of nobly elevating national histories are astonishing, or so it seems to those of us who write for the academic market. I am frustrated by what passes for history in much of our popular culture. My mother got so fed up with the History Channel's fascination with the Third Reich that she declared "No Nazis at Night" a household rule. Yet at the same time, I am inspired by the desire to learn more and see more and understand more about the past that I witness in bookstores, at megaplexes, and in my friends' living rooms. Those of us who think about history for a living, who teach and write about it for students and scholars, can do a better job connecting with this deeply-rooted historical passion. (Please, let us not leave it to Martin Scorsese, who would have us believe that the United States Navy responded to the draft riots of the Civil War by shelling lower Manhattan.) Furthermore, we can make these connections without sacrificing our hard-won insights into plural perspectives, multiple causality, and general complication in the worlds of the past.[1]

Luckily, environmental history offers excellent ways to write good his-

Conevery Bolton Valencius is a Senior Fellow at the Dibner Institute for the History of Science and Technology and author of *The Health of the Country: How American Settlers Understood Themselves and Their Land* (2002).

1. Martin Scorsese, *Gangs of New York*, Miramax Films, 2002. I greatly appreciate the comments of S. Charles Bolton, Brian Donahue, Nicholas B. King, Harold Cleveland May, Ted Steinberg, Mart Stewart, Matthew G. Valenčius, Robert T. Vinson, and students in my Spring 2004 seminar "Sagebrush and Suburb: Writing the Environmental History of the United States."

tory that engages public interest. The landscape, terrain, and human ecology of the American western states provide abundant material for work that will challenge, inform, and involve our neighbors as well as each other.

The American West has some colossally Big Stuff: big deserts, big mountains, big dams, big plains, big waves, big dust storms, big mansions. There's an epic quality to much of the weather and topography west of the Mississippi. Subtle detail can be crucial for historical insight, but largeness of scale can also be tremendously exciting. Big Stuff has innate drama, and much of it has inherently narrative qualities. Big Stuff also yields great visuals. Dramatic narrative and images capture people's imaginations and fire their curiosity. I think if we—that is, people who would use their hard-earned time to read an article like this—include more drama, narrative, and imagery in our work, we will end up writing stronger histories that advance our fields and also engage our fellow citizens.

I see four main themes through which western environmental history can help us do this. For the sake of alliteration (the kind of popular technique that works even if professional historians think it's kind of cheesy), I'm calling these Disease, Disaster, Desiccation, and Dystopia. In the coming years, I'd like to read more about each of these. Here's what I mean.

Start with disease. Bad bugs make good copy. Everyone likes reading about disease—the more loathsome, the better. This is why Richard Preston in his "Trilogy of Dark Biology" can move back and forth between historical journalism and fiction without losing any of his audience: his prose terrifies us, it fascinates us, and it makes us feel informed about our present-day world. Moreover, Elizabeth Fenn's recent *Pox Americana* demonstrates that excellent (and much-better-documented) history can get immense air-time in our popular culture when it is about something that we all fear, like smallpox. Disease and sickness have massive gross-out appeal. This paradox makes horror movies sell, and I think it can also expand the sales and readership of histories that embrace the sometimes unpleasant realities of the human form.[2]

---

2. Since Preston rarely includes any but the breeziest source citation, emphasis here is on *feeling* informed. Richard Preston, *The Hot Zone* (New York, 1994); *The Cobra Event: A Novel* (New York, 1997); and *The Demon in the Freezer: A True Story* (New York, 2002). Elizabeth Anne Fenn, *Pox Americana: The Great*

The search for health in various places reveals the complicated history of regional identity in this country. Emigrants to the West struggled to avoid "sickly" places and claim "healthy" ones. Yet as successive regions became defined as healthy with respect to illnesses like malaria or tuberculosis, the "healthful West" moved along at quite a good clip. In turn, health concerns influenced how generations of Americans shaped and engineered their Wests. Paying attention to the history of sickness and health can both reveal why we see region as we do and perhaps push us to question our early-twenty-first-century boundaries of region.[3]

To look at disease is to confront central themes in human history. Sickness and its consequences reveal social disparities and ethnic prejudice in all their ugly detail. Prevalent illnesses determine what groups win wars, plant farms, or get their languages spoken. Looking at the history of disease also forces us to acknowledge a dynamic and sometimes un-knowable "nature." Bacteria are no more static than human societies; diseases themselves evolve over time, growing in virulence or sputtering off into insignificance. Acknowledging such change can help keep us environmental historians honest about our ability to pin down too exactly any aspect of "nature" at a given time.[4]

Smallpox Epidemic, 1775–82 (New York, 2002), provides an enlightening contrast. On histories of the human form: as a press's editor once observed to me about Elliott West's excellent *Contested Plains*, "who wouldn't like a book where one chapter starts with a book about farting?" Elliott West, *The Contested Plains: Indians, Goldseekers, and the Rush to Colorado* (Lawrence, KS, 1998), chap. 9.

3. On health and place, see Gregg Mitman, Michelle Murphy, and Christopher Sellars, eds., *Landscapes of Exposure, Osiris,* 19 (Winter 2004); Billy M. Jones, *Health-Seekers in the Southwest, 1817–1900* (Norman, 1967); Gregg Mitman, "Hay Fever Holiday: Health, Leisure, and Place in Gilded-Age America," *Bulletin of the History of Medicine,* 77 (Fall 2003): 600–35; Sheila M. Rothman, *Living in the Shadow of Death: Tuberculosis and the Social Experience of Illness in American History* (New York, 1994); Conevery Bolton Valenčius, *The Health of the Country: How American Settlers Understood Themselves and Their Land* (New York, 2002). Recent work on health and region in the United States includes Martha L. Hildreth and Bruce T. Moran, eds., *Disease and Medical Care in the Mountain West: Essays on Region, History, and Practice* (Reno, 1998); and Margaret Humphreys, *Malaria: Poverty, Race, and Public Health in the United States* (Baltimore, 2001). On engineering and health concerns, see Linda Nash, "Finishing Nature: Harmonizing Bodies and Environments in Late-Nineteenth-Century California," *Environmental History,* 8 (2003): 25–52.

4. On ethnic conflicts and disease, see Alan M. Kraut, *Silent Travelers: Germs, Genes, and the "Immigrant Menace"* (New York, 1994). On evolution as a force

Second, consider disaster. Historians need to take more account of the "Weather Channel Effect": everyone wants to see a good tornado. Environmental history represents a way to take back some of the popular readership captured so thoroughly by military history and its sidekick, Great Men. Unlike other forms of cultural history, environmental history has the advantage of dealing with tangible—and thus inherently pictureable—things. Rather than shying away from this, we can involve the public by responding to the widespread interest in catastrophe.[5]

Cataclysm can reveal cracks in social structure as well as mountainsides. The American West has some especially good disasters: fires, floods, mudslides, earthquakes. To people reading contemporary newspapers, these concerns can sound quite recent—the problems of southern California movie stars—but these events helped shape the very early history of the West. In the winter of 1811-1812, for instance, what are now known as the New Madrid earthquakes rolled out east and south from the Missouri bootheel, leveling nearby forests, creating swampland and a sizable lake, changing the course of the Mississippi, waking up people in the Ohio Valley, shaking crockery on the East Coast, and badly frightening John James Audubon's horse. Close to the epicenter, damage was catastrophic: one village in what is now southeast Missouri was done in, and the thriving town of New Madrid was largely abandoned. For my current book, I am exploring the historical impact of these quakes, particularly their role in reinforcing American influence in a critical period in the Mississippi Valley. The tremors were centered on a trading and mining area that had long been the site of French/Native American interaction but would thereafter be little more than a way station for steamboats needing more cordwood. As with many (perhaps all?) environmental calamities, the New Madrid earthquakes appear to have done uneven harm to disparate communities, harming some but advantaging others, in historically lasting ways.[6]

---

in history, see Edmund Russell, "Evolutionary History: Prospectus for a New Field," *Environmental History*, 8 (2003): 204-28.

5. Recent literature on disaster includes Louis A. Perez Jr., *Winds of Change: Hurricanes and the Transformation of Nineteenth-Century Cuba* (Chapel Hill, 2001); Theodore Steinberg, *Acts of God: The Unnatural History of Natural Disaster in America* (New York, 2000); Simon Winchester, *Krakatoa: The Day the World Exploded: August 27, 1883* (New York, 2003).

6. Myron L. Fuller, *The New Madrid Earthquake* (1912; rep., Cape Girardeau, MO, 1958); James Lal Penick Jr., *The New Madrid Earthquakes* (1976; rev. ed., London, UK, 1981).

"Wild" fires that sweep across the western states grip us as a nation every couple of years, but we still have more people working on the average Civil War battle than on the history of western fire and its causes and consequences (Stephen Pyne may be indefatigable, but he can't carry a field alone). Paradoxically, those of us working in institutions that get massive public financing are almost completely uninvolved in great civic memorializations, many of which center on catastrophe. Historians can help bring structure and context to reflections on public disaster—and perhaps doing so might help us respond to the vast public hunger for commemoration that seems to exist in contemporary American society alongside profound and selective historical amnesia.[7]

Many disasters are not even remotely acts of God, as Ted Steinberg's recent book so well demonstrates. Human hands have created or helped along a number of catastrophes, from the Johnstown flood to the potential inundation of many of our coastal areas. Studying disaster helps us to see the complicated ways in which human beings have changed—as well as having been changed by—our environments.[8]

Calamities create gripping images on which historians can build. Nowadays, disasters are documented both by official sources and by crazy people with camcorders. Every time I roll my eyes at footage of another endangered house on an impossibly steep hillside or another line of palm trees bending in the latest hurricane, I try to remind myself that such visual images offer rich possibilities for responsible historical investigation—they could be used to convey insight, rather than sheer hype. If every book published in environmental history had about five times as many pictures as most now do, I think we'd see a lot more people also reading the text.

Disasters possess an innately Aristotelian structure: they have a beginning, a middle, and an end. It is easier to write narrative about events that unfold through time, and that's a help to historians for whom narrative seems like a cherry lollipop, awfully appealing but way too sweet and likely to leave us all sticky when we're ready to put it down. Our skepticism is indeed warranted. Books that call themselves histories but that tell a series of stories and nothing else are not good history. But

---

7. The latest installment in Stephen J. Pyne's "Cycle of Fire" is *Fire: A Brief History* (Seattle and London, 2001).

8. Steinberg, *Acts of God*.

histories that tell good stories nevertheless get read and remembered. Historians need to get over the notion that "a story" is something you read to small children. Perhaps writing about disasters is one way for us to use story-telling to create powerful history.

What about desiccation? Histories of western waters helped create the field of environmental history, and it would behoove us to stay watery. More precisely, we need more accounts of water and its *absence*. Worldwide lack of water and fights over water will, I fear, characterize our coming century. This environmental reality can help direct our attention to the centrality of water and aridity in making, using, and allocating past American landscapes. Good histories can tell us how the United States became a society where a twenty-minute-long private shower with filtered and chlorinated water is considered a daily right (if not obligation). I suspect that this will soon be regarded as a historical aberration along the lines of binding feet.[9]

Even rain-soaked Atlanta is having water scarcity troubles; much of the United States is beginning to experience the vanishing of the water we long have taken for granted. Since many of the bitterest fights in the western United States have been over scant water supplies, environmental history of the West has the potential to lead American historiography in grappling with worldwide concerns over lack of water. Looking at—perhaps looking *for*—water can help us draw much-needed links between U. S. history and the history of other countries and regions.[10]

Visual images may not seem as obvious a theme of this kind of topic, yet stories of water can present us with telling images—Dorothea Lange's photographs of Dust Bowl families against parched, blowing fields haunt viewers seventy years later. Such images present an alternative to conventional historical narratives in which only certain subjects are presented as worthy of being photographed. Too many "documentaries" consist of World War II footage loosely strung together by deep-voiced

---

9. Patricia Nelson Limerick, *Desert Passages: Encounters with the American Deserts* (Albuquerque, 1985); Marc Reisner, *Cadillac Desert: The American West and Its Disappearing Water* (New York, 1986); Donald Worster, *Rivers of Empire: Water, Aridity, and the Growth of the American West* (1985; rep., New York, 1992).

10. As in, for instance, Ian Tyrrell, *True Gardens of the Gods: Californian-Australian Environmental Reform, 1860–1930* (Berkeley, 1999).

narration. Keen environmental history can help use historical imagery as something other than a recycling project.[11]

Finally, consider dystopia. When I think of "environmental history of the American West," the image that comes to mind is not mountains, seashores, or sweeping grasslands, but a poster for the 1993 film *Falling Down*. Actor Michael Douglas appears in one of his average-guy-gets-tough roles. Holding a briefcase in one hand and a shotgun in the other, he stands against a backdrop of spray paint and distantly looming sky-scrapers. The poster offers a disturbing image of urban frustration and violence. It also reminds me that cities and places—*especially* in the American West—are products of imagination, hype, dreaming, and media, as well as of land grants, market roads, sewer systems, tax poli-cies, immigration restrictions, freeways, and so on.[12]

We need to understand spaces and places as the creation of our fears, hopes, and dreams. From Washington Irving to Charles Dickens to Jules Verne, nineteenth-century reporters on the American landscape under-stood the projections of utopia against which civic success and failure would play out. Environmental historians would do well to emulate our predecessors' respect for worlds of the imagination. "Dystopia" is too strong a term here (but the alliteration is nice); I don't mean to suggest that all of American experience of cities is characterized by Michael Douglas. Nonetheless, much of how cities are imagined does foretell apocalyptic futures, and that's important for how we understand the past.[13]

Looking at the perceptions of places, at the ways in which music and graffiti and boosterism and Fox News have woven important strands in the fabric of place, we can understand much about the American West, and especially about its cities. We might try to come to terms with Los Angeles, for instance, as a physical space *and* as the place of Tom Petty's

---

11. *Dorothea Lange: Photographs of a Lifetime* (Millerton, NY, 1982). The "Gallery" feature of the journal *Environmental History* highlights and discusses often off-beat visual images, making this point far better, of course, than I can in words.

12. Joel Schumacher, *Falling Down*, Warner Brothers, 1993.

13. Washington Irving, *The Western Journals of Washington Irving*, ed. J. F. McDermott (1873; rep., Norman, 1944); Charles Dickens, *Martin Chuzzlewit* (1844; rep., Hertfordshire, UK, 1994); Jules Verne, *Around the World in Eighty Days* (1873; rep., New York, 1988), 150.

wry laments and Mexican workers' pragmatic hopes. Dealing with L. A., as well as with border zones like San Diego or the conjoined twins of Brownsville and Matamoros, can push us into work that does not stop at the "medicine line" of borders on a map, even though government documents so regrettably do.[14]

Environments are created by murky combinations of physical and imaginative work. Recent environmental history by Michelle Murphy has established the "sick building" as a kind of space; Jennifer Price has defined the Nature Company as an expression of American ideas of nature. The 1990s fears of "emerging disease" reveal stories about places—jungled Africa, vulnerable jet hub cities—as well as about societies and their microorganisms. Looking at cultural imagination can lead us into environmental history that grapples with the full range of "environment."[15]

These exhortations and urgings leave out a great deal. What about race relations? munitions depots? federal land policies? Where are national parks and toxic waste sites? What of Native American use of land, not just in the past but up to the present day? And what about Alaska and Hawai'i, each fascinating in environmental terms in its own right? These and other questions don't fit into my broad conceptualizations, nor should they—the most interesting work in history often takes place in between categories. I offer my impatience with how we've dealt with disease, disaster, desiccation, and dystopia as an entry into unknown future terrain.

To reach ordinary people around us, to respond in more satisfying ways to the hunger for history that so many hucksters use to sell so much junk, environmental historians need to write better while remaining true to the principles of excellent historical scholarship. Embracing drama, drawing on narrative, and making better use of visual images are some of the tools we can use to bring our business into the public's in ways that will make us proud.

---

14. Love it or hate it, anyone dealing with these themes and this city has to wrestle with Mike Davis, *Ecology of Fear: Los Angeles and the Imagination of Disaster* (New York, 1998). "The Medicine Line" in Wallace Stegner, *Wolf Willow: A History, a Story, and a Memory of the Last Plains Frontier* (1955; rep., New York, 1966).

15. Michelle Murphy, "White Noise, Race, and the Privilege of Imperception at the U. S. Environmental Protection Agency," in Mitman, Murphy, and Sellars, eds., *Landscapes of Exposure*; Jennifer Price, *Flight Maps: Adventures with Nature in Modern America* (New York, 1999), chap. 4; Nicholas B. King, "The Scale Politics of Emerging Diseases," in Mitman, Murphy, and Sellars, eds., *Landscapes of Exposure*.

Down, Down, Down, No More
Environmental History Moves Beyond Declension

TED STEINBERG

There is a saying that I once heard that goes something like this: twenty years from now you will be the same person you are now. The only difference will be the people you get to know and the books you read along the way.

Twenty years ago I sat down with William Cronon's *Changes in the Land*, by all accounts today the seminal work in early American environmental history. I was already somewhat familiar with the community studies tradition practiced by social historians such as Philip Greven, Kenneth Lockridge, John Demos, and others. These historians produced an impressive body of literature that forever changed the way we viewed life in the period before 1800. Cronon's book, however, broke new ground—literally. The environment had never been more than a backdrop to these earlier social histories, but as John Demos has written recently: "*Changes in the Land* reversed all that. Following its publication, the environment would be much more than a stage—would become, indeed, an important actor in its own right. . . . The 'community' of community studies would never again look quite the same."[1]

Ted Steinberg is the author of *Down to Earth: Nature's Role in American History* (2002) and *Acts of God: The Unnatural History of Natural Disaster in America* (2000). His new book, *American Green: The Obsessive Quest for the Perfect Lawn*, is forthcoming.

1. William Cronon, *Changes in the Land: Indians, Colonists, and the Ecology of New England* (New York, 2003), xiii. Examples of the community studies tradition include, Philip J. Greven Jr., *Four Generations: Population, Land, and Family in Colonial Andover, Massachusetts* (Ithaca, 1970); Kenneth A. Lockridge, *A New England Town: The First Hundred Years, 1636-1736* (New York, 1970); and John Demos, *A Little Commonwealth: Family Life in Plymouth Colony* (New York, 1970).

There is no question that, from a historiographical standpoint, *Changes* constituted a radical departure from the earlier community studies tradition. To begin with, Cronon made the ecosystem, not the arbitrary town boundary, his locus of study. These ecosystems, Cronon argued, had a history every bit as important as the political and social history that unfolded within them. Indeed, environment and culture, he argued, existed in a "dialectical" relationship with each other. As he wrote: "Environment may initially shape the range of choices available to people at a given moment, but then culture reshapes environment in responding to those choices. The reshaped environment presents a new set of possibilities for cultural reproduction, thus setting up a new cycle of mutual determination."[2]

If such statements were not radical enough, the overall political message contained in the book seemed to me a very progressive one. Adopting a comparative approach, Cronon highlighted the important differences between how the Indians and the colonists related to the land: usufruct versus private property, subsistence strategies versus market relations, and so forth. In coming to grips with the driving forces behind the ecological changes he deduced in the book, Cronon was careful to point out that history is rarely the result of a single cause. Still, it is hard to read the book and not come away convinced that economic structures played the leading role in explaining the decline in trees and wildlife and the substitution of "a world of fields and fences" in their place. "Ultimately," Cronon wrote, "English property systems encouraged colonists to regard the products of the land—not to mention the land itself—as commodities, and so led them to orient a significant margin of their production toward commercial sale in the marketplace. . . . Capitalism and environmental degradation went hand in hand."[3]

Those last words were fighting words. After Demos reviewed the book in the *New York Times*, economic historian Robert Higgs wrote in to protest. He objected to what he termed the "antihumanism" and "present-mindedness" of environmental history. "This capitalism that the modern environmentalists hate so deeply is nothing more than the liberty of individual humans to express their own values as the supreme determinants of resource use," he wrote. And as for Cronon's claim that capi-

---

2. Cronon, *Changes in the Land.*, 13.
3. *Ibid.*, 161.

talism and ecological degradation went together, he remarked: "I wonder how he [Cronon] would have viewed the matter had he lived among those wresting a precarious livelihood from the rocky soils of New England two or three centuries ago."[4]

Cronon set out to chart the ecological changes that occurred as the Indian land-use regime gave way to one dominated by Europeans with their markets and private property. But he implied that, for the most part, the changes were overwhelmingly negative, a point that may have been reinforced by the book's cover, which shows a fence behind which appear a bunch of tree stumps. The book thus begs the question, what exactly do we mean by ecological degradation? It turns out that evaluating the ecological degradation (or health) of a landscape, as Brian Donahue points out, is infinitely more complicated than it seems at first glance, not least because even ecologists can't seem to agree on these matters.

Nevertheless, the changes in the land described in Cronon's book (whether they are ecologically negative or not) do seem to grow out of the economic imperatives associated with the rise of an alienated market in land and the increasing dominance of market relations. Certainly, the evidence Cronon marshaled points to that conclusion. The problem (which Cronon himself identified) lies in his approach: founded on comparing Indian interactions with the land to those of the Europeans who came after seems unavoidably deterministic. In other words, his conclusion about the relationship between capitalism and ecology was in part the product of his approach. *Changes in the Land* may well be, as Demos argues, "a foundational work."[5] It certainly has energized an entire generation of environmental historians; but it also contributed in fundamental ways to the field's emphasis on telling stories that centered on the environmental decline and fall of the American republic.

In fact, the relationship between market relations and environment is a good deal more complex than Cronon's work suggests. Brian Donahue, who calls himself "a confirmed declensionist," argues that the market economy's effect on ecological relations remains a vital and important

---

4. Letter to the editor, *New York Times*, June 17, 1984, sec. 7, 31; Demos's review can be found in "A New World of Fields and Fences," *ibid.*, May 20, 1984, sec. 7, 3.

5. Cronon, *Changes in the Land*, xi.

area of study. Yet he also notes that a lot of time elapsed between the two points on Cronon's time line—the world of the Puritans and that of Henry Thoreau. As he writes, "Seven generations is a long time to go on ravaging a farm—or to degrade it twice, first as extensive patriarchs and then again as intensive entrepreneurs." Cronon's two-point approach (New England before and after colonization) seems to lead us down a path of ecological implausibility.

Instead, it appears possible that the colonists, whom Cronon features in the book as ecological evildoers, may have had a little stewardship in their bones as well. The diverse agrarian form that New Englanders called "husbandry" involved the successful balancing of pasture, cropland, livestock populations, and woodland. In his microhistory of Concord, Massachusetts, Donahue finds that, by roughly the time of the American Revolution, demographic expansion had put significant stress on the community. Still, population growth did not lead, inevitably, to an ecological crisis. The system of husbandry in place was resilient enough to tolerate the stress of increasing numbers. Then the intervention of the market revolution seemed to push Concord over the ecological edge, though the tradition of stewardship did not by any means disappear among farmers in the nineteenth century.

The stewardship tradition persisted even in the face of market imperatives, as Sean Cadigan has pointed out in his work on the Newfoundland cod fishery (1815-1855). People there had a keen sense of customary rights of access to fishing grounds. When new technologies, involving large amounts of capital, entered the picture and a more exploitative approach to the common resource emerged, the fishing people objected. The protests, involving the destruction of the new generation of equipment and other forms of dissent, were carried out in the name of preserving an equal right of access to the fishery. In addition, the protestors advocated the wise use of the resource so as to preserve the stake that future generations had in it. Cadigan argues that the fishing people in this area acquired some sound, if not entirely perfect, knowledge of the region's fishery ecology. From at least the 1840s, if not before, they used that knowledge to object to those who employed relatively expensive seines to exploit the codfish more aggressively. Their objections, in turn, brought ridicule from those associated with "progress." To oppose the new cod seining technology, said one, was to flirt with the idea of returning "to the days of our ancestors, put on with all speed our bear skin coats, and with bows and arrows in our hands betake ourselves to the forests." Still, it seems clear that these ecological Luddites understood something about the exhaustible nature of the resource. "For these fishers," writes Cadigan, "the desire to preserve a customary and equitable right of access to fish for all implied a need to conserve that marine resource for future generations. The preservation of equitable access may be seen as an ecological norm of a moral economy that ran counter to the individualistic and accumulative values of a nascent local capitalist political economy."[6]

It seems clear that some Americans assumed the role of conservationists well before Theodore Roosevelt, Gifford Pinchot, and the other Progressives, who set out to rein in rampant natural resource use. Mart Stewart notes that in the South, conservation emerged in response to declining soil fertility, a development that threatened the entire slave-based system. Conservation, Stewart argues, was simply another name for "agricultural improvement." The southern reformers pioneered the use of various techniques for rejuvenating the soil, including new methods for using both manure and marl, though the results were far from what the improvers had hoped. This development was part of a larger process of rationalization applied to the slave system. Deploying a paternalist creed, southern reformers tried to conserve soil fertility at precisely the same time that they introduced techniques for better managing slave labor. Stewart rightly points out that historians have been slow to recognize the incipient conservation in the South because it was tied so closely to the racist ideas around which the slave system revolved. Social oppression and conservation may have gone hand in hand in the slave South. Yet there is historical evidence that refutes this conjunction in other times and places.[7]

Even if southern agriculture was spiraling downward, ecologically speaking, the efforts of these reformers seem to suggest that it may not have been one straight line down. What is valuable about this insight is that it allows for historical complexity. The trick, however, will be to preserve the moral force associated with the declension narrative and its

6. Sean Cadigan, "The Moral Economy of the Commons: Ecology and Equity in the Newfoundland Cod Fishery, 1815–1855," *Labour/Le Travail*, 43 (1999): 6, 35.

7. See, for example, Donald Worster, *Rivers of Empire: Water, Aridity, and the Growth of the American West* (New York, 1985), which argues that the West's water problems are, at their root, problems that stem from power inequalities.

critique of market economics. For as Conevery Bolton Valenčius notes, if environmental historians are to build an audience for their work, outside the walls of the academy, they must pay special attention to story telling and the drama associated with it. Historians, she seems to argue, need to spend more time taking seriously what they see when watching television and going to the movies.

Her title, "Mudslides Make Good History," suggests that somehow the main message of environmental history is still not getting across. Of course mudslides or earthquakes make for legitimate topics of historical inquiry, or so thinks the environmental historian. But for many in the history profession and even more people outside of it, history is still about politics and social life. For them, the environment remains little more than a backdrop to these other stories. That is an unsettling realization given that environmental history's most important achievement to date has been to show how ecological forces shape history—even politics and social life. As a field, environmental history still has a ways to go to convince people that nature really does matter; perhaps emphasizing the drama of the tumultuous ecological world, as Valenčius suggests, will help get our message across.

In principle then, I am all for good writing and gripping historical narratives. And I believe that disease, disaster, dehydration, and dystopia make for important topics of study. But it would be a terrible shame if historians spent too much time sitting around trying to figure out which topics are likely to "help expand the sales and readership of histories that embrace the sometimes unpleasant realities of the human form." It might be more useful, instead, for historians to take note of the realities of the book business and the fact that it has become over the last few decades a far more concentrated industry centered on some of the same market principles that governed the lives of the New England colonists of whom Cronon wrote so eloquently. (As of 2000, five conglomerates published 80 percent of all books sold in the United States.)[8]

What then should the environmental historian do when she wakes up in the morning? To which issues should she turn her attention? It seems to me that perhaps the only way of answering these questions is simply to put forth still more questions. How do we evaluate the ecological

---

8. André Schiffrin, *The Business of Books: How International Conglomerates Took Over Publishing and Changed the Way We Read* (London, UK, 2000), 2–3.

degradation of a particular locale? What exactly, in other words, is ecological health? What role has the environment played in shaping how the past has unfolded? How do we avoid the trap of presentism and still use environmental history to address concerns of pressing contemporary relevance? And perhaps most pressing of all: How do we say goodbye to the declension narrative without losing the moral force associated with it? If we do a good job of grappling with these issues, the question that Valenčius poses—how to get readers to pay attention to us—may be solved.

PART IV

Commodification of People

... in which people are bought and sold or otherwise reduced to ciphers in a marketplace increasingly structured by capitalist principles.

WALTER JOHNSON, CHAIR

Few problems have consumed as much historical attention and spilled so much ink (not to mention blood) as the problem of slavery in the modern world. The political economy of agrarian versus commercial and industrial societies, the moral and social character of the master-slave relationship, the developmental trajectories of slave-labor and free-labor systems, the "rationalization" of social relations within regimes of free enterprise capitalism—all these questions and more have kept the last two generations of historians working feverishly and quarreling bitterly. Although the polarization of analysis that once posited very stark contrasts between slavery and free labor systems seems to be relaxing, there is likely no neat consensus waiting in the wings. Asked to interrogate this problem in very broad terms of the commodification of persons, Walter Johnson recruited three scholars whose own work is migrating toward the center of this issue. David Waldstreicher offers here a contrasting look at the thoughts of Benjamin Franklin and Venture Smith on freedom and slavery in America. Amy Dru Stanley directs our attention to the intersections of evangelical Protestant theology and the personal moral problem of slavery—both wage slavery and chattel slavery. Stephanie Smallwood probes the concept of commodification itself as it pertains to human beings. Finally, Walter takes us back to the source of much of the debate to review what Karl Marx really said, and why, about slavery and the emergence of capitalism.

The Vexed Story of Human Commodification Told by Benjamin Franklin and Venture Smith

DAVID WALDSTREICHER

In the pages of this journal and elsewhere two of our most accomplished historians, Joyce Appleby and Gordon S. Wood, have depicted qualms about capitalism in the early republic as figments of historians' fervid imaginations. They associate the rise of capitalism with democracy and freedom, not with its more disturbing and, arguably, ubiquitous results: human commodification. While Appleby especially takes pains to distinguish this early liberal capitalism from later industrial, rapacious varieties, the impression given is that ordinary people did not view the spread of market relations or the cash nexus as a problem. On the contrary, they embraced it as their salvation, an alternative to empire and aristocracy. Republicanism, with its anti-commercial uprising of political man, was for Wood at best a halfway house with diminishing significance in the nineteenth century. Economic and political factors combined to create a democratic society of relative equals whose very free and democratic spirit are sufficient to explain the entrepreneurial zeal with which people in the new nation took up all manner of causes from abolitionism to evangelical religion.[1]

David Waldstreicher is Professor of History at Temple University and the author of *In the Midst of Perpetual Fetes: The Making of American Nationalism, 1776–1820* (1997), *Runaway America: Benjamin Franklin, Slavery and the American Revolution* (2004), and *Beyond the Founders: New Approaches to the Political History of the Early American Republic* (2004), which he has coedited with Jeffrey L. Pasley and Andrew W. Robertson.

1. Gordon S. Wood, "The Enemy Is Us: Democratic Capitalism in the Early Republic," *Journal of the Early Republic,* 16 (1996): 293–308; Joyce Appleby, "The Vexed Story of Capitalism Told by American Historians," *ibid.,* 21 (2001):

Much, in their accounts, rests on the testimony of eyewitnesses who made good, such as Benjamin Franklin. Franklin serves in Wood's *Radicalism of the American Revolution* and his more recent work on Franklin as a kind of prophet who does not get to see the promised land. In Appleby's revolutionary generation, he is the father everyone can embrace, the author of the model memoir or how-to book for a do-it-yourself generation. In his defining statement about the new nation written for an international audience, "Information to those who would Remove to America" (1782, 1784), Franklin did indeed depict the quintessential American as a freeholder who works for himself, with his own hands. Wages paid to immigrants, some of whom first come over bound for a period of years to pay their passage, translated directly into their ownership of landed property: in Franklin's words, "Multitudes of poor people from England, Ireland, Scotland and Germany, have by this means in a few Years become wealthy Farmers." The "commodity" of "high birth" was worth next to nothing in the United States: what mattered about a man was *"What can he DO?"* It was the very opposite of an old world order based on the aristocratic extraction of all agricultural profit. For this reason, European nobles could not take their rank—their property in themselves—to a "worse market."[2]

1–18; Wood, *The Radicalism of the American Revolution* (New York, 1992); Appleby, "The Popular Sources of American Capitalism," *Studies in American Political Development,* 9 (1995): 437–57; Appleby, *Inheriting the Revolution: The First Generation of Americans* (Cambridge, MA, 2000). Of course, much turns on how capitalism is defined; and while I do not have space to explain why I think that neither customary conflation of markets and capitalism or the narrow stress on wage labor as capitalism's essence are sufficient for U. S. history, I would point out that one increasingly promising definition—promising because it makes it possible to understand better the place of modern slavery in the history of capitalism, and to come to grips with contemporary "hypercapitalism"—stresses how capitalism tends to commodify everything, including human relations, for the purpose of building capital reserves, i.e., liquid profits. This tends to economic (and political) compulsions that force people into the marketplace on terms often not of their own choosing; it also tends toward geographic expansion in search of cheap labor and new markets. For useful recent accounts, compare Immanuel Wallerstein, *Historical Capitalism, with Capitalist Civilization* (1983; rev. ed., London, UK, 1995), esp. 13–16, 39; Ellen Meiksins Wood, *The Origins of Capitalism: A Longer View* (New York, 2002); Antonio Negri and Michael Hardt, *Empire* (Cambridge, MA, 2000); and Susan Strasser, ed., *Commodifying Everything: Relationships of the Market* (New York, 2003).

2. Benjamin Franklin, *Writings*, ed. J. A. Leo LeMay (New York, 1987), 976–77.

It is interesting that Franklin would place aristocratic titles inside of a world market. While some early modern regimes, including the British one, did informally sell off titles, the metaphor does not really work. And that was Franklin's point. Insofar as the corrupt system of rank did operate as a market, that market breaks down in North America. These observations of Franklin's introduced the larger argument, that those who came to America as commodities in a rather different labor market—that is, indentured servitude—ended up happily beyond it. The American system, in short, de-commodified people. Work, land, and demographics combine to turn aristocrats and redemptioners alike into free middling folk. Franklin's American story seems straightforward, its results humane, and, like Wood and Appleby's transition to capitalism, unvexed by contradiction or even by nostalgia for the past.

And yet even while he was still talking about the misconceptions of European aristocrats, there is more to the story as Franklin tells it. And that more is slavery—or at least the necessity of rhetorically (if not otherwise) doing away with it. It does not take much reading between the lines to see the presence of slavery, for Franklin himself brought it up twice. He artfully unvexed American freedom by associating its underside, African slavery, with the old world, which he had elsewhere blamed for bringing slaves to America.[3] Europeans had read false reports that "the [American] Governments . . . not only pay the Expence of personal Transportation, but give Lands gratis to Strangers, with Negroes to work for them, Utensils of Husbandry, and Stocks of Cattle." The real America was different: slaves did not solve the labor problem, the immigrants themselves did.

---

3. Richard B. Morris mentioned Franklin's evasion of plantation slavery in *Information*; Ormond Seavey is the only other scholar I know of to observe how "deliberately provincial," and not antislavery, Franklin chose to be in this defining statement. Richard B. Morris, *The Forging of the Union, 1781–1789* (New York, 1987), 9; Seavey, "Benjamin Franklin and Imperialist and Provincial," in Gianfranca Balestra and Luigi Sanpietro, eds., *Benjamin Franklin: An American Genius* (Rome, Italy, 1993), 30–31. A contemporary who knew Franklin's politics and writings very well responded at length on the occasion of Franklin's death and insisted that emigration to America actually produced not progress but instead, "white Negroes." *Memoirs of the late Dr. Benjamin Franklin: With a Review of his Pamphlet, Entitled 'Information to those who would wish to remove to AMERICA'* (London, 1790), 68.

Two paragraphs later, the African presence recurs, but ventriloquized, in West Indian dialect, in a comment on the Americans' propensity to work. "[The Americans] are pleased with the Observation of a Negro, and frequently mention it," Franklin asserted,

that *Boccarorra* (meaning the Whiteman) make de Blackman workee, make de Horse workee, make de Ox workee, make ebery ting workee; only de Hog. He de Hog, no workee; he eat, he drink, he walk about, he go to sleep when he please, *he libb like a Gentleman.* According to these Opinions of the Americans, one of them would think himself more oblig'd to a Genealogist, who could prove for him that his Ancestors & Relations for ten Generations had been Ploughmen, Smiths, Carpenters, Turners, Weavers, Tanners, or even Shoemakers, & consequently that they were useful members of Society; than if he could only prove that they were Gentlemen, doing nothing of Value, but living idly on the Labour of others, mere *fruges consumere nati,* and otherwise *good* for *nothing,* till be their Death, their estates like the Carcase of the Negro's Gentleman-Hog, come to be *cut up.*

Franklin's ventriloquism here repays close attention. The slave trickster tale embedded in his essay depicts whites as exceptional slave drivers who become hog-like in the process.[4] There is an unmistakable criticism of slavery here, voiced in an Afro-Caribbean accent readers would have recognized as such.

But who is being criticized? By implanting the black dialect story in a paragraph contrasting the hardy *North* American citizenry with a European aristocracy that derives land and wealth from birth, new world slavery is compared to old world tyranny and the American yeomanry emerges as the antithesis of both. Some white people may be gentlemen-hogs—maybe in the West Indies, as in Europe—but not in our America. The larger comparison of Europeans versus Americans distinguishes the

---

4. This anecdote actually derived from a tract celebrating the progress and profits of Barbados and the suppression of a slave revolt there. *Great Newes from Barbadoes, or a True and Faithful Account of the Grand Conspiracy of the Negroes Against the English and the Happy Discovery of the Same* (London, 1676); Marcus Rediker and Peter Linebaugh, *The Many Headed Hydra: Sailors, Slaves, Commoners, and the Hidden History of the Revolutionary Atlantic* (Boston, 2000), 125, 372n; Jack P. Greene, "Changing Identity in the British Caribbean: Barbados as a Case Study," in Nicholas Canny and Anthony Pagden, eds., *Colonial Identity in the Atlantic World* (Princeton, 1987), 229.

United States of America from the Americas, from the slave societies that the West Indian accent of the Negro tale-teller otherwise signals. Americans are whites, yet not true slave-drivers like Caribbean whites. The way they drive "de Blackman" reflects only their own greater national industry, not their historical and continuing debt to slavery. In other words, Franklin's minstrelization did more than miss the point of the slave's tale. It actually appropriated the stories being told by new world slaves and obscured their very different understanding of whose labor had made America (not to mention their rather different prediction of who, in the end, might justly find themselves under the knife and "cut up" into pieces). The slave himself goes from being a victim and, in the telling, moral victor to being, in essence, an alibi.

With the commodified aristocrat-hog, we come full circle. The disturbing fact of human commodification is simultaneously blamed on the European aristocracy and visited upon them. Mere projection becomes outright fantasy. We can also see how important it was to Franklin's revolutionary ideology—or perhaps we should say, with Francis Jennings, wartime propaganda—to project the human commodification actually going on in the United States onto the old world.[5] If the reputedly most antislavery of the founding fathers dodged or reframed the issue so artfully while representing America to the world, we surely have license to wonder whether the commodification of humans played a greater role in post-revolutionary culture, society, and politics than Wood or Appleby allow. Franklin's text is artful; if you believe implicitly its vision of American freedom, as we are schooled to do, it is likely to be damned near inspiring—especially if you can ignore or enjoy the literary blackface that helps it work. We might wish it were factual, but we cannot call it unvexed.

Wood and Appleby have not easily incorporated the reality of slavery or the presence of African Americans into their synthetic frameworks. Wood considers the issue of slavery anachronistic and prefers to emphasize, as his mentor Bernard Bailyn did, the antislavery effects of revolutionary ideology. Appleby discerns the entrepreneurial ethos among free northern blacks and defines the intransigent South out of the northern liberal capitalist culture she describes in light of its success stories. Race,

---

5. Francis Jennings, *The Creation of America: Through Revolution to Empire* (New York, 2000), 9, 203–05.

for Appleby, functions as a tragic bar to market activity—to whites' recognition of the human potential in African Americans. The published memoirs of its victims before they themselves, like Frederick Douglass, became success stories did not make it into her database. But as Ann Fabian has argued, the emergence of plebian storytellers in the marketplace of print testified doubly to harsh economic necessities. These people, the less successful members of Appleby's first generation, took up the opportunity to commodify their own stories as a kind of last chance to salvage some measure of freedom in a market that otherwise systematically devalued them, often because of their sex or race.[6]

The first memoir by a former slave published in the post-revolutionary North also suggests a far more vexed relationship between the rise of capitalism and the commodification of human beings than exists in the dominant paradigm. Where Franklin invents a free market of free persons in which the imagined absence of blacks is offered as proof, Venture Smith shows how flexibly whites applied the supposedly neutral rules of the marketplace to keep blacks tethered to their status as commodities, even during and after their very gradual emancipation.[7]

The first third of Smith's *Narrative* covers his five years in his native country, the despoliation of his nation, the murder of his father, and his journey to the coast in an enslaving war "instigated by some white nation." The middle part describes his own middle passage on a Rhode Island vessel across the Atlantic, with a stop in Barbados. He avoided the West Indies death trap after being bought by a ship's mate named Robert Mumford "for four gallons of rum and a piece of calico." Mumford named him "VENTURE, on account of his having purchased me with his own private venture," and brought Smith to his family home on Fisher's Island, New York.[8]

---

6. Ann Fabian, *The Unvarnished Truth: Personal Narratives in Nineteenth-Century America* (Berkeley, 2000).

7. Joanne Pope Melish, *Disowning Slavery: Gradual Emancipation and "Race" in New England, 1780–1860* (Ithaca, 1998), 105.

8. *A Narrative of the Life and Adventures of Venture, a Native of Africa: But resident above sixty years in the United States of America. RELATED BY HIMSELF* (New London, CT, 1798), reprinted in Vincent Carretta, ed., *Unchained Voices: An Anthology of Black Authors in the English-Speaking World of the Eighteenth Century* (Lexington, KY, 1996), 369–85. For an excellent discussion of the background, see Robert R. Desrochers Jr., " 'Not Fade Away': The Narrative of Venture Smith, an African American in the Early Republic," *Journal of American*

The Mumfords were the epitome of the mixed economy of the eighteenth-century coastal North. They farmed; they fished; they carded wool for home use; they sailed the Atlantic; and they traded in slaves. Three generations shared in one household, and it was generational tensions among the Mumfords that Smith emphasized because of how they put the eight-year-old slave at personal risk. The eldest Mumford patriarch demanded that Venture hand over the key to his venturesome, seagoing son's trunk. Refusing, the young slave earned the "confidence" of his master, but soon had trouble with Robert Mumford's teenage son, who gave him contradictory orders whenever he had the chance. Smith makes it clear that the honorable slave could not expect good treatment in a land of ventures, where fathers had questionable power and sons had questionable prospects. His labor was a weapon—his own and others'—in the battles among men.[9]

In 1754, at the age of twenty-six, Smith decided to join the white indentured servant Joseph Heday and two fellow slaves in a fantastic plan to sail all the way to "the Mississippi." This rebellion came to little, though, because Heday betrayed the others, taking the valuable clothes they had run away with, which the master listed in great detail in a newspaper ad. During this episode Smith, although naïve about geography and perhaps still too willing to trust whites, showed for the first time an awareness of the economic system that would later make a significant difference in his life. He himself successfully "advertised" for the thief Heday's capture! When Heday was brought to them the other fugitives decided to turn themselves in and Heday as well.[10]

History, 84 (1997): 40–66. Desrochers's emphasis on Smith's African roots—more rhetorical than actual, as his essay deals with a range of contexts—apparently licenses Joseph J. Ellis to dismiss Smith, with Laurel Ulrich's Martha Ballard, as interesting common folk whose experience social historians have overemphasized at the expense of the statesmen "at the center of the national story." Joseph J. Ellis, *Founding Brothers: The Revolutionary Generation* (New York, 2000), 12–13.

9. Smith, *Narrative*, 375–76; Desrochers, " 'Not Fade Away,' " 58n.

10. Smith, *Narrative*, 375–77; *New York Gazette and Weekly Post-Boy*, Apr. 1, 1754. This ad is also reprinted in Graham Russell Hodges and Alan Edward Brown, *"Pretends to be Free": Runaway Slave Advertisements from Colonial and Revolutionary New York and New Jersey* (New York, 1994), 49–50. The existence of the ad and its closeness to what Smith says can be taken to document the whole. It adds to Desrochers's documentation of other accurate references to Africa the fact that Venture had been "mark'd in the Face, or scar'd with a Knife in his own Country."

In Smith's mind, the honesty, ingenuity, and hard work he displayed in this episode—characteristics that would make him legendary in his community in the years to come—should have been enough to guarantee his forgiveness. Instead, he found himself sold away from his wife and infant daughter within the year. Thus began a series of removals, abuses, and negotiations throughout coastal Long Island and Connecticut, in which Smith tried again and again to hang on to what cash he made "by cleaning gentlemen's shoes and drawing boots, by catching muskrats and minks, raising potatoes and carrots, &c. and by fishing in the night, and at odd spells." He got his new master to buy his wife and daughter, only to get caught in violent disputes between his wife and mistress. By the time he was thirty-six, he "had already been sold three different times, made considerable money with seemingly nothing to derive from it, been cheated out of a large sum of money" by another master, who held it for him and then sold him away, "lost much by misfortunes," but finally managed to buy, with an "enormous sum," his own freedom.

Narrating his free years, Smith begins to sound like the "Franklin and a Washington in a state of nature, or rather in a state of slavery," that the editor of his memoir discerned in the self-made African. He wears homespun and counts the cost of everything in a desperate and ultimately successful quest to buy his wife, his sons, his daughter, and some land with which to support them. His consciousness of the cash nexus is almost a parody of Franklin's playful awareness of the relationships between people and capital in *Poor Richard's Almanack*.[11] When his teenage son Solomon was enticed by an employer to go whaling and died of scurvy aboard ship, he recorded the loss as "equal to seventy-five pounds" he had paid for the boy. When he purchased his pregnant wife for forty pounds in 1772, he saved "having another child to buy." There is something deeply disturbing about Smith's absorption of the cash nexus in his society, as disturbing, perhaps, as his self-liberation is inspiring.[12]

---

11. For more on this theme, see my *Runaway America: Benjamin Franklin, Slavery and the American Revolution* (New York, 2004), chap. 4; and "Capitalism, Slavery and Benjamin Franklin's American Revolution," in Cathy D. Matson, ed., *The Early American Economy: New Directions* (University Park, PA, forthcoming).

12. William L. Andrews, *To Tell a Free Story: The First Century of Afro-American Autobiography, 1760–1865* (Urbana, 1986), 51–53, 59–60; Philip Gould,

That, however, was not his main message. What Smith emphasized, again and again, was not his own worries about the bottom line, or even his adaptation of whites' pecuniary strategies, but how whites (and, sadly, a few blacks with no other resources at their disposal) took advantage of his marginal status to steal the fruits of his labor. To Venture Smith, the American North harbored nothing but confidence men—and race was not the exception but the name of the game. The problem was epitomized for him in a favor he agreed to do for a Native-American boatman who sailed the Long Island Sound, and Elisha Hart, a Saybrook shipmaster who owned a barrel of molasses on board. At the request of the boatman, with granddaughter in tow, Smith went to tell Hart of the boat's arrival after it docked. Meanwhile, at the wharf, the barrel fell overboard and sank. The Indian could not pay for it, and Hart took Smith to court, making him pay ten pounds damages. Afterwards, Hart "insultingly taunted me with my unmerited misfortune." Memories of Africa, in this context, gave Smith more than an identity. They gave him the means to criticize: "Such a proceeding as this, committed on a defenceless stranger, almost worn out in the hard service of the world, without any foundation in reason or justice, whatever it may be called in a christian land, would in my native country by branded as a crime equal to highway robbery. But Captain Hart was a *white gentleman*, and I a *poor African*, therefore it was *all right, and good enough for the black dog*."

In the end, Franklin and Smith had things other than their entrepreneurship in common, something very important about the problem of capitalism in the early republic. Both understood that human commodification was a live issue and a result of new world settlement. Both depicted alternatives to it: for Franklin, an idealized free America itself; for Smith, in the passage above, both Christian and African standards of ethical behavior. And both conveyed, albeit differently, that even for northerners slavery and race both created and put limits on the commodifying, inhumane tendencies of nascent capitalism.

What this suggests to me is that the proper attitude for the historian is not Wood and Appleby's optimism and near-celebration of capitalism qua liberal democracy but rather early national Americans' own ambiva-

---

"Free Carpenter, Venture Capitalist: Reading the Lives of the Early Black Atlantic," *American Literary History*, 12 (2000), 677.

lence about capitalism's effects. As Laurel Thatcher Ulrich, Richard Bushman, Catherine Kelly, and others increasingly suggest, even small property holders (like Smith) displayed a striking ambivalence about the effects on their human relationships of a capitalistic orientation toward the world. As a result, they often engaged in innovative, entrepreneurial activities in order to preserve real (or imagined) realms apart from the market. Extended to the South, such a perspective supports accounts that reconcile the rapacious capitalism in slaveholder expansionism with the paternalistic ethos more established planters made central to their culture. Precisely because their most important property was people, planters had to invent traditions that emphasized their distance from the most dehumanizing of marketplaces.[13]

Moreover, far from seeing capitalism as the root cause of antislavery (as Thomas Haskell would have it), we must remember that world capitalism created modern slavery, even if its slaveholding outposts, when viewed in isolation, did not always look like what we tend to think of (in a set of teleologies that would put any Marxist to shame) as what true (*i.e.* industrial or consumer) capitalism looks like. Such an interpretation might place the abolitionists—who repeatedly emphasized how slavery was a highly developed *market* in persons, in which slaves functioned as a flexible form of capital as well as of labor—much closer to the center of early republic and antebellum political culture. Although the political party system was reconstructed during the Jacksonian era in part to marginalize them, abolitionists repeatedly called white Americans to account the contradictions in their self-conceptions. When William Lloyd Garrison described a citizen who could not eliminate slavery as branded chattel, and when Thoreau depicted a trip to town itself as a cattle drive, they continued the dialogue about republicanism, economic arrangements, and human commodification that Franklin himself engaged in as a way of justifying, and salvaging, the American Revolution. In this as in

---

13. Richard Bushman, "Markets and Composite Farms in Early America," *William and Mary Quarterly*, 55 (1998): 351–74; Laurel Thatcher Ulrich, *The Age of Homespun: Objects and Stories in the Creation of an American Myth* (New York, 2001); Catherine E. Kelly, *In the New England Fashion: Reshaping Women's Lives in the Nineteenth Century* (Ithaca, 1999); James Oakes, *Slavery and Freedom: An Interpretation of the Old South* (New York, 1990); Jeffrey Robert Young, *Domesticating Slavery: The Master Class in Georgia and South Carolina, 1670–1837* (Chapel Hill, 1999).

other things they were less outside the consensus than they were inside the cultural logics of the time.[14]

And in the end, their fellow citizens failed to marginalize them as much as historians' syntheses have. Perhaps it is time for historians to take their cues from the abolitionists and the slaves, rather than from the Benjamin Franklins.

---

14. Thomas Haskell, "Capitalism and the Origins of the Humanitarian Sensibility," in Thomas Bender, ed., *The Antislavery Debate: Capitalism and Abolitionism as a Problem in Historical Interpretation* (Berkeley, 1993), 107–60; Eric Williams, *Capitalism and Slavery* (Chapel Hill), 1944; Barbara L. Solow, "Capitalism and Slavery in the Exceedingly Long Run," in Solow and Stanley L. Engerman, eds., *British Capitalism and Caribbean Slavery: The Legacy of Eric Williams* (New York, 1987), 51–77; Solow, "Slavery and Colonization" and David Richardson, "Slavery, Trade, and Economic Growth in Eighteenth-Century New England," in Solow, ed., *Slavery and the Rise of the Atlantic System* (New York, 1991), 21–42, 237–64; Robin Blackburn, *The Making of New World Slavery: From the Baroque to the Modern, 1492–1800* (New York, 1997); Joseph Inikori, *Africans and the Industrial Revolution in England: A Study in International Trade and Economic Development* (Cambridge, UK, 2002); Seth Rockman, "The Unfree Origins of American Capitalism," in Matson, ed., *The Early American Economy*; Walter Johnson, *Soul by Soul: Life Inside the Antebellum Slave Market* (Cambridge, MA, 1999), 25–27, 230–31n20; Robert Fanuzzi, *Abolition's Public Sphere* (Minneapolis, 2003), 26; Henry David Thoreau, *Walden and Civil Disobedience*, ed. Owen Thomas (New York, 1966), 113; Paul Goodman, *Of One Blood: Abolitionism and the Origins of Racial Equality* (Berkeley, 1998).

Wages, Sin, and Slavery
Some Thoughts on Free Will and Commodity Relations

AMY DRU STANLEY

In what ways did the problem of human commodification represent a problem of religion for Americans in the early republic? That question, I shall suggest, ought to become a significant part of the agenda of the future study of commodity relationships. Indeed, it is a line of inquiry that runs against the grain of my own prior work, which has tended more to the secular than the sacred, to political economy rather than theology in exploring the problem of human commodification—its moral ambiguities, ideological complexities, legal boundaries, and cultural legitimacy. Necessarily, therefore, these observations will be quite preliminary. Perhaps, at some level, the daily evidence from across the world of religion's momentous, often fatal, contemporary sway has evoked these reflections. Or perhaps, at a very different level, they arose from contemplating sin and regeneration while teaching David Brion Davis's *The Problem of Slavery in Western Culture* in a graduate history course last autumn.[1] My intent here, though, is to think about outcomes not origins—to mark at least some of the value gained by studying the religious dimensions of issues of power and dependence, freedom and unfreedom, virtue and sin at the very heart of the problem of human commodification. The question embraces both chattel slaves and free persons. Amid emergent industrial capitalism in the North and burgeoning plantation slavery in the South, what resources—both spiritual and

---

Amy Dru Stanley is Professor of History at the University of Chicago and author of *From Bondage to Contract: Wage Labor, Marriage, and the Market in the Age of Slave Emancipation* (1998).

1. David Brion Davis, *The Problem of Slavery in Western Culture* (Ithaca, 1966). The course was in U. S. cultural history.

intellectual—did new Christian doctrines of personal moral agency afford Americans absorbed in debating what kinds of commodities should be put up for sale?

Consider the significance of the propositions set forth by two of the nation's most influential evangelical ministers, the Yankee Presbyterian critic of slavery, Charles Grandison Finney, and the southern Presbyterian defender of slavery, James Henley Thornwell. An Arminian who celebrated individual free will, Finney rejected the tenets of predestination and human depravity and presided over revivals where multitudes achieved conversion. A Calvinist who deplored northern heresies, Thornwell adhered to the orthodoxy of original sin and echoed the social theory of George Fitzhugh. In 1851 in his *Lectures on Systematic Theology* Finney wrote that his Christianity rested on two axioms: "that the will is free, and that sin and holiness are voluntary acts of mind." Free will was the essence of "moral agency." And of slavery he wrote that it was "revolting wickedness" to deprive an innocent human being "of liberty . . . rob him of himself—his body—his soul." For Finney, seeking to justify slavery in terms of moral law was the "greatest absurdity." Conversely, Thornwell lamented the "dreary night of Arminian darkness." And in an 1850 sermon he declared that slavery was absolutely consistent with Christian morality, for it converted neither individual will nor conscience to property: "the moral and responsible agency of one person . . . can never be owned by another—it is not an article of barter or exchange." Even the slave retained his or her "will," and the "soul" was "beyond all price." For Thornwell, the "absurdity" lay in the notion that slavery degraded "voluntary agents to the condition of tools or brutes." Although differing over the extent of human ability to achieve grace, on at least one thing the two preachers could agree—some degree of free will was "a sacred bestowment," and treating the soul as a commodity was blasphemy.[2]

---

2. J. H. Fairchild, ed., *Lectures on Systematic Theology by Rev. Charles Grandison Finney* (New York, 1878), x, 15, 228; "Antinomianism," in John B. Adger, ed., *The Collected Writings of James Henley Thornwell* (2 vols; Richmond, 1889), 2:383; James Henley Thornwell, *The Rights and Duties of Masters. A Sermon Preached at the Dedication of a Church, Erected in Charleston, S.C., for the Benefit and Instruction of the Coloured Population* (Charleston, 1850), 22, 23. See Nathan O. Hatch, *The Democratization of American Christianity* (New Haven, 1989), esp. 170–201, 205–09; Daniel Walker Howe, "Charles Sellers, the Market Revo-

The new, evangelical faith in personal moral agency, therefore, transcended regional divisions. Indeed, that faith, like the Bible itself, might be invoked either to oppose or to defend chattel slavery. It has been well established that by the late eighteenth century new conceptions of human nature, sin, and agency figured decisively in the rise of antislavery opinion on both sides of the Atlantic. "There was nothing unprecedented about chattel slavery, even the slavery of one ethnic group to another," David Brion Davis has written. "What was unprecedented by the 1760s and early 1770s was the emergence of a widespread conviction that New World slavery was deeply evil." Because sin traditionally was likened to slavery, and bondage was said to stem from sin, "any change in the meaning of sin would be likely to affect attitudes toward slavery. . . . The point is that men could not fully perceive the moral contradictions of slavery until a major religious transformation had changed their ideas of sin and spiritual freedom." For over three thousand years slaves had been reckoned commodities; the transformation lay in "moral perception," which made slavery newly appear as a problem to be eradicated.[3]

But what of forms of human commodification other than chattel slavery—forms that were unprecedented, that lacked slavery's ancient lineage, that instead were new to the world of capitalism? What ideological consequences did the new religious faith in personal moral agency hold for the traffic in the faculties of free persons that was created by the advent of capitalist industry? This is not simply to ask again about the Protestant ethic and the spirit of capitalism. For Weber mainly was concerned with orthodox Calvinism and the cultural meaning of the dire anxiety about salvation inspired by doctrines of predestination and origi-

---

lution, and the Shaping of Identity in Whig-Jacksonian America," in Mark A. Noll, ed., *God and Mammon: Protestants, Money, and the Market, 1790–1860* (New York, 2002), 54–74; Eugene Genovese, *The Slaveholders' Dilemma: Freedom and Progress in Southern Conservative Thought, 1820–1860* (Columbia, SC, 1992), 28–29, 35–36, 60–63; Eugene Genovese, *A Consuming Fire: The Fall of the Confederacy in the Mind of the White Christian South* (Athens, GA, 1998), 115–21; and Mark A. Noll, *America's God: From Jonathan Edwards to Abraham Lincoln* (New York, 2002), esp. 293–315, 382–445.

3. David Brion Davis, *The Problem of Slavery in the Age of Revolution 1770–1823* (Ithaca, 1975), 41, 42; David Brion Davis, *In the Image of God: Religion, Moral Values, and Our Heritage of Slavery* (New Haven, 2001), 131; Davis, *Slavery in Western Culture*, 292, 32, vii. See also Walter Johnson, *Soul by Soul: Life Inside the Antebellum Slave Market* (Cambridge, MA, 1999).

nal sin among Puritans confronting an infinitely powerful and inscrutable God. Here, though, the question centers on a different sensibility, rooted in spreading assurance about human moral agency, and its bearing specifically on the rectitude of the buying and selling of free labor. And the stakes of the question were heightened by the fact that in antebellum America the debates over the legitimacy of capitalism coincided with the debates over the legitimacy of chattel slavery.[4]

Unlike chattel slavery, however, the commodification of free labor long had posed a problem in Anglo-American traditions of thought. At least a century before Thomas Jefferson famously derided manufactures in his 1787 *Notes on the State of Virginia*, wage labor had been associated with the hierarchies of the household and carried the stigma of dependence. Hirelings—no matter how voluntarily they put up their labor for sale or what the price they were paid—were considered not fully free. To be sure, the cash nexus, contract, and the play of the free market in labor eroded the personal relations of dominion and submission characteristic of the customary bonds of paternalism between the gentry and laboring people. Nevertheless, though masterless and free to dispose of their own labor as they chose, hirelings (like paupers and wives) ostensibly lacked both the autonomy and virtue presumed to be based on independent ownership of property. Throughout the seventeenth and eighteenth centuries, plain folk, patricians, political theorists, and members of Parliament joined in expressing "hostility to the status of wage-labourer," according to Christopher Hill's classic study of the subject. For the hireling had lost his birthright, "that property in a man's own labour and

---

4. See Seymour Drescher, *Capitalism and Antislavery: British Mobilization in Comparative Perspective* (New York, 1986); Seymour Drescher, *The Mighty Experiment: Free Labor Versus Slavery in British Emancipation* (New York, 2002); Robert Steinfeld, *The Invention of Free Labor: The Employment Relation in English and American Law and Culture, 1350–1870* (Chapel Hill, 1991); Sean Wilentz, *Chants Democratic: New York City & the Rise of the American Working Class, 1788–1850* (New York, 1984); Max Weber, *The Protestant Ethic and the Spirit of Capitalism*, ed. Talcott Parsons (1930; rep., New York, 1992); Davis, *Slavery in the Age of Revolution*; Thomas Bender, ed., *The Antislavery Debate: Capitalism and Abolitionism As a Problem in Historical Interpretation* (Berkeley, 1992); and Amy Dru Stanley, *From Bondage to Contract: Wage Labor, Marriage, and the Market in the Age of Slave Emancipation* (New York, 1998).

person," which was the badge of a free man. In Jefferson's words, "Dependance [*sic*] begets subservience and venality, suffocates the germ of virtue."[5]

The question raised, then, by analyzing the commodification of free labor in light of religious transformation is hardly identical to that raised by viewing slaves' commodification in the same light. As Davis bluntly stated, regarding slavery, "The central question is: What led men to see the problem?"[6] But here the point of interest lies not in the sudden, new awareness of a problem, since the animus against wage labor already had existed for centuries by the time of the Second Great Awakening and Finney's theological innovations. Regarding free labor's commodification the question must be put differently: What convictions about moral agency led men and women to see that problem differently—or, perhaps, no longer to see it at all?

Much recent scholarship has addressed the problem of commodification, a line of inquiry to which this symposium itself testifies. But to my knowledge, the questions have not been broached quite as I have tried to do so here. The tendency has been to explore the pervasiveness of commodity relations, their penetration beyond the market, their symbiosis with seemingly antithetical social forms and systems of values, their sway over alternative ways of living and thinking. And this despite the notable efforts of contemporaries, who witnessed capitalism's development alongside slavery's expansion, to make sense of the transformation by erecting literal and imaginative boundaries around commodity relations (the market versus the home) as well as between different kinds of commodification (slavery versus wage labor, or prostitution versus

---

5. Christopher Hill, "Pottage for Freeborn Englishman: Attitudes to Wage-Labour," in Christopher Hill, *Change and Continuity in Seventeenth-Century England* (1974; rep., New Haven, 1991), 219, 232, 234; Thomas Jefferson, *Notes on the State of Virginia* (1787; rep., New York, 1972), 165; E. P. Thompson, "Patrician Society, Plebeian Culture," *Journal of Social History* 7 (1974); Amy Dru Stanley, "Home Life and the Morality of the Market," in Melvyn Stokes and Stephen Conway, eds., *The Market Revolution in America: Social, Political, and Religious Expressions, 1800–1880* (Charlottesville, 1996), 74–96; C. B. Macpherson, *The Political Theory of Possessive Individualism: Hobbes to Locke* (Oxford, UK, 1962).

6. Davis, *Slavery in Western Culture*, 337.

marriage) in order to understand the nature of a culture where everyone became, as Adam Smith had expected, "in some measure a merchant."[7]

Scholarly findings about the past, then, in some ways run counter to contemporaries' own endeavors to order their world. There are landmark studies of chattel slaves who owned slaves and other property, and who also engaged in market activities—studies that blur the line between slavery and freedom by demonstrating that chattel were proprietors and that human commodities themselves acted as buyers and sellers in the marketplace. Some historians contend that the Old South was so thoroughly capitalist in its ethos, slaveholders so fully attuned to market rationality, and the plantation economy so entirely enmeshed in industrial ones to the North and across the Atlantic, that nothing was really so peculiar about its institutions after all. Others show how closely tied the fortunes of the free-soil North were to those of the slave South and that antebellum Americans should not be seen as a nation "sharply divided between slavery and freedom." Still others illuminate the interdependence of New World slavery and capitalist development in the Atlantic World, pointing to the linkage between bound labor and wage labor as well as to the staple production of commodities such as sugar, whose exquisite sweetness supplied a mass market of hireling consumers due to the toil of chattel slaves. Meanwhile, historians of the antebellum North have found that commodity relations pervaded not simply family farms and artisan workshops but also street culture (as laboring girls exchanged sex for consumer pleasures) and the intimacies of home life (as tenement kitchens became sweatshops). Neither religion nor emotion was insulated from the market. Even things closest to the heart were for sale.[8]

---

7. Adam Smith, *An Inquiry into the Nature and Causes of the Wealth of Nations*, ed. Edwin Cannan and Max Lerner (1776; rep., New York, 1937), 22. See also Stanley, *From Bondage to Contract*.

8. Ira Berlin, *Generations of Captivity: A History of African-American Slaves* (Cambridge, MA, 2003), 18. See Dylan C. Penningroth, *The Claims of Kinfold: Africa American Property and Community in the Nineteenth-Century South* (Chapel Hill, 2003); Robert Fogel, *Without Consent or Contract: The Rise and Fall of American Slavery* (New York, 1989); James Oakes, *The Ruling Race: A History of American Slaveholders* (New York, 1982); Douglas R. Egerton, "Markets Without a Market Revolution: Southern Planters and Capitalism," *Journal of the Early Republic*, 16 (1996): 207–21; Robin Blackburn, *The Making of New World Slavery: From the Baroque to the Modern, 1492–1800* (New York, 1998); Davis, *In the Image of God*, 151–64, 178–88, 205–16; David Brion Davis, *Chal-*

Amidst the profusion and promiscuity of commodity relations, both advocates and critics of capitalist transformation clung fast to the disparate boundaries they created or aspired to maintain, a theme I have explored elsewhere. They insisted that some things must never be for sale—that the very legitimacy of human commodification rested on its boundaries; and they argued incessantly over where those boundaries should fall. The intent of abolitionists, for example, was hardly to discredit all commodity relations but rather to isolate the market in slaves as a unique and singularly evil form of human commodification. Rejecting Thornwell's justification (that the slave's service but not the person or soul was marketable), abolitionists countered that the slave's entire being constituted a commodity, and they decried "the traffic in the bodies and souls of men and women who are 'made but a little lower than the angels.'" Like Finney, they protested that slavery violated the sovereignty of soul and self granted by God. In other words, such an extreme form of human commodification negated the Christian doctrine of personal moral agency.[9] Yet, in other cases, the moral dualisms were less clear-cut.

Especially ambiguous was the problem of free labor's commodification, and the terms of its vindication or renunciation. Over the course of

---

lenging the Boundaries of Slavery (Cambridge, MA, 2003), 15–33; Christopher Clark, *The Roots of Rural Capitalism: Western Massachusetts, 1780–1860* (Ithaca, 1990); Winifred Barr Rothenberg, *From Market-Places to a Market Economy: The Transformation of Rural Massachusetts, 1750–1850* (Chicago, 1992); Wilentz, *Chants Democratic*; Paul Faler, "Cultural Aspects of the Industrial Revolution: Lynn, Massachusetts, Shoemakers and Industrial Morality, 1826–1860," *Labor History*, 15 (1974): 367–94; Charles Sellers, *The Market Revolution: Jacksonian America, 1815–1846* (New York, 1991); Stokes and Conway, eds., *The Market Revolution in America*; Christopher Tomlins, *Law, Labor, and Ideology in the Early American Republic* (New York, 1993); Christine Stansell, *City of Women: Sex and Class in New York, 1789–1860* (New York, 1986); Stanley, "Home Life and the Morality of the Market"; Stanley, *From Bondage to Contract*; R. Laurence Moore, *Selling God: American Religion in the Marketplace of Culture* (New York, 1994); John Corrigan, *Business of the Heart: Religion and Emotion in the Nineteenth Century* (Berkeley, 2002); Kathryn T. Long, "'Turning . . . Piety into Hard Cash': The Marketing of Nineteenth-Century Revivalism," in Noll, ed., *God and Mammon*, 236–61; Viviana A. Zelizer, "The Purchase of Intimacy,"*Law and Social Inquiry*, 25 (2000): 817–48.

9. Remond cited in Stanley, *From Bondage to Contract*, 243; and see Stanley, "Home Life and the Morality of the Market."

the nineteenth century, with the rise of metropolitan and rural factories, independent commodity producers slid increasingly into the dependent condition of hirelings, owning nothing but themselves, having nothing to sell but their own labor. And the ranks of hireling men were joined by hireling women—seamstresses, washerwomen, textile operatives—as well as by immigrants from diverse nations. Yet countervailing ideological developments, rooted in the construction of moral boundaries and the affirmation of cultural differences, gradually lent legitimacy to the condition of the hireling. A wealth of studies have demonstrated how antislavery itself, by establishing the slave as the absolute symbol of unfreedom, thereby vindicated the freedoms of wage laborers vested with formal rights. So too, it has been argued, did the prerogatives ("wages") of whiteness elevate ostensibly unfree proletarians far above the status of black chattels. Similarly, the shibboleth of wage slavery rang false as long as hireling men could claim dominion at home as well as title to their wives and children. And so too did consumption practices—commodities purchased through wages—supposedly afford a new measure of status and dignity to even the lowliest free laborers by the turn of the century. Simultaneously, the argument goes, hirelings became inured to the new industrial discipline through the new evangelical churches, the revivals, and the promises of salvation to all Christians who chose to heed the call and obey the new moral order.[10]

In England, the acceptance of the traffic in free labor took a long time, according to Christopher Hill. That was true also in America, where protest against wage slavery endured into the late nineteenth century

---

10. Davis, *Problem of Slavery in the Age of Revolution*; Jonathan Glickstein, "'Poverty Is Not Slavery': American Abolitionists and the Competitive Labor Market," in Lewis Perry and Michael Fellman, eds., *Anti-Slavery Reconsidered: New Perspectives on the Abolitionists* (Baton Rouge, 1979), 195–218; David Roediger, *The Wages of Whiteness: Race and the Making of the American Working Class* (London, 1991); Stanley, "Home Life and the Morality of the Market"; Jeanne Boydston, "The Woman Who Wasn't There: Women's Market Labor and the Transition to Capitalism in the United States," *Journal of the Early Republic*, 16 (1996): 183–206; Lawrence B. Glickman, *A Living Wage: American Workers and the Making of Consumer Society* (Ithaca, 1997); Paul E. Johnson, *A Shopkeeper's Millennium: Society and Revivals in Rochester, New York, 1815–1837* (New York, 1978); Bruce Laurie, *Working People of Philadelphia, 1800–1850* (Philadelphia, 1980); George M. Thomas, *Revivalism and Cultural Change: Christianity, Nation Building, and the Market in the Nineteenth-Century United States* (Chicago, 1989).

and after, as labor advocates continued to object that labor was "not a commodity" and spoke of recovering the "lost ownership of self." Although the forces of legitimation were powerful, so too did traditions of renunciation run deep. Which is why the question of moral values is so particularly important. Perhaps the fundamental issue at stake in the debate over free labor's commodification involved subjectivity: Was human labor distinct from the self and therefore alienable and as proper to sell as an inanimate object? Or was human labor a part of the self and therefore inalienable and as improper to sell as the soul, thereby amounting to slavery? Bound up with ideas of freedom and unfreedom and the nature of selfhood, this problem of subjectivity necessarily involved the problem of human agency. It was at once philosophical and spiritual. And as such it implicated themes at the marrow of the religious transformation.[11]

In the 2002 anthology, *God and Mammon: Protestants, Money, and the Market, 1790–1860*, the religious historian Mark Noll points to a vast uncharted terrain. In the era from the American Revolution to the Civil War, he writes, "the relationship of money and Protestantism . . . must be regarded as a mountain where exploration has reached only to the foothills." Precisely the same might be said for the relationship of human commodification and Protestantism. For all that has been written about the market revolution in the early nineteenth century, on the one hand, and about the transformation of Protestantism, on the other, not much attention has been directed to the religious aspects of the cultural problems posed by the spread of the market in free human labor—as opposed to the expanding market in inanimate commodities and the mere ascendance of money transactions. It is clear that between 1776 and 1860 church membership increased at a rate more than twice that of national population growth, especially among the Methodists and Baptists and Presbyterians who turned away from Calvinism, and that hirelings certainly numbered among the new congregants, although in cities most adults still remained unchurched. Two decades ago historians pointed to the "scattered and fragmentary church records" that would have to be sifted painstakingly to ascertain the religious affiliations of the rank and file of the early labor movement. That undertaking is now well underway. Analytical approaches have grown more nuanced, and interpretations of the meaning

---

11. Hill, "Pottage for Freeborn Englishmen," 238; cited in Stanley, *From Bondage to Contract*, 95, 97, 263.

of Christian faith for wage laborers' response to capitalist transformation accordingly have become more complex. Questions of cultural hegemony remain foremost. Nonetheless, initial accounts of the role of Protestant revivalism in vindicating new class relations in the workshops, promoting an entrepreneurial ethic, and inculcating labor discipline have been refined by more recent studies of insurgent Christian laboring people who joined trade unions and workingmen's parties and used religious language and imagery to criticize the terms and conditions of work.[12]

Less clear, though, is still the relationship of consciousness and commodification. As preachers of the new Arminian gospel denounced the wickedness of southern masters robbing slaves of their souls, what lessons did their teachings hold for hirelings who perhaps wondered about the condition of their own souls and the nature of their own free will and moral agency? Was the traffic in their labor in some way tantamount to slavery—and sin—or not? "Christ has said 'sell what thou hast and give to the poor'," declared a textile operative at a labor reform meeting in Lowell in 1847. "Many of our *professed* christians [*sic*] have their thousands and millions of dollars hoarded by them, while thousands are compelled to sell their very lives for bread."[13] By her lights, did the sale of labor—life itself—dissolve or sustain the capacity to choose grace?

---

12. Noll, ed., *God and Mammon*, 12; Wilentz, *Chants Democratic*, 237. Even historians who doubt that capitalist development posed a cultural problem or a rupture involving a new acquisitive ethos and new social relations of authority and submission, nonetheless acknowledge that the changing status of the laborer did pose a problem for contemporaries; see Gordon Wood, "The Enemy Is Us: Democratic Capitalism in the Early Republic," *Journal of the Early Republic* 16 (1996): 293–308. On popular religious adherence, and the complexities of laboring people's religious consciousness, see, Noll, ed., *God and Mammon*, 11 and *passim*; Jon Butler, *Awash in a Sea of Faith: Christianizing the American People* (Cambridge, MA, 1990), 283; E. P. Thompson, *The Making of the English Working Class* (New York, 1966), 350–401; Laurie, *Working People of Philadelphia*; Wilentz, *Chants Democratic*, 80–87, 145–60, 226–27, 277–79, 305–11; Teresa Murphy, *Ten Hours' Labor: Religion, Reform, and Gender in Early New England* (Ithaca, 1992); Johnson, *Shopkeeper's Millennium*; Ronald Schultz, "Alternative Communities: American Artisans and the Evangelical Appeal, 1780–1830," in Howard B. Rock, Paul A. Gilje, and Robert Asher, eds., *American Artisans: Crafting Social Identity, 1750–1850* (Baltimore, 1995), 65–76; Jama Lazerow, *Religion and the Working Class in Antebellum America* (Washington, DC, 1995); and William R. Sutton, *Journeymen for Jesus: Evangelical Artisans Confront Capitalism in Jacksonian Baltimore* (University Park, PA, 1998).

13. Cited in Lazerow, *Religion and the Working Class*, 2.

Commodified Freedom

Interrogating the Limits of Anti-Slavery Ideology in the Early Republic

STEPHANIE SMALLWOOD

Historians have long understood the relationship between slavery and freedom in western culture as a "problem" to be explained, a paradox to be resolved. Whereas the long-held view has explained the relationship as one in which "freedom in the Western world" is understood to have been "dependent to some degree on the slave systems that western Europe also developed," David Eltis recently has offered a convincing argument that the relationship can be better understood in properly historical terms by reversing that formulation: "the rise of slavery in the Americas," Eltis argues, "was dependent on the nature of freedom in western Europe."[1] If Eltis is right about the direction of the causal link between slavery and freedom (and I believe he is), it remains for us to learn more about precisely *how* the one produced the other. One of the difficulties we face in our effort to better understand the relationship between slavery and freedom derives, I believe, from our tendency to treat these as fixed, stable categories when, in fact, the fuzzy boundaries and unclear content of these categories was precisely what fueled debate about "slavery" and "freedom" in the eighteenth century.

Stephanie Smallwood is Assistant Professor of History at the University of California at San Diego. She is working on her first book, *Saltwater Slavery: A Narrative of Captivity and Diaspora in the Anglo-Atlantic World*.

1. Eltis, *The Rise of African Slavery in the Americas* (Cambridge, MA, 2000), 279, commenting on the work of Orlando Patterson, David Brion Davis, and Edmund Morgan.

My goal in this essay is to explore the diverse and contradictory strands of "freedom" that were at play in the early modern Atlantic world. There may have been a political consensus against royalist absolutism in that world, but the parameters of the various individualist freedoms unleashed by the triple crown of Protestantism, post-Restoration constitutionalism, and mercantilism—"shifts in European thought," writes Eltis, "that helped the rights of the individual against group or state to evolve into recognizably modern form"—remained unclear.[2] In this essay, I suggest that commodification can serve as an important category of analysis for interrogating what we might call "the problem of freedom" in the early republic. I first will make the case for commodification as an appropriate category for analysis and interpretation of the politics of slavery; next I will suggest what we can learn from this approach; and finally, I will suggest why it matters.

*n.*Commodity—*v.*Commodify—*n.*Commodification: It has been useful for me to begin this essay by pondering the word "commodification." Although commodification interests us greatly in the era of late capitalism (enter the word in any search engine and you will get a large and fascinating variety of "hits"), neither this action-noun nor the verb from which it derives was much on the minds of those who inhabited the world of early capitalism—the Atlantic world in the sixteenth, seventeenth, and (long) eighteenth centuries. It was in the sixteenth and seventeenth centuries, Douglas Bruster observes, that "the word 'commodity' itself— once connoting something like 'convenience,' a meaning now obsolete— referred instead with more frequency to *concrete* things, exchangeable goods and wares."[3] And it was at this time (the turn of the seventeenth century) that John Wheeler's 1601 *Treatise of Commerce* mapped the great degree to which all the world had come to be enclosed in the grip of the market:

The Prince with his subjects, the Master with his servants, one friend and acquaintance with another, the Captain with his soldiers, the Husband with his wife,

---

2. Eltis, *Rise of African* Slavery, 8. In particular, see also David Brion Davis, *The Problem of Slavery in the Age of Revolution, 1770–1823* (Ithaca, 1975); *idem*, *The Problem of Slavery in Western Culture* (Ithaca, 1966); Richard W. Davis, ed., *The Origins of Modern Freedom in the West* (Stanford, 1995); and Eric Foner, *The Story of American Freedom* (New York, 1998).

3. Douglas Bruster, *Drama and the Market in the Age of Shakespeare* (Cambridge, UK, 1992), 41–2 (quotation at 41, emphasis added).

Women with and among themselves, and in a word, all the world choppeth and changeth, runneth and raveth after Marts, Markets and Merchandising, so that all things come into Commerce, and pass into traffic (in a manner) in all times, and in all places: not only that, which nature bringeth forth, as the fruits of the earth, the beasts, and living creatures, with their spoils, skins and cases, the metals, minerals, and such like things, but further also, this man maketh merchandise of the works of his own hands, this man of another man's labor, one selleth words, another maketh t[r]affic of the skins and blood of other men, yea there are some found so subtle and cunning merchants, that they persuade and induce men to suffer themselves to be bought and sold . . .[4]

Since it attained its place as the seed of wealth in western society, far more attention has been paid (by early moderns and continuing to this day) to the "riches and power" that derive from commodities and their circulation ("how the commodities of this land may be vented"[5]) than to the processes by which things become commodities. Although our notions of morphology tell us that the derivation of verbs from nouns signifies a process of conversion or transformation, the action or process embedded in the life of the thing, the commodity, is difficult for us to pin down. We know a great deal about commodities and their fetishization, but *commodification*—the process by which things are made into commodities—remains less rigorously interrogated.

The general function of commodification is understood well enough: defined according to generic qualities, enormously diverse kinds of things can be rendered commensurable with other things, giving the market its capacity to accommodate an infinite number and variety of transactions. But how, precisely, is this achieved? Where, exactly, is the *action* implied in the word "commodification" to be found?

Mary Poovey has tried to help us isolate what kind of activity this process entails. As Poovey explains it, the logic of commodification requires that "a thing or an experience . . . must be *broken down* into units whose commensurability is more important than any features that might distinguish these units," so that the thing is "*conceptually subdivided* into

---

4. Wheeler, *Treatise of Commerce*, cited in Bruster, *Drama and the Market*, 41–42.

5. "John Locke's Notes on Trade, c. 1674," in Joan Thirsk and J. P. Cooper, eds., *Seventeenth-Century Economic Documents* (Oxford, UK, 1972), 96; "Instructions to the Council of Trade, 1650," *ibid.*, 501.

units that are equivalent" and thus can in turn "be evaluated according to the common (and apparently noninterpretive) scale of number." Thus quantified, enormously diverse things can be grouped by infinite categories of abstraction, according to terms that "ignore or devalue the particulars that enable us to distinguish the unique qualities of things in favor of features whose primary function is to permit grouping or generalization. These grouping categories," Poovey goes on to explain, "like the infinitely divisible scale of number, seem to be noninterpretive in and of themselves, but they allow us to apply various kinds of explicitly interpretive systems to the things they group. For example, if we think of a chair and a table in terms of their most common function in houses, we can group them together as 'furniture' even though they differ from each other in obvious ways."[6] In sum, the logic of commodification secures particular ways of seeing, evaluating, classifying, and representing things that emphasize fixed, uniform, stable characteristics, so as to render their commensurability self-evident and thereby facilitate their easy circulation and exchange as commodities in the market economy.[7]

These effects embedded in the logic of commodification are awkward to describe because their operation is neither material nor visible. I find Poovey's language especially useful for this reason, as it draws (and holds) our attention to the fact that commodification is fundamentally a *representational* act. The "breaking down" and "subdividing" Poovey describes is not a material process—the chair is not physically disassembled as it is being commodified. Rather, the action involved in commodi-

---

6. Mary Poovey, "For Everything Else, There's . . . ," *Social Research*, 68 (2001): 2 (emphasis added).

7. My thinking on these cultural dimensions of economic systems has been especially influenced by Arjun Appadurai, "Introduction: Commodities and the Politics of Value," in *The Social Life of Things: Commodities in Cultural Perspective*, ed. Appadurai (Cambridge, UK, 1986), 3–63; Igor Kopytoff, "The Cultural Biography of Things: Commoditization as Process," *ibid.*, 64–91; Mary Douglas and Baron Isherwood, *The World of Goods: Toward an Anthropology of Consumption* (New York, 1979); Jane I. Guyer, ed., *Money Matters: Instability, Values and Social Payments in the Modern History of West African Communities* (Portsmouth, NH, 1995); Margaret Jean Radin, *Contested Commodities: The Trouble with Trade in Sex, Children, Body Parts, and Other Things* (Cambridge, MA, 1996); Joyce Oldham Appleby, *Economic Thought and Ideology in Seventeenth-Century England* (Princeton, 1978); and Michel Callon, ed., *The Laws of the Markets* (Oxford, UK, 1998).

fication is entirely conceptual—it occupies a "provisional" realm "which is neither wholly subjective nor quite objective," one whose operation we cannot witness, as the only evidence we have of it is its effect, the representation of the thing as a commodity.[8] Simply put, when things become commodities, it is their representational qualities—or rather those representational qualities that are regarded as most meaningful— that undergo transformation. Commodification's power resides in language, in discursive forms (ledgers, bills of sale) carefully crafted to define and imagine things in the terms that best facilitate their exchange and circulation. Thus, for example, rather than signifying a social or cultural value, a slave's gender is made to signify an economic value— quantified labor power: 1 male slave *equals* a Portuguese "peça," or Spanish "pieza de India."[9]

The life of the commodity, then, begins not with its material production through labor but rather with its epistemological constitution through discourse in the political economic thought of early modern Europe. When we deploy the action-noun derived from the word "commodity" we are concerned to isolate a discursive process that makes things "commoditable," or "fit" for market exchange.[10] We are pursuing the idea, then, that the commodities Marx identified as the root of capitalism have their own history—a history to which we have not paid sufficient attention. If commodities and their fetishization are the necessary beginning point of an understanding of industrial capitalism, then com-

---

8. Appadurai, "Commodities and the Politics of Value," 3, commenting on Georg Simmel's discussion of "value" in *The Philosophy of Money* (1907; London, 1978).

9. "A pieza de India," Philip Curtin writes, "was a measure of potential labor, not of individuals. For a slave to qualify as a pieza, he had to be a young adult male meeting certain specifications as to size, physical condition, and health. The very young, the old, and females were defined for commercial purposes as fractional parts of a pieza de India. This measure," he continues, "was convenient for Spanish imperial economic planning, where the need was a given amount of labor power, not a given number of individuals." Philip D. Curtin, *The Atlantic Slave Trade: A Census* (Madison, 1969), 22.

10. *Oxford English Dictionary,* definition given for "commoditable," an obsolete usage illustrated with a late eighteenth-century quotation. Interestingly, the *OED* shows no quotations earlier than 1975 to illustrate usage of "commodification."

modification is the necessary starting point for understanding capitalism's murky pre-history.

If it is in the discursive domain of market rhetoric that things are constituted as commodities—if it is through certain kinds of ascriptive language and the power it acquired in the early modern Atlantic world, in other words, that the representation of things as commodities is stabilized and secured—it is also for this reason that it is difficult to subject the process of commodification to sustained analysis. We are only able to approach commodification from the vantage point of its end result— the thing already commodified, already represented as a commodity in the ledger, bill of sale, or political economic treatise. Thus made evident to us only by those systems of representation that pronounce completion of the act, commodification is especially impervious to analysis by the methods of social science. When we see the end of the process—the thing already represented as a commodity in the ledger—through the various positivist lenses of social science (and I include here the scientific aspirations that infuse the discipline of history), we too easily take its place there for granted as something natural or given. We have much to learn, then, from those who have recognized important epistemological contests at play in the various modes of early modern economic discourse, as it is this kind of "thick description" that will help us see the opacity in a seemingly transparent text like the ledger, to question it and treat it as a form of language or discourse.[11] Paying closer attention to the process, we can see the power commodification derives from the status that accrued to certain kinds of representational systems (for example, ledgers) when they came to be understood as embodiments of incontrovertible "facts."[12]

---

11. Here I am thinking of, among others, Michel Foucault, *The Order of Things: An Archaeology of the Human Sciences* (1966; rep. New York, 1971); Jean-Christophe Agnew, *Worlds Apart: The Market and the Theater in Anglo-American Thought, 1550–1750* (Cambridge, UK, 1986); Bruster, *Drama and the Market*; Appleby, *Economic Thought and Ideology*; Mary Poovey, *A History of the Modern Fact: Problems of Knowledge in the Sciences of Wealth and Society* (Chicago, 1998); Walter Johnson, *Soul by Soul: Life Inside the Antebellum Slave Market* (Cambridge, MA, 1999); and more generally, economic anthropology as a useful literature for historians engaged in what I like to think of as the "cultural history of economic systems" (see note 7 above).

12. See Poovey, *History of the Modern Fact*, who notes that "numbers have come to epitomize the modern fact, because they have come to seem preinterpretive or even somehow noninterpretive at the same time that they have become the bedrock of systematic knowledge" (xii).

As a discursive system however, commodification always exists alongside other, competing systems of representation, meaning commodification is always a political process. It is always a contest between different systems of representing or articulating value. The more relevant subject of analysis, then, is not the fact of commodification, but rather its politics—when, how, and to what effect does the logic of commodification "win," that is, effectively silence the other systems of representation with which it competes? If people can be rendered convincingly as commodities where circumstances provide that competing systems of representation are silenced or disavowed, then how were such circumstances produced or discovered?

This silencing could be achieved by physically removing people from the reach of other registers of meaning (as in the case of the transatlantic traffic in African captives), or through ideology, as in the construction of racial categories of representation. And in turn, writing—commanding dominant systems of representation—was a necessary tool for those who would resist their commodification.[13] This, as Henry Louis Gates and other critics of black self-narration have shown, was something slaves in the early republic understood intuitively. Phillis Wheatley, Olaudah Equiano, and other black Atlantic figures who wrote themselves into western notions of subjectivity knew that the only way to get out from under the shadow of the commodity form was to write, to represent their own selves. The "record[ed]" black voice, writes Gates, was "a voice of deliverance from the deafening discursive silence which an enlightened Europe cited to prove the absence of the African's humanity," and was "the millennial instrument of transformation through which the African would become the European, the slave become the ex-slave, brute animal become the human being."[14]

---

13. This calls to mind Simmel's important observation regarding the tension, the politics, inherent in commodification: thus Appadurai notes Simmel's suggestion that "objects are not difficult to acquire because they are valuable, 'but we call those objects valuable that resist our desire to possess them.'" Appadurai, "Commodities and the Politics of Value," 3, commenting on and citing Simmel, *The Philosophy of Money.*

14. Henry Louis Gates, Jr., "Writing 'Race' and the Difference it Makes," in *"Race," Writing, and Difference,* ed. Gates (Chicago, 1986), 11–12. Also see especially Katherine Fishburn, *The Problem of Embodiment in Early African American Narrative* (Westport, CT, 1997), for the important call to recover "what the body knows" of its commodification. "Rather than seeing the ex-slaves' embodiment as something to be denied, underplayed, or overcome," Fishburn writes, "I

These questions all point to a familiar place: the terrain John Locke long has occupied in Anglo-American political thought. What did the triumph of Locke's liberal political philosophy mean for the relationship between people and markets in the early American republic? What did Locke's emphasis on the protection of property rights mean in a system where the market was the key regulator of social relations—in a social order, that is, where none but the gentry could hold themselves securely outside the bounds of the market? Space permits me to do more to ask than to answer these questions, but let me briefly outline where I think the line of inquiry and analysis I have charted might lead.

If the logic of commodification is one of "quantification" and "abstraction,"[15] then presumably people—the most singular of beings—should represent the greatest challenge to that logic, should be the most resilient in the face of its homogenizing impulse. In the first instance, then, we confront the difficult truth that the modern freedom envisaged by Locke and produced by Anglo-Atlantic capitalism not only easily accommodated and protected slavery, but in fact found its fullest expression in the commodification of the person—in the lesson learned that the logic of commodification *could* be extended to cloak even human beings in its shadow. The striking thing, the problem to be solved, is how the early modern spread of the market economy produced that discovery.

In the second instance, we confront the necessary limitations of antislavery ideology, by which I mean the impossibility of sustained critique of commodification as such within the particular articulations of liberal political economic theory taking root in early republican America. In other words, for all of its impassioned discourse about the meanings of liberty and slavery, it is striking how much antislavery ideology targeted the effects of slavery rather than the process—the act—that made the person into a slave (or free?) *subject*.

What was at issue fundamentally was not whether slaves were property or human, or whether human beings could be property, but rather what *property* itself would be in the new nation—in other words, how

---

began to see it as the route to a new kind of knowing—one based in the body, or, as I prefer to call it, one based in the body-self. The more I reread the narratives themselves, the more I became convinced that the ex-slaves were not trying to write themselves into Western metaphysics as equal to whites, but were instead, more radically and daringly, rethinking metaphysics itself" (xii).

15. Poovey, "For Everything Else, There's . . . ," 2.

questions fundamental to the European enlightenment would resolve themselves in the particular terrain of the new republic. I am less interested, then, in how ideas about property shaped debates over slavery than in how the presence of half a million slaves shaped understandings of property in the American republic. How did their commodification demand particular kinds of articulations of basic Lockean liberal principles? How did the understandings of property underwritten and authored by slavery shape relationships between people and the market in the modern West independent of the abolition of the institution of slavery? This points of course to the important relationship between capitalism and slavery—between, in other words, market relations and commodification of humans, whether that be the self-commodification of the free wage laborer or the denial of self-commodification suffered by the slave laborer.

If the most significant boost slavery gave to capitalism came not from a quotient of labor (that had run its course by the nineteenth century) but rather from the lesson that the power of representation was sufficient to commodify people, then arguably the most important relationship we need to interrogate and understand is not the empirical relationship between industrial capitalism and slave labor, but rather the epistemological relationship between markets and "freedom" in the modern western society that the Atlantic system made. In other words, I suspect that what underlies concern about the relationship between social life and economic life is the unspoken awareness of what I have called the "problem of freedom" in modern western society: that problem being the inescapable shadow of commodification encoded in Lockean definitions that whittled "freedom" down (from all the liberties it might embody) to the ability to whittle things (and people) down (from all that they might be) to their own-able characteristics.[16]

Viewed through the lens of commodification it becomes apparent that those who insisted there was a contradiction between American liberty and American slavery stood on shaky ground. American slavery was more deeply rooted in property relations than at any other time or place in recorded history, and property relations here were more sacrosanct than at any other time or place. In this sense, the relationship of liberty to slavery in America seemed so compelling because the contradiction was in fact more apparent than real. Well before American independence was actually achieved it had become apparent that the liberty Anglo-

---

16. My thanks to Walter Johnson for help on this point.

Americans sought would require a very high price of some members of society. It was apparent, in other words, that there was an unresolvable tension between the lofty ideal of political liberty and the material reality of economic liberty. Human equality and economic liberty were mutually exclusive, yet they were antagonistically interdependent. The combination was ironic, to be sure, but it was hardly a contridiction. In a society founded on the sanctity of property rights, slavery for some was an unfortunate if distasteful fact of legitimate property rights.

My point is not to question the meaning or impact of antislavery thought, or to question why contemporary actors did not themselves critique commodification. I aim, rather, to suggest why it matters that we probe a critique of the commodifiying element of modern slavery. Generally it has been taken as a truism that where there is slavery there is also the slave market. The coexistence of the two institutions may be universal, but the relationship between the two can vary substantially. The American colonies, for example, had the distinction of being the only societies to embody an institution of slavery built entirely and exclusively on a foundation of market relations. Here, in other words, not only did the slave market coexist alongside slavery: it was the slave market that alone gave birth to institutionalized slavery. In this important regard, the commodification of people holds a powerful and special place in American slavery.

In place of the slave-free paradox that has guided us for so long, then, perhaps it is important for us to turn greater attention to the slave-free continuum: to expose the continuity between black chattel slavery and indentured Asian servitude in plantation systems; to bring critical historical perspective to the unavoidable trueism that slavery, far from being dead and gone, is growing in our modern western (and now global) capitalist system.[17]

---

17. Pursuing these lines of inquiry will lead historians of the early republic into terrain that crosses disciplinary boundaries and refigures the temporal frames by which we narrate the diverse kinds of commodification that shaped the politics of selfhood in the modern West. See Walter Johnson, "Time and Revolution in African America: Temporality and the History of Atlantic Slavery," in *Rethinking American History*, ed. Thomas Bender (Berkeley, 2001); Lisa Lowe, "The Intimacies of Four Continents," in *Tense and Tender Ties: North American History and Postcolonial Studies*, ed. Ann Stoler (Durham, NC, forthcoming); Saree Makdisi, *William Blake and the Impossible History of the 1790s* (Chicago, 2003); and Jeffrey Sklansky, *The Soul's Economy: Market Society and Selfhood in American Thought, 1820–1920* (Chapel Hill, 2002).

The Pedestal and the Veil

Rethinking the Capitalism/Slavery Question

WALTER JOHNSON

What does it mean to speak of the "commodification of people" as a domain of historical inquiry? Why put it that way? What does it mean to say that a person has been commodified? Is this about slavery? Prostitution? Wage labor? The sale of donated organs, fetal tissue samples, and sections of the human genome? Is it about the way that my personal data is sold without me knowing anything about it? Is it about the Coke machine in my kid's school cafeteria—the sale of her unwitting little field of vision, her tiny stomach, and her enormous desire to be grown-up? At first glance, the phrase seems impossibly baggy: inviting all sorts of comparisons of the incommensurable, and posing questions that sit at odd angles to the standard categories of historical inquiry. But perhaps that's the point: by inviting comparisons, the editors have framed a question that draws attention to the connections and similarities between historical processes that are usually analyzed as if they were distinct—slavery, wage labor, and prostitution, say—and calls attention to the historically embedded distinctions that separate them from one another as ethical, legal, and analytical subjects.

In reflecting on these wonderful essays, I want first to review the older version of the question out of which this one seems to have been conjugated: the question of the relation of "capitalism" to "slavery." And I

Walter Johnson is Associate Professor of History and American Studies at New York University and the author of *Soul by Soul: Life Inside the Antebellum Slave Market* (1999) and the forthcoming *River of Dark Dreams: Slavery, Capitalism, and Imperialism in the Mississippi River Valley.*

want to do so with particular attention to the work of Karl Marx and the most influential of those who have written about slavery in the United States in orthodox Marxian terms; for it is, after all, this intellectual tradition that has most actively kept alive the idea that when you talk about "capitalism" and "slavery" you are talking about two things, rather than one. Finally, I want to propose a heterodox reading of a short section of *Capital* that foregrounds the question, which Marx so insistently repressed throughout the rest of the text: the question of slavery.

If it is hard to think about slavery as capitalism, that is because it is supposed to be: slavery is, in some sense, "unthinkable" in the historical terms that frame western political economy.[1] In both Smithian and Marxian economics, slavery serves as an un-theorized historical backdrop to the history of capitalism, an un-thought (even when present) past to the inevitable emergence of the present. This foundational exclusion of the fact of slavery from the framing of political economy, I would argue, has had consequences that bedevil us down to the present moment.

James Oakes recently has argued that Adam Smith and the "bourgeois" political economists who followed him spent a great deal of time and energy trying to reconcile what everybody knew—that slavery would inevitably give way to "free" labor because of the superior capacity of self-interest as a tool of labor discipline—with what seemed nevertheless to be everywhere the stubborn fact: slaveholders were making a great deal of money. Smith resolved this problem, according to Oakes, by passing it off to other regions of intellectual inquiry. Perhaps it was the "pride" of man that made "him love to domineer," combined with the excessive fertility of the tropics, that accounted for the persistence of slavery in the face of its inherent inefficiency and inevitable decline.[2] Perhaps, that is, the persistence of slavery was a question to be answered by psychology or geography (by moral philosophy or natural history, to use terms Smith would recognize) but certainly not political economy.

---

1. See, especially, Cedric J. Robinson, *Black Marxism: The Making of the Black Radical Tradition* (London, 1983). For the idea of histories "unthinkable" in the terms of western political thought, see Michel-Rolph Trouillot, *Silencing the Past: Power and the Production of History* (Boston, 1995); and Dipesh Chakrabarty, *Provincializing Europe: Postcolonial Thought and Historical Difference* (Princeton, 2000).

2. James Oakes, "The Peculiar Fate of the Bourgeois Critique of Slavery," in Winthrop D. Jordan and Annette Gordon-Reed, eds., *Slavery and the American South* (Jackson, MS, 2003), 29–33.

If Smith displaced the question of slavery, it might be said that Marx simply evaded it. The magnificent critique of the commodity form with which Marx began *Capital*, for instance, unfolds from a detailed consideration of the nature of a bolt of linen. Out of the dual character of that linen as an object and a commodity—having a use value and an exchange value—Marx develops the notion of "the fetishism of commodities," the habit of mind by which things are made to seem as if they exist in relation to one another (compared according to their prices) rather than to their uses and the circumstances of their production (which reflected the larger matrix of social relations).[3] But wait: *a bolt of linen?* At a moment when English mill hands expended the (few) calories they gained from American sugar on the work of processing American cotton?[4] Describing an economy that shipped sterling debt to the new world to pay for slave-grown products and then received it back again in exchange for the finished textiles produced in British factories?[5] In the shadow of a bloody Civil War in which the Confederate foreign policy had been premised on the (almost true) idea that the disruption of the cotton trade would cause such suffering in England that the British would be forced to support secession?[6] A bolt of linen?[7]

Marx's substitution of (British) flax for (American) cotton as the emblematic raw material of English capitalism enabled him to tell what in essence was a story of the commodity form artificially hedged in by Brit-

---

3. Kark Marx, *Capital: A Critical Analysis of Capitalist Production* (3 vols., New York, 1967), 1: 43–87. For a reading of *Capital* that outlines a helpful (if doxological) set of interpretations, see David Harvey, *The Limits to Capital* (1982; rep., London, 1999).

4. See Sidney Mintz, *Sweetness and Power: The Place of Sugar in Modern History* (New York, 1985).

5. See Edwin J. Perkins, *Financing Anglo-American Trade: The House of Brown, 1800–1880* (Cambridge, MA, 1975).

6. See Frank Lawrence Owsley, *King Cotton Diplomacy: Foreign Relations of the Confederate States of America* (Chicago, 1959), 134–53; Thomas Hietala, *Manifest Design: Anxious Aggrandizement in Late Jacksonian America* (Ithaca, 1985), 55–94.

7. The substitution of linen for cotton seems even more remarkable in light of the facts that Marx was subsisting during the period he wrote *Capital* largely on loans from Engels, who was working as the manager of a cotton mill partly owned by his family. See Peter Stallybrass, "Marx's Coat," in Patricia Spyer, ed., *Border Fetishisms: Material Objects in Unstable Spaces* (London, 1998), 190–94.

ish national boundaries. This unacknowledged spatial specificity surfaces again in the chapter on "primitive accumulation," which provides the ground in which most of those seeking to apply Marxian historical categories to the story of American slavery have rooted their ideas. The bloody story that Marx told in this chapter is of the expropriation of the commons through the process of enclosure (the forcible imposition of private property on the landscape through the planting of hedges and violent enforcement of exclusive rights), which prevented the landless from providing for themselves in any way other than working for wages they would then use to pay for things they once had made (here specified as yarn, linen, and woolens). "The expropriation and eviction of a part of the agricultural population," Marx explained, "not only set free for industrial capital, the laborers, their means of subsistence, and material for labor; it also created the home market."[8] With its emphasis on laws from the reign of the Tudor monarchs, domestic products, and the "home" market, this is an unabashedly provincial story. It is the story of feudalism succeeded by capitalism in England, Anglo-centric in its spatial parameters and teleological in its temporal framing.

And yet this is the section of *Capital* upon which historians of slavery have relied when they have attempted to situate their histories in that of capital. For among the very few remarks that Marx made about slavery he did include in the historical account of capitalism at the back of the book the following amazing sentence: "The veiled slavery of the wage-workers in Europe needed, for its pedestal, slavery pure and simple in the new world."[9]

Those claiming the mantel of Marx have generally read this sentence according to the framing of the material on European history that surrounds it, as if it makes a claim about historical development. "Veiled slavery," of course, refers to the commodification of labor power (the sectioning of the human body's capacities into time-scaled units of labor that can be "freely" sold on the open market) as opposed to "slavery pure and simple," the commodification of the laborer (the sale of a human being at a price that made that person comparable to all manner of things). In the standard reading, this is the passage where Marx refers to the inevitable succession of the latter by the former. Thus, in answer

---

8. Marx, *Capital*, 1: 667–712 (quotation at 699).
9. *Ibid.*, 711.

to the question as it is commonly put—what does Marx say about capitalism and slavery?—there can only be one answer: slavery in Marx is not, properly speaking, "capitalist." As Elizabeth Fox-Genovese and others have argued, in American slavery there was no separation of labor from the land; it was labor rather than labor power that was being commodified; capital and labor did not stand in relation to one another counterpoised by contract but cohabited in the same exploited body; the domination of labor was not abstract but concrete, etc. According to the indicia of orthodox Marxism (at least as it is represented by those who have invoked it to study slavery in the United States), slavery was, like feudalism, "pre-capitalist," "archaic," a "conservative" residuum; its super-cession by "capitalism" (here defined as an industrial mode of production characterized by wage labor) was inevitable and its theorization beyond that fact (for Marx at least) unnecessary.[10] So, that's what (they say) Marx says about slavery. But what does slavery say about Marx?

By attempting to frame the history of slavery within categories derived from writings that self-consciously treated slavery as a historical and conceptual backdrop for the main event—the history of industrial capitalism in Europe—historians writing as orthodox Marxists have, understandably, ended up in a bit of a mess. If slavery was not capitalist how do we explain its commercial character: the excrescence of money changers and cotton factors in southern cities who yearly handled millions and millions of pounds of foreign exchange; the mercantile ambitions of southern slaveholders who wanted to take over Cuba and Mexico and Nicaragua so as to insure their commercial dominance and greatness; the thriving slave markets at the centers of their cities where prices tracked those that were being paid for cotton thousands of miles away? The standard answer has been to say that slavery was "in but not of" the capitalist economy, a beguilingly otiose formulation, which implies some sort of spatial

---

10. See Eugene D. Genovese, *The Political Economy of Slavery: Studies in the Economy and Society of the Slave South* (New York, 1965); Elizabeth Fox-Genovese and Eugene D. Genovese, *The Fruits of Merchant Capital: Slavery and Bourgeois Property in the Rise and Expansion of Capitalism* (New York, 1983); Elizabeth Fox-Genovese, *Within the Plantation Household: Black and White Women of the Old South* (Chapel Hill, 1988). The temporal unevenness of the succession story is generally smoothed by the invocation of the category of "contradiction": see Mark V. Tushnet, *The American Law of Slavery: Considerations of Humanity and Interest* (Princeton, 1981).

unity of process ("in") which it defines only negatively in relation to an orthodox definition of "capitalism."[11]

The existing discussion, that is to say, has devolved into a set of more-or-less tautological propositions about how you define the categories of historical analysis (if "capitalism" is defined as that-mode-of-production-characterized-by-wage-labor then slavery was, by definition, not "capital-ist"). But doesn't it make more sense to think about the political econ-omy of the eighteenth- and nineteenth-century Atlantic as a single space, its dimensions defined by flows of people, money, and goods, its nested temporalities set by interlocking (though clearly distinct) labor regimes, cyclical rhythms of cultivation and foreign exchange, and shared stan-dards of calculability and measurement?[12] Try for just a minute to imag-ine the history of that bolt of cotton that Marx left out of *Capital*. It had been bought before it even existed by a British buyer who extended credit in sterling to an American factor. It had been put in the ground, tended, picked, bagged, baled, and shipped by an American slave. It had graded out well and brought a premium price because it was free of "trash" (leaves, stems, sticks, rocks, etc.) and "stains" (which resulted from cotton being left in the field too long after it bloomed); its condi-tion, that is, reflected the palpable presence of standards of the exchange in Liverpool in the labor regime that governed Louisiana. It had been shipped in the name of a planter who was thus liable for any difference between the price he had received in advance and the price for which it was eventually sold—a planter, that is, who was legally present at the exchange on which his cotton was sold. It had been summed out in the accounts between planters and factors in dollars that the factors had bought with the sterling they had received from English buyers and sold to northern merchant bankers who would pass it on to those seeking to

---

11. Fox-Genovese, *Within the Plantation Household*, 53–58.

12. For a reading of Marx that dovetails with my reading of the political econ-omy of the Atlantic world, see David Kazanjian, *The Colonizing Trick: National Culture and Imperial Citizenship in Early America* (Minneapolis, 2003), 14–24. See also Stuart Hall, "Race, Articulation, and Societies Structured in Dominance," in Philomena Essed and David Theo Goldberg, eds., *Race Critical Theories: Text and Context* (Oxford, UK, 2002), 38–68. For the emphasis on time, space, and "calculation," see David Harvey, "Money, Space, Time, and the City," in his *The Urban Experience* (Baltimore, 1989), 165–99.

buy English manufactures. And had been finished in an English mill, made into a coat, and ended up on the back of an English millhand who paid for it with his wages.[13]

In trying to reframe the capitalism/slavery discussion as a set of questions about eighteenth and nineteenth-century Atlantic political economy, it might be worth just for a second (because that is all it will take) to see what Marx did say about the history of slavery in *Capital*. Right before the business about the veil and the pedestal he wrote this: "Whilst the cotton industry introduced child-slavery in England, it gave in the United States a stimulus to the transformation of the earlier, more or less patriarchal slavery, into a system of commercial exploitation."[14] What is striking about this sentence is the first word: "whilst." It frames the relation of what we have been calling "capitalism" and what we have been calling "slavery" in terms of dynamic simultaneity rather than simple super-cession, though it does so with careful attention to the historically different relations of production—slavery and wage labor—which characterized the two poles of this single Atlantic economy. In so doing, it frames the pedestal metaphor that directly follows it as a structural (or spatial) metaphor rather than a temporal one. Rather than focusing on the specifics of capitalist development in Europe, this sentence treats the Atlantic economy as its ground of analysis, a spatial unit over which economic practice had differential but nevertheless related forms and effects.

And the name that Marx gives this trans-Atlantic political economy at this moment very close to the end of *Capital* is not "capitalism" but "slavery"—"child-slavery," "veiled slavery," "slavery pure and simple."

---

13. For money and credit, see Harold Woodman, *King Cotton and His Retainers: Financing and Marketing the Cotton Crop of the South, 1800–1925* (Lexington, KY, 1968), 3–198; and Perkins, *Financing Anglo-American*. For slaves, labor, discipline, and cotton, see Walter Johnson, *River of Dark Dreams: Slavery, Capitalism, and Imperialism in the Mississippi River Valley* (forthcoming). For the increasing identification of the English working class with cotton clothing, see Stallybrass, "Marx's Coat," 193–94.

14. Marx, *Capital*, 1: 711. Marx also used the idea of "commercial slavery" when he compared the interstate slave trade in the United States to the importation of Irish workers to England: "*Mutato nomine de te fabula narratur*," he wrote: "with the name changed, the story applies to you" (254).

It would strain credibility to argue that the hundreds upon hundreds of pages of *Capital* in which Marx ignored the question of slavery should be re-read in the light of the several moments at the end where he seemed to suggest that "slavery" was *the* essential form of exploitation in the nineteenth-century economy and that the forms it took in Manchester or in Mississippi were simply variant manifestations of a shared essence. Safer to understand the invocation of "slavery" as a rhetorical effect, designed to pierce the illusion that wage-workers were in any sense "free." "Slavery" was, after all, an often-invoked metaphor in the nineteenth-century. The term served as a sort of universal comparison for disparate injustices, and in the process it lost some of its meaning and most of its historical specificity. But the very metaphorical promiscuity of the term "slavery" as Marx used it, calls us to pay close attention to both the pattern of its deployment and the maneuvers by which its seemingly universal applicability was contested and controlled. To pay attention, that is, to historical process by which the boundaries between slavery and "freedom" were drawn, and to the character of the "veil" that separated them.

The "veil" to which Marx refers is most simply imagined as "contract freedom": the idea that wage-labor contracts (by which "free" workers sold control over the capacities of their bodies by the hour) reflected freely given "consent" to the bargain (and thus elided the deeper histories of expropriation and coercion that, according to Marx, actually structured the bargain).[15] It refers, that is, to the historical process by which the commodification of laborers and the commodification of labor power came to be understood as two entirely separate and, indeed, opposite things—slavery and freedom, black and white, household and market, here and there—rather than as two concretely intertwined and ideologically symbiotic elements of a larger unified though internally diversified structure of exploitation.

This formulation of functional unity veiled by ideological separation

15. See David Brion Davis, *The Problem of Slavery in the Age of Revolution, 1770–1823* (Ithaca, 1975); David R. Roediger, *The Wages of Whiteness: Race and the Making of the American Working Class* (London, 1991); and Amy Dru Stanley, *From Bondage to Contract: Wage Labor, Marriage, and the Market in the Age of Slave Emancipation* (Cambridge, UK, 1998).

entails several interesting avenues of inquiry taken up by these essays. They commend us, first, to try to think about the economies of Europe, America, Africa—so long divided by historiographies framed around national boundaries and hard-and-fast distinctions between modes of production—in all of their concrete interconnection.[16] This emphasis on the concrete and practical seems to me to have the virtue of allowing for the use of some of the most powerful categories produced by western political economy—the idea of commodification, the labor theory of value, the notion of variability (across space and race) of the socially necessary cost of the reproduction of the laboring class, and the calculation of surplus value—without having first to engage a long doctrinal dispute about the capitalism question. Once the teleology of the "slavery-to-capitalism" question has been set aside, that is, we still have an enormous amount to learn from what Marx had to tell us about the work of capitalists as we try to diagram the historical interconnections and daily practices of the global economy of the eighteenth and nineteenth centuries.

These essays likewise suggest a second set of topics as we try to think of the enormous work involved in categorizing and containing all of those interconnections in notions of process and history structured by the oppositions of slavery and freedom, black and white, and coercion and consent. As they argued about where to draw the line between proper and improper forms of political economy—about whether wage work was wage slavery, whether slaveholding was slave trading, and whether marriage was prostitution—capitalists and anti-capitalists, employers and employees, masters and slaves, husbands and wives argued over the character of freedom, right, and personhood, over where they began and where they ended, where these things could be said to be salable and where they must be held to be sacred. These violent arguments were eventually settled on a frontier where we live today: "slavery" was defined by the condition of blacks in the South before 1865 and "freedom" was defined as the ability to choose to work for a wage or a share of the crop (though not to choose not to work for a wage or a share of the crop

---

16. See Eric Williams, *Capitalism and Slavery* (Chapel Hill, 1944); Mintz, *Sweetness and Power*; and Joseph Miller, *Way of Death: Merchant Capitalism and the Angolan Slave Trade, 1730–1830* (Madison, 1988).

or, indeed, to choose not to be "free"), and "the household" was defined as "in but not of the market."[17] "So massive was the effort" wrote Marx, "to establish 'the eternal laws of Nature' of the capitalist mode of production."[18] And so began the history of "freedom," which is apparently hurtling toward such a fearful conclusion all over the world today.

17. See Daniel T. Rodgers, *The Work Ethic in Industrial America, 1850–1920* (Chicago, 1978); Thomas C. Holt, *The Problem of Freedom: Race, Labor, and Politics in Jamaica and Britain, 1832–1938* (Baltimore, 1992); Stanley, *From Bondage to Contract*; Saidiya V. Hartman, *Scenes of Subjection: Terror, Slavery, and Self-Making in Nineteenth-Century America* (New York, 1997); Kazanjian, *The Colonizing Trick*, 35–138.

18. Marx, *Capital*, 1:711. In the original: "*Tantae molis erat. . . .*"

PART V

Public, Private, and Spirit Worlds

. . . at the intersections of which, we think, culture is constructed, contested, and negotiated.

DAVID S. SHIELDS, CHAIR

Now cultural history is everything—and it is, predictably, in danger of losing its way altogether. Once naïvely conceived as the spread of arts and letters into the Ohio Valley (remember Louis B. Wright, Culture on a Moving Frontier?), cultural history got a facelift from the anthropologists one generation back, and a whole-body makeover more recently from literary scholars of every description. As editors this past decade we have labored to aerate the soil of early republic studies with offerings from scholars whose questions (and answers) differ sharply from the traditional centers of our field in constitutional and political history. In that spirit we decided to close this forum on needs and opportunities by asking David Shields, a SHEAR stalwart whose work is always unorthodox and extremely creative, to coordinate reflections on culture and how we approach it. He invited Bernard Herman, Leigh Schmidt, and Patricia Cline Cohen to think about the intersections we had laid out for him. Their essays suggest three very different points of view and avenues of further investigation. David then closes the show with twenty-eight questions for which you, gentle reader, must supply the answers in the decade ahead.

Sex and Sexuality

The Public, the Private, and the Spirit Worlds

PATRICIA CLINE COHEN

Historians of sex in early America have long attended to a public/private dichotomy, for the simple reason that most sexual behavior in past times was confined to a very private realm, usually beyond direct observation, while the rules, norms, prescriptions, and laws—all the ways a society attempts to regulate sex—had to be part of the public realm to be effective. The news that a third realm, the spirit world, offers another metaphorical arena bearing on the history of sex at first sounds rather strange; but in the mid-nineteenth century such was the case. This essay first highlights both classic and recent scholarship exploring private behavior and public regulation of sexuality in the early republic, and then it turns to ideas about sex inspired by (or, more accurately, justified by) a spirit world invoked to challenge the institution of marriage starting in the years around 1850. The spirit-inspired challenge ultimately failed to attract many adherents, but while it was garnering headlines it generated a remarkable debate about sexual desire built around a distinction between sexual love and lust.

Foundational work on the history of early American sex emerged some forty years ago in the field of demographic history centered on the colonial experience. Practitioners drew on large data sets to capture change over time in reproductive behavior, to be sure a very imperfect proxy for sexual behavior. While the quantitative approach is out of fashion of late, in its heyday it produced very useful studies based on the good vital records kept by New England towns. Averages, such as average age at

Patricia Cline Cohen is professor of history at the University of California, Santa Barbara. She is currently working on a book about Mary Gove Nichols and Thomas Low Nichols, two antebellum marriage reformers and advocates of free love.

marriage or average family size, allowed inferences about marital sex, and rates of fornication, bastardy, and prenuptial pregnancy gave us baseline measures of the frequency of non-marital sex. The news that perhaps a third or more of New England brides were pregnant at the point of marriage in the mid- to late eighteenth century seemed stunning back in the 1960s, since it so sharply contradicted traditional assumptions about pious New Englanders.[1] Since then, we have developed greater caution about equating premarital pregnancy in 1790 with 1950s dating behaviors; the numbers produced by historical demography still need sensitive interpretation. The ever-terse Martha Ballard eschewed judgmental comments in her long-term midwifery diary as the numbers of "early" births mounted up in Hallowell, Maine; but did that mean she approved of premarital sex?[2] Some 1830s ministers active in the Seventh-Commandment Society (a male moral reform group) expressed astonishment at their own church records from fifty years earlier, with lists of births and marriages that manifested the pattern of high early first births. Their astonishment over the ministerial silence of that earlier era says a lot about a half-century sea change in attitudes toward female chastity that we are still struggling to make sense of.

Early demographic studies clustered in seventeenth- and eighteenth-century towns where vital records allowed for family reconstitution. The early republic, with its population mobility and less complete vital records, has proved more resistant to the local study approach, which requires a stable universe of people out of which averages and rates can be calculated. Still, my hunch is that with all the new genealogical and local history sources on the web now, the time may arrive when future scholars will reengage with quantitative methods and find a way to apply them to small towns of the early republic. Perhaps there will be new surprises then, maybe not in prenuptial pregnancy rates but, I'm guessing, bigamy.[3]

---

1. The classic work is probably ripe for restudy now: Daniel Scott Smith and Michael Hindus, "Premarital Pregnancy in America, 1640–1971: An Overview and Interpretation," *Journal of Interdisciplinary History*, 5 (1974–75): 537–70.

2. Laurel Thatcher Ulrich, *A Midwife's Tale: The Life of Martha Ballard, Based on her Diary, 1785–1812* (New York, 1990).

3. Two recent works point in this direction: Hendrik Hartog, *Man and Wife in America: A History* (Cambridge, MA, 2000); and Beverly J. Schwartzberg, "Grass Widows, Barbarians, and Bigamists: Fluid Marriage in Late Nineteenth-Century

Beyond numbers, a second classic approach to learning about sexual activity in the past has been the study of manuscripts in search of mention of deeply private intimacies. Letters and diaries are the bread and butter of historical work, but men and women of the early republic were reticent about committing personal sexual stories to paper, both due to modesty and to prudent self-protection, since the only licit form of sex was the marital relation. Karen Lystra uncovered great riches in a study of courtship letters, *Searching the Heart*.[4] Written by men and women on the verge of marriage decisions, their letters express covert and even overt sexual desire along with attention to whatever forces put a brake on courting couples' intimacies.

Lystra's evidence often came from prominent families whose sense of self-importance caused their papers to be saved. A valuable addition is Karen V. Hansen's article on two African-American women who exchanged a remarkable set of love letters in the 1850s and 1860s. Letters also form the basis for the pathbreaking 1975 essay by Carroll Smith-Rosenberg on intimate female friendships of the late eighteenth to mid-nineteenth centuries.[5] While private letters about sex might well be pruned from family manuscript collections, one untapped source of such material was generated in breach of marriage and seduction suits, two legal actions of accelerating occurrence in the early republic. Entered into evidence to establish a couple's relationship (and therefore probably pruned by the plaintiff), such letters were not usually preserved by the court; but sometimes they found their way into the hands of newspaper editors wishing to print them for their entertainment value.

A third pathway to the history of private sex in the early republic has come from close studies of records of houses of refuge, where unwed mothers showed up in need, or local courts and justices of the peace,

---

America" (Ph.D. diss., University of California, Santa Barbara, 2001). It is a challenge to quantify illegal behavior when it was not prosecuted; Schwartzberg used Civil War pension records of competing widows in her study.

4. Karen Lystra, *Searching the Heart: Men, Women, and Romantic Love in Nineteenth-Century America* (New York, 1992).

5. Karen V. Hansen, " 'No Kisses like Youres': An Erotic Friendship Between two African American Women During the Mid-Nineteenth Century," *Gender & History*, 7 (1995): 153–82; Carroll Smith-Rosenberg, "The Female World of Love and Ritual: Relations between Women in Nineteenth-Century America," *Signs*, 1 (1975): 1–29.

adjudicating paternity suits and family law. Clare Lyons's research, *Sex Among the Rabble,* pulls together many inventive sources to get at a working-class culture of sex in postrevolutionary Philadelphia. Two other excellent recent works grounded in court records show the intricate ways that sexual relations structured race and class: Kirsten Fischer's *Suspect Relations* focuses on colonial North Carolina and Ann Marie Plane's *Colonial Intimacies* looks at Native-American marriage under the pressure of English colonization.[6] It is striking that these (and several other) rich regional studies are anchored in the pre-1800 period. Is it a paucity of data, a change in record keeping, or just the massively growing and moving population that deter scholars of the early republic from attempting similar studies?

Instead, many of those scholars turn to writing microhistories as a compelling way of exploring sexuality in the early republic, taking off from some transgressive event that brought private sex into public notice (hence the documentation). Irene Quenzler Brown and Richard D. Brown do this wonderfully for an 1806 family drama, *The Hanging of Ephraim Wheeler,* about a Massachusetts man executed for raping his daughter. Two other quite different examples are Doron Ben-Atar's essay on an elderly Connecticut man accused of repeated bestiality and my own essay on an Episcopal bishop's sexual harassment trial of 1845. Microhistories make good teaching tools, as several recent anthologies demonstrate. But they often skew our attention to sexual misbehavior, without giving us a sense of how common that misbehavior was.[7]

---

6. Clare Lyons, *Sex Among the Rabble* (forthcoming in 2005 from the Omohundro Institute for Early American History and Culture); Kirsten Fischer, *Suspect Relations: Sex, Race, and Resistance in Colonial North Carolina* (Ithaca, 2001); Ann Marie Plane, *Colonial Intimacies: Indian Marriage in Early New England* (Ithaca, 2000).

7. Irene Quenzler Brown and Richard D. Brown, *The Hanging of Ephraim Wheeler: A Story of Rape, Incest, and Justice in Early America* (Cambridge, MA, 2003); Doron Ben-Atar, "Reflections on Bestiality in the Early Republic: The Case of Gideon Washburn," presented at the SHEAR annual meeting, University of California, Berkeley, July 2002; Patricia Cline Cohen, "Ministerial Misdeeds: The Onderdonk Trial and Sexual Harassment in the 1840s," *Journal of Women's History,* 7 (1995): 34–57. Anthologies include Merrill Smith, ed., *Sex without Consent: Rape and Sexual Coercion in America* (New York, 2001); Martha Hodes, ed., *Sex, Love, Race: Crossing Boundaries in North American History* (New York, 1999); Elizabeth Reis, ed., *American Sexual Histories* (Malden, MA, 2001); and

Two studies of another kind of transgressive sex, interracial, have advanced our understanding of the instability of race in a southern society erected on racial categorization. Martha Hodes's *White Women, Black Men* presents tantalizing evidence that before the Civil War, the far less common pairing of white women with black men not only happened on occasion, but was apparently countenanced by whites. Joshua D. Rothman explores the opposite case, of white men and black women in coercive or adulterous relationships, in *Notorious in the Neighborhood*. Rothman uncovers many fascinating examples of Jefferson/Hemings-like relationships in the larger Virginia planter community Thomas Jefferson inhabited, widely tolerated (by whites, anyway), and existing directly at odds with laws and sentiments about miscegenation.[8]

Medical writings about sex are an obvious place to go for information about how sexual knowledge was produced and disseminated. For four decades scholars have quoted the ever-growing sexual advice literature in the early republic as if it were unproblematic prescriptive literature expressing popularly-held ideas. Two recent studies tell us much more about the authors and their contrasting points of view. Janet Farrell Brodie's *Contraception and Abortion in Nineteenth-Century America* covers not only family limitation practices but brings to life the various health writers themselves to uncover their sometimes hidden agendas. And Helen Lefkowitz Horowitz's *Rereading Sex: Battles over Sexual Knowledge and Suppression in Nineteenth-Century America* takes it all several big steps further in her notion that a "sexual conversation" in at least four parts was in progress in antebellum America, involving evangelical religious types, popular health reformers, free thinkers and free lovers, all with new and conflicting ideas to compete with what she calls the "vernacular culture" with its male-defined approach to sex as a bodily function. No longer is it possible to speak of merely a two-sided sexual system of polite Victorian repression versus a sexual underworld.[9]

Kathy Peiss, ed., *Major Problems in the History of American Sexuality: Documents and Essays* (Boston, 2001).

8. Martha Hodes, *White Women, Black Men: Illicit Sex in the Nineteenth-Century South* (New Haven, 1997); Joshua D. Rothman, *Notorious in the Neighborhood: Sex and Family across the Color Line in Virginia, 1787–1861* (Chapel Hill, 2003).

9. Janet Farrell Brodie, *Contraception and Abortion in Nineteenth-Century America* (Ithaca, 1994); Helen Lefkowitz Horowitz, *Rereading Sex: Battles over Sexual Knowledge and Suppression in Nineteenth-Century America* (New York, 2002).

That urban sexual underworld is getting ample coverage, as it always has, ever since the first "lights and shadows" and city mystery books were published in the 1840s. But lately the research is deepening our knowledge not just of the low life as seen through the eyes of the police or the moral reformers, but now the low life as it saw itself. Horowitz's book, as well as new work by legal scholar Donna Dennis, traces the world of early pornography and the printers who tangled with obscene libel charges thirty years before vice crusader Anthony Comstock masterminded a federal obscenity law in 1873. In the last decade, a set of remarkable weekly New York newspapers has come to light with titles like *Rake*, the *Whip*, the *Flash*, the *Libertine*, the *Sporting Whip*, and the *Scorpion*, published in the 1840s by young men intent on mapping the licentious culture of the brothel world and luring city newcomers (both male and female) into its orbit. Here we find the opinions, jokes, and worldly philosophies of sporting or "flash" youth full of bravado, temporarily on leave from their respectable communities of origin. Female companions participated as well in this sporting life; but their voices are harder to recover. Mostly they lived by prostitution, and while it is no surprise that prostitution flourished in the big cities (as books by Timothy Gilfoyle, Marilyn Hill, and myself have shown), it seems to have been endemic in towns and smaller cities as well; a forthcoming book by Sharon Wood expertly maps the cartography of vice in Davenport, Iowa.[10]

From the netherworld to the spirit world: it would seem an impossible leap, and yet the idea of promiscuous sex summed up by the phrase "Free Love" was associated with both in the middle 1850s. About the time when the brothel world got its own trade press, numbers of other Americans took flight from the commercial and licentious stew of the cities and sought respite and renewal in utopian communities that turned

10. The flash newspapers are held by the American Antiquarian Society in Worcester, Massachusetts. Donna Dennis, "Obscenity Law and the Conditions of Freedom in the Nineteenth-Century United States," *Law and Social Inquiry*, 27 (2002): 369–99; Timothy Gilfoyle, *City of Eros: New York City, Prostitution, and the Commercialization of Sex, 1790–1920* (New York, 1992); Marilynn Wood Hill, *Their Sisters' Keepers: Prostitution in New York City, 1830–1870* (Berkeley, 1993); Patricia Cline Cohen, *The Murder of Helen Jewett: The Life and Death of the Prostitute in Nineteenth-Century New York* (New York, 1998); Sharon Wood, *The Freedom of the Streets: Work, Citizenship, and Sexuality in American Urban Life, 1875–1910* (Chapel Hill, forthcoming 2005).

their backs on the profit motive, cultivated "attractive industry," and, in some cases, reorganized sexual and familial relations. Lawrence Foster has taught us much about the Oneida Community of Christian Perfectionists with their group marriage practices. Carl Guarneri has mastered the Fourier challenge, and in an article not contained in his masterful book he explores the utopians' flirtation with unconventional marital arrangements. Sarah Gordon has the most recent word on Mormon polygamy with its spiritual wives, and Ann Braude has dissected Spiritualism and its Free Love component.[11]

A thread connecting some members in all these alternative groups is the seventeenth-century Swedish mystic Emanuel Swedenborg, whose writings were published in the United States starting in the 1830s. Swedenborg wrote of a deep crisis that brought him clairvoyant visions of an alternate post-life spiritual universe that could communicate with humans. One of his works, a ponderous 400-page tome called *Conjugial Love*, set forth a complex view of a spiritual married love opposed to what he termed adulterous or scortatory love, loveless sex within marriage.[12] In the 1840s his term "spiritual marriage" turns up in essays in the Fouriers' *Phalanx* and in essays by the Oneidan leader John H. Noyes. In 1842 at least one woman, a Brook-Farm fellow traveler named Mary S. Gove, surprised her unsympathetic husband with the news that they were not "spiritually married," rendering earthly legal and religious marriage ties null and void.

Central to "spiritual marriage" was a belief that profound love, expressed in the physicality of sex, was all-important, for men and for women. From there, opinion divided on what recourse existed if earthly

---

11. Lawrence Foster, *Religion and Sexuality: The Shakers, the Mormons, and the Oneida Community* (Urbana, 1984); Lawrence Foster, ed., and George Wallingford Noyes, comp., *Free Love in Utopia: John Humphrey Noyes and the Origin of the Oneida Community* (Urbana, 2001); Carl J. Guarneri, *The Utopian Alternative: Fourierism in Nineteenth-Century America* (Ithaca, 1994); Carl J. Guarneri, "Reconstructing the Antebellum Communitarian Movement: Oneida and Fourierism," *Journal of the Early Republic*, 16 (1996): 463–88; Sarah Barringer Gordon, *The Mormon Question: Polygamy and Constitutional Conflict in Nineteenth-Century America* (Chapel Hill, 2002); Ann Braude, *Radical Spirits: Spiritualism and Women's Rights in Nineteenth-Century America* (Boston, 1989).

12. Emanuel Swedenborg, *Delights of Wisdom Concerning Conjugial Love; after which Follow Pleasures of Insanity concerning Scortatory Love* (Boston, 1833).

marriage partners no longer felt "passional attraction" (a Fourier phrase imported into the sex debate). The timid counseled patience, to be rewarded in heaven where according to the Bible there would be no husbands and wives. Others, taking their cue from Swedenborg, felt that sex in a loveless marriage was a form of adultery, requiring an end to the marriage. All reformers on this spectrum abhorred *sensualism*, a lustful engagement in sex undertaken solely for bodily pleasure. (The modern use of *sensualism* is not pejorative; we must take care to recover older meanings of words.) The most radical of this spectrum began to call earthly marriage into question, to defend the right to leave any union that had ceased to be fully satisfying, in both spiritual and sexual terms, and seek one's affinity in a new union—and perhaps repeatedly.[13]

By the early 1850s, a marriage reform movement sparked lively discussion. Key books by Henry C. Wright and Thomas L. Nichols were the focus of many columns and letters to editors in the Spiritualist, free thought, and utopian presses of the day. A debate over Free Love erupted in the columns of the New York *Tribune* in 1852, with its defenders claiming it would actually purify sex in America: husbands in spiritual unions would not resort to prostitutes.[14] The bravest advocates of the woman's rights movement found the climate of debate opened the way to talk about sexual abuse within marriage. The whole heady tangle gained coverage in the mainstream press; it is hard to think of another occasion in pre-Civil War America when qualities of sexual desire—love versus lust—were up for discussion in print. The moralists who tagged

---

13. Matthew 22:30: "At the resurrection people will neither marry nor be given in marriage; they will be like the angels in heaven"; Braude, *Radical Spirits*; John C. Spurlock, *Free Love: Marriage and Middle-Class Radicalism in America, 1825–1860* (New York, 1988); Joanne E. Passet, *Sex Radicals and the Quest for Women's Equality* (Urbana, 2003).

14. Henry Clarke Wright, *Marriage and Parentage, or The Reproductive Element in Man as a Means to His Elevation and Happiness* (New York, 1854); Thomas L. Nichols, *Esoteric Anthropology* (New York, 1853), and with wife Mary S. Gove Nichols, *Marriage: Its History, Character, and Results* (New York, 1854). The *Tribune*'s free love debate was published as a pamphlet by one participant, Stephen Pearl Andrews, *Love, Marriage, and Divorce, and the Sovereignty of the Individual* (New York, 1853). For scholarly discussions, see Nancy F. Cott, *Public Vows: A History of Marriage and the Nation* (Cambridge, MA, 2000); and Norma Basch, *Framing American Divorce: From the Revolutionary Generation to the Victorians* (Berkeley, 1999).

Free Love as immoral vice whether practiced in brothels or in utopian or Spiritualist enclaves missed the point. For many people, the spiritual world added a new authority to the sanctity of marriage debate and opened up a space to reconfigure heterosexual sex.

The literature on sex and sexuality in the early republic is burgeoning right now, as the very recent publication dates of works cited here attests. The closest thing to a synthesis at present is Helen Horowitz's book, but for some time to come there will be more microhistories of transgressive individuals, more social and cultural histories of groups, and more attention to the serious religious component of changes in sexuality. The field has advanced enormously from its inception forty years ago, and my surest prediction is that as more serials and newspapers of the period go online, making it far easier to locate the tiny sidebars where sex intruded into public notice (of seduction suits adjudicated, cross-dressers arrested), there will be much new and exciting work in the future.

Space in the Early American City

BERNARD HERMAN

It remains an astonishing fact that historians of all stripes continue to wrestle with the evidential legitimacy and interpretive opportunities afforded by the worlds of objects and images people made and the ways in which the critical space of "things" can shape and direct our understanding of the past in new and important ways. Despite notable contributions, the interpretation of urban life in the early republic remains curiously detached from the material substance of the lives of those who lived in the early American city. Our challenge is twofold. First, we need to commit ourselves with greater confidence to the integration of the evidence of material culture into the history of the early republic. Second, our ability to make this happen demands that we truly embrace interdisciplinary approaches—and this means that we embrace different strategies for the consideration of evidence as well as underutilized bodies of evidence.

A 2003 roundtable discussion on how best to incorporate the lives of George Washington's enslaved servants into the interpretation of his house and the larger contexts, both historical and political, of Independence National Historical Park in Philadelphia illustrates the problem and points to the need to incorporate material culture more effectively. George Washington's Philadelphia presidential mansion has been the subject of a thoroughgoing research effort. Edward Lawler's detailed his-

Bernard L. Herman is Edward F. and Elizabeth Rosenberg Professor of Art History and Director of the Center for Material Culture Studies at the University of Delaware. His books include *The Stolen House* (1992) and *Architecture and Rural Life in Central Delaware, 1700–1900* (1987), both of which received the Abbott Lowell Cummings Award. His forthcoming books *Town House: Architecture and Material in the Early American City, 1780–1830* and *Bricklayers and Housetops: The Architecture of Gee's Bend Quilt* will appear in 2005.

tory of the house mapped out the physical history of the site and the evolution of the building over time, and it is his work that provides the basis for the observations about the layout and appearance of the house.[1] Lawler reconstructed plans of the house as it stood at the time the Washingtons lived there. Coupled with the information on the house, Lawler also charted Washington's lodging assignments for his household, including free and enslaved servants. His discussion of the location of the principal reception rooms on the ground floor and the president's private chambers in the upper stories is well grounded in the documentary record. Similarly, the National Park Service invested considerable effort in researching the site and its occupants. Their work extended beyond the written record and included archaeological explorations with particular attention to an icehouse that stood near the rear of the property. The combined evidence—written, architectural, and archaeological—for the first president's urban mansion is extraordinary in its variety, depth, and, significantly, its ambiguities.

What we do not know about the president's house focuses on the ways in which its many and varied residents inhabited those spaces and what those spaces signified to them and to those around them. Given the historic proximity of the president's house to Independence Hall (less than 500 feet) and all the buildings and public spaces that housed the operations of the newly formed federal government, we are compelled to consider the broader interpretive implications of urban space and culture. An issue that underscores the difficulty and importance of these considerations for writing inclusive histories of the early American republic is how we narrate the lives of the occupants of the president's house. Washington's correspondence, for example, clearly documents the presence of the enslaved Africans forced to accompany the president's family from Mount Vernon to the streets of Philadelphia, but it provides no commentary on their lives in the Washington household. Washington wrote at length about the remodeling of the house in preparation for his tenure, and in those letters he described changes he wished undertaken for the accommodation of his servants. Prominent among the renovations were provisions for servant housing and work spaces includ-

---

1. Edward Lawler Jr., "The President's House in Philadelphia: The Rediscovery of a Lost Landmark," *The Pennsylvania Magazine of History and Biography*, 136 (2002): 5–95.

ing the conversion of a smokehouse, the division of the attic into additional lodging rooms, and the construction of a servants' hall for dining.[2]

The interpretive debates engendered by the lives of servants (slave and free) in George Washington's presidential mansion cannot be resolved in a single narrative strand. Rather, those debates respond to narrative demands—the need to relate specific histories to particular, all too often unarticulated ideological ends. In essence, we write the histories that for varying political and narrative reasons need telling at a given moment in time. Moreover, the question of free and enslaved servants is not just one of presences, but of experiences, contributions, and legacies. The need to convey this history invites the development of new strategies for writing the spatial history of the urban world of the early republic. At the heart of any strategy, however, is the attainment of specified goals. We can readily craft multiple narratives that incorporate all of the actors, but which of those stories should receive privilege of place? Narrative preeminence is situational and ideological—we advance the narratives that most need telling at a given moment in time. So it is with the Washington household's extended sojourn in the Philadelphia presidential mansion and what it tells us about the deeply conflicted and contested terrain of urban space, social interaction, and political ideologies. I do not propose to resolve those ongoing debates here but instead to offer observations on how we might begin to think about the materiality of experience as an opportunity to develop open-ended approaches to research on and interpretations of the city in the early republic.

Among Washington's many penned observations about the remodeling of his Philadelphia residence and the relocation of his household to the new capital were a series of comments about servant staffing and accommodations. In a letter written from Baltimore in September 1790, the president noted: "In my last I left it with you to decide on the propriety of bringing the Washer women. I do so still. But with respect to Mrs. Lewis and her daughter, I wish it may not be done, especially as it is in contemplation to transplant Hercules and Nathan from the Kitchen at Mount Vernon to that in Philadelphia; and because the dirty figures of Mrs. Lewis and her daughter will not be a pleasant sight in view (as

2. Mark A. Mastromarino, ed., *The Papers of George Washington, Presidential Series* (Charlottesville, 1996), 6: 397.

the Kitchen always will be) of principal entertaining rooms in our new habitation."[3]

Even as a fragment taken from an extensive correspondence, this brief passage encourages us to think about the character of spatial experience in Philadelphia at the close of the eighteenth century. First, Washington identifies a set of actors: himself, Tobias Lear (his on-site representative in Philadelphia), Mrs. Lewis and her daughter (white household servants who worked in the Washington household in New York City), Hercules and Nathan (enslaved African servants from Mount Vernon), and the implied guests in the "principal entertaining rooms."[4] Second, Washington notes a network of connected domestic spaces, specifically the kitchen and entertaining rooms, implicitly the back garden and kitchen dooryard. His expressed anxiety about actors and spaces focuses on the ways in which spaces could become transgressive. To gain a larger sense of the ways in which urban domestic space worked relies on an understanding of the president's house as an object.

Despite debates over the details, our understanding of George Washington's presidential townhouse is generally resolved. Extensively reworked and enlarged within its eighteenth-century lot lines, the house reflected upon in Washington's correspondence began its life in the mid-eighteenth century. Two rooms deep, the brick dwelling occupied by the Washington household stood a full three stories in height and was organized around a variation of a formal side-entry plan supported by a complex array of back buildings including kitchen, wash house, stable, and ice house. In form, appearance, and detailing, it was an urban house closely identified with city elites in every English-speaking seaport city on both sides of the Atlantic. Houses of this quality and organization stood in London, Bristol, Hull, Boston, and Charleston. They were primarily the residences of families grown wealthy and powerful through trade. The first spatial contexts that concern us here, however, are those identified with Mrs. Lewis, her daughter, Hercules, and Nathan—the kitchen—and those with the polite guests in the "principal entertaining rooms"—the state dining room and adjacent family dining room on the

---

3. *Ibid.*, 409.

4. The Washingtons ultimately left Nathan at Mount Vernon and brought Hercules's son Richmond to Philadelphia in his stead. Edward Lawler Jr., personal communication (Jan. 22, 2004).

ground floor and "two public (drawing) Rooms" in the second story.[5] In addition to these rooms, Washington identified the sightlines across the paved yard that linked them, fearing that the view of the "dirty" Mrs. Lewis and her daughter might offend his guests. Significantly, Washington's enslaved servants do not figure into this statement of offensive visibility.

In Washington's view, the best rooms in the house—those set aside for formal receptions and entertainments—were also the most vulnerable domestic spaces. As settings for the display of power and ritualized events such as levees or state dinners that bound elites together and provided them the means of distinguishing themselves from each other and *hoi poloi*, but these spaces were ritualized through performance and generally accessible only by invitation or service. The view from Washington's nineteen-foot bow window, an improvement he added in the remodeling of the house, took in the kitchen, the dooryard, and a range of other service structures. The kitchen dooryard and paved yard were functionally conflicted spaces. Envisioned as an occasional entertaining space and visible through the dining room bow window during levees, the area was kept well swept and reflected Washington's concern with the symbolic representation of regularity and order in every aspect of domestic, social, military, and political life. Still, the proximity of the paved yard to the kitchen and the inevitable overflow of tasks related to cooking, washing, and cleaning along with service traffic including deliveries and temporary storage left the area within the gaze of the bow window vulnerable to the disorderly aspects of everyday life. The amenity of a paved yard enabled servants to sweep these workspaces—a definite visual enhancement over the common alternative of a packed-earth yard scattered with broken ceramics, shell, bone, and other household debris. Washington's concern with the view through his bow window from his "principal entertaining rooms" was precisely one of the threat of dirtiness and disorder. What was deemed "dirty," however, was not so much the physical space of the kitchen dooryard but of the people who stood there. Moreover his notion of the offending denizens of his space appears to have extended in this brief passage only to his white servants and not to the enslaved Hercules and his son Richmond who traveled to Philadelphia in Nathan's place.

---

5. Mastromarino, ed., *The Papers of George Washington, Presidential Series*, 6: 397.

My intent here is not to interpret the dynamics of the domestic spaces within and around Washington's Philadelphia townhouse but to suggest strategies through which we might think about those spaces and their place in larger social, political, and cultural contexts. Space—both architectural and experiential—lies at the heart of interpreting the lives of all the residents within Washington's Philadelphia house. Spatiality, however, is an idea that entails much more than the re-creation of physical settings for the placement of individual events. At its most basic level space superintends notions of form in its physical sense. We can think of urban spaces as very formal constellations; the plan of the city, for example, at its largest, or the arrangement of objects within a particular room at its most intimate and specific. These are the kinds of urban space with which we are most familiar and comfortable—spaces that are tangible. Space also is an abstract construction based on perceptions of borders and bodies: those objects that bound as well as those objects that inhabit. Space is experiential. We know space, even in its most abstracted sense, as a category of experience within which the body and/or the imagination works. Space is inscriptive. That is, space can never be empty in the sense that it is always meaningful in some context, especially in the context of describing how people organized and made sense of their lives simultaneously at their most intimate level and most public. Given all these qualities of space (and there are surely others), then we can imagine overlapping categories of space, for example, critical space, contested/conflicted space, invasive space, negotiated space. And, we can use terms like silence, noise, anonymity, fiction, and history to describe spatial "content."

A significant element in Washington's statement is his perception of the dirtiness of Mrs. Lewis and her daughter. In Washington's comments we can deduce that her dirtiness was personal and invasive. The very idea of dirtiness and women's bodies was deeply ingrained in the popular imagination of the early modern world, and its appearance in the context of Washington's remark immediately engages a broader constellation of associations. Although we cannot explore these connections here, we should realize that the perception of dirtiness constituted a visible expression of cultural and social disorder that could be read as a metaphor for civic tensions with the larger society. The appearance of irregularity in a spatial setting (composed of the principal entertaining rooms, the kitchen, and the sightlines that connected them) that was simultaneously public and private preyed on Washington's acute awareness of the symbolic impact of his actions, the creation of precedent, and his insecurities about the ways in which his own person refracted perceptions of the new nation. The dirty Mrs. Lewis and her daughter, when viewed from the formal environs of the president's public rooms, reflected badly not just on the president and his family but on the turbulent, fractious character of the new nation.

Washington's brief commentary reveals the ways in which perceptions of the physical realities of urban space implicate and are implicated by larger concerns. Robert Blair St. George provides a way for us to engage and unravel these relationships through his notion of the "poetics of implication":

Implication opens to view much of what we normally term the symbolic; however, it exposes it not by reifying "meaning" in isolated events but by suggesting an open-ended skein of entangled, involved descriptive passages that loop back continually and bring normally latent tissues that tie one referent to another, and another, and another, and . . . into public view. [6]

Key to St. George's poetics are the notions that cultural productions are systemically related and possess the capacity to convey an array of meanings symbolically. St. Georges's poetics of implication owes much to the concept of "haunting" advanced in Susan Stewart's writings on poetry. Stewart observes that, "The poet needs a continuing reader—both the social and historical context in which the poem is on a continuum with other poems, making it intelligible" as "knowledge of reference necessarily withers, the poem does not lose fullness or complexity but rather acquires a residue of accrued meanings that expand the possibilities for poetry's significance."[7]

The spatialities of the new republic, however, were experiential in nature—and it was the body that both occupied and defined those spatialities. The polite sensibilities of Washington and his guests were offended, not by the prospect of the kitchen dooryard itself but by the prospect of the "dirty" Mrs. Lewis in it. Thus, Washington's letter in its discussion of people, spaces, and views communicates the symbolic

---

6. Robert Blair St. George, *Conversing by Signs: Poetics of Implication in Colonial New England Culture* (Chapel Hill, 1998), 3.

7. Susan Stewart, *Poetry and the Fate of the Senses* (Chicago, 2001), 117.

substance of experience only in implicit terms. What Washington's letter also communicates is the subjective nature of urban space as a category of social and symbolic experience. His immediate concerns are his own, but they quickly expand to include his perception of those who share his sensibilities. It is their space that is threatened by the physical presence of the "dirty" Mrs. Lewis and her daughter. But what of Mrs. Lewis's view from the dooryard looking up to the best rooms in the house visible from her station through the bow windows that break the plane of the rear elevation? And, what of Hercules and Richmond—the enslaved Africans who are present but not included in the same perceptions of dirtiness that condemn Mrs. Lewis?

The tension between individual experience and collective sense remains problematic at the center of these discussions. Numerous scholars have investigated the dynamics of place that create sense of space and in doing so have demonstrated the ways in which actions and objects that seem profoundly singular in fact provide windows into larger patterns of association. Dell Upton provocatively addresses the issues of the "practice of place" and the interplay of its many subjectivities.[8] "Everyday life," Upton observes, "can be oppressive or liberating, depending on the ways it is organized temporally and spatially." It shaped, he continues, "selfhood and personhood through material, and particularly bodily, practices." Practice, in turn, is shaped by routine, repetition, occasion, and significantly unpredictability. Thus, the spatialies of everyday life achieve the status of actors in shaping our understanding of broader, more abstract ideological, social, and economic contexts in the urban worlds of the early republic. In the end we can begin to imagine how the prospect of the "dirty Mrs. Lewis" returning the gaze of the Washingtons' guests as she stood in the kitchen dooryard of the president's Philadelphia townhouse played to the cultural anxieties and political tensions that attended the struggle to shape the discourses of the new nation.

---

8. Dell Upton, "The City as Material Culture," in Mary C. Beaudry and Ann Yentsch, eds., *The Art and Mystery of Historical Archaeology* (Boca Raton, FL, 1992); Upton, "Another City: The Urban Cultural Landscape in the Early Republic," in Catherine E. Hutchins, ed., *Everyday Life in the Early Republic* (Winterthuir, 1994); Upton, "Architecture in Everyday Life," *New Literary History*, 33 (2002): 707–23.

9. Upton, "Architecture in Everyday Life," 720.

A History of All Religions

LEIGH E. SCHMIDT

In *Aids to Reflection*, which Samuel Taylor Coleridge published in 1825 and which James Marsh made available in an American
edition in 1829, the poet commented on one exercise that was especially
conducive to forming "a *habit* of reflection." "Accustom yourself to reflect on the words you use, hear, or read, their birth, derivation and
history. For if words are not THINGS, they are LIVING POWERS, by
which the things of most importance to mankind are actuated, combined,
and humanized." Coleridge's spiritual aid is by now a reflexive habit that
most scholars instinctively cultivate and perhaps even live by as a linguistic and genealogical imperative. As Daniel Dubuisson remarks in his
postcolonial screed on *The Western Construction of Religion*, "All scientific study today ought to have as its *sine qua non* the critical, uncompro-
mising study of its own language."[1]

The history of the early republic is an ideal domain for further devel-
oping this practice of reflection, especially with regard to the study of
religion, its keywords, and critical terms. The period from the end of the
eighteenth century to the middle of the nineteenth century is one of the
most fecund in all of Euro-American history for the generation of new
classifications by which to map the religious world. From a long-standing

Leigh E. Schmidt, a Professor in the Department of Religion at Princeton University, is the author of *Holy Fairs: Scottish Communions and American Revivals
in the Early Modern Period* (1989); *Consumer Rites: The Buying and Selling of
American Holidays* (1995); and *Hearing Things: Religion, Illusion, and the American Enlightenment* (2000). He is currently working on a book on the making of
American "spirituality."

1. Samuel Taylor Coleridge, *Aids to Reflection*, ed. John Beer (Princeton,
1993), 10; Daniel Dubuisson, *The Western Construction of Religion: Myths,
Knowledge, and Ideology*, trans. William Sayers (Baltimore, 2003), 197.

four-pronged diagram of Jewish-Christian-Muslim-pagan traditions, the categories for organizing religion—especially those of the heathen world—underwent massive and decisive expansion. Between 1801 and 1862, Buddhism, Hinduism, Taoism, Zoroastrianism, and Confucianism all were added to the lexicon as differentiated species of religion.[2] More than that, crucial categories for re-imagining the relationship among religion, the state, and an enlightened civic society also came into being in these decades: most notably, liberalism, voluntarism, and secularism. At the same time, mysticism and spirituality were revised as terms to emphasize the riches of solitary interiority and to lay claim to a universal and essentialized form of religious experience. In other words, the scope of religious invention in the era extended well beyond the evangelical Protestant resourcefulness of retrospectively creating "the Great Awakening" or gradually redefining Jonathan Edwards's "true virtue" in republican and common-sense terms. The new nation was a laboratory for the pluralization of knowledge about religions and for the negotiation of shifting views on religion's place within "public" and "private" spheres—two processes that were intimately interconnected. Further cultivating Coleridge's reflective habit on the birth and derivation of words would be a good (not to say spiritual) exercise for historians of religion and the early republic.

The historian Frank E. Manuel insisted in his classic study of the radical Enlightenment that Americans remained "ill-prepared for serious original reflection on the nature of man and his gods," but citizens of the new nation hardly sat out the growing production of knowledge about the history of all religions. The most prevalent model they inherited was a didactic one that descended from seventeenth-century Anglican divines—Samuel Purchas, Alexander Ross, and William Turner among them—who compiled sources from around the globe to demonstrate *inter alia* the fundamental importance of orthodox religious belief, practice, and hierarchy to the smooth functioning of English society. In 1820 the first American edition of John Bellamy's *The History of All Religions* appeared, having been published initially in London in 1812. Bellamy's

---

2. Wilfred Cantwell Smith, *The Meaning and End of Religion: A New Approach to the Religious Traditions of Mankind* (1963; rep., Minneapolis, 1991), 61; Jonathan Z. Smith, "Religion, Religions, Religious," in Mark C. Taylor, ed., *Critical Terms for Religious Studies* (Chicago, 1998), 276.

compendium retained the Christian apologetic purposes of its forebears and placed the growing welter of reports about other religions within "the order of sacred history" from Genesis forward. Luther, Calvin, Fox, Whitefield, and Wesley graced its frontispiece, and the vindication of Jesus as the Messiah formed its crucial subtext.[3]

If clericalism and the Anglican establishment were usually lost in translation, much of this British genre was still readily imported. David Benedict, a Baptist historian from Rhode Island, was best known for his denominational histories; but that did not keep him from attempting his own *History of All Religions,* a volume he published in 1824. What looked on its face like another compendious history of paganism, Judaism, and Islam quickly gave way to a history of "all the denominations of Christendom," particularly in service of the "Holy Alliance" of evangelical churches. Akin to Bellamy's triumphant Protestant frontispiece, Benedict's volume pictured six American divines, carefully chosen to represent the leading Protestant denominations of the early republic. He wanted to make his history of religions "as modern and American as possible," which for him meant serving evangelical Protestantism and its sundry projects of benevolent empire. Benedict's approach to the genre—Protestant curiosity about the depraved diversity of religions and hope for containing that variety through the extension of evangelical Christianity—prevailed in the United States beyond the Civil War.[4]

A somewhat less predictable Protestant rendering came from outside the ranks of the clerisy. Hannah Adams, a New England Congregationalist with increasingly Unitarian leanings, first published her *Alphabetical Compendium of the Various Sects* in 1784 and kept working on it through a fourth edition in 1817, which appeared under the title *A Dictionary of All Religions and Religious Denominations.* Adams expressly criticized the inherited Anglican model, mediated to her through Thomas Broughton's work of the 1740s, and upheld instead denominational vari-

---

3. Frank E. Manuel, *The Eighteenth Century Confronts the Gods* (Cambridge, MA, 1959), 10; John Bellamy, *The History of All Religions* (Boston, 1820), viii, 39.

4. David Benedict, *A History of All Religions* (Providence, 1824), 4–5. See also Thomas Robbins, *All Religions and Religious Ceremonies: In Two Parts* (Hartford, 1823); Samuel Schmucker, *History of All Religions* (Philadelphia, 1859); and Charles A. Goodrich, *A Pictorial Descriptive View and History of All Religions* (New York, 1860).

ety and Protestant dissent against schismatic and enthusiast labels. Significantly, she dedicated the second through fourth editions to John Adams, a distant relation who had opened to her his own considerable library on religion and the religions.[5] Hannah Adams pursued in a more modest and orthodox vein what John Adams fantasized about achieving in his old age. As he wrote to Thomas Jefferson in 1817:

Now Sir! please to hear a modest Proposal. Let me go back to twenty. Give me a million of Revenue, a Library of a million Volumes, and as many more as I should want. I would devote my Life to such an Œ[u]vrage as Condorcet tells us, that Turgot had in contemplation, all his Lifetime. I would digest Bryant, Gebelin, Dupuis, Sir William Jones and above all the Acta Sanctorum of the Bolandists.[6]

Adams's dream of composing a universal history of religions breathed the barely tempered spirit of the radical Enlightenment. Charles Dupuis, an author John Adams read closely late in life, was notorious for seeking the naturalistic origins of all religions, proclaiming that "the genius of a man capable of explaining religion" is of "a higher order than that of a founder of religion. And this is the glory to which I aspire."[7]

Clearly, not everyone in the early republic wanted to bathe the world in gospel light. Freethinkers, who seem to have been all but lost in the recent inundation of work on the rise of evangelicalism, were crucial in imagining religion as an object of philosophical inquiry and critique. In January 1827, the deist George Houston, for example, started up a journal in New York called *The Correspondent*, which had as its announced purpose "A Strict Enquiry into the Origin of Religion" and which took as its heroes Hume, Paine, Gibbon, and Volney. Houston, along with allies such as Frances Wright and Abner Kneeland, promoted free inquiry into religion as a means of independence and improvement. The emancipations were sundry: from the authority of revelation, from the cunning of religious leaders, from ignorance and prejudice, from Sunday

---

5. Thomas A. Tweed, "Introduction," in Hannah Adams, *A Dictionary of All Religions and Religious Denominations: Jewish, Heathen, Mahometan, Christian, Ancient and Modern* (Atlanta, 1992), xi, xiii, xvii.

6. John Adams to Thomas Jefferson, July 15, 1817, in Lester J. Cappon, ed., *The Adams-Jefferson Letters: Complete Correspondence between Thomas Jeffersson and Abigail and John Adams* (Chapel Hill, 1959), 518–19.

7. See Manuel, *Eighteenth Century Confronts the Gods*, 243, 272, 276–78.

Schools, from popery, from the clamor of creeds, from Calvinism especially. In some sense, the Enlightenment came late to the United States,
and admittedly much of it was made so thoroughly Protestant as to be
toothless. Still, freethinkers in the early republic portended various liberal projects in the critical remapping of religion in the second half of
the nineteenth century, including substantial aspects of the agenda of the
Free Religious Association, the Radical Club, the Positivist Society, and
the wider "science of religions." Their voices should not be drowned
out in all the Methodist and Baptist hoopla. The evangelicals hardly won
every battle and debate (in that regard, it is perhaps worth recalling
Francis Asbury's descendant Herbert Asbury, a freethinker, who wrote
a memoir called *Up from Methodism* and who wanted nothing more than
to liberate Americans from evangelical taboos).[8]

Still, freethinkers were modest in number, even in liberal circles. It
would be ill-conceived to revive any thesis that suggests a relentless
march of secularism and demystification, since it has become clear by
now that "Christianization" and "sacralization" make more sense of
American religious and cultural history than the reverse narratives. Liberalism hence needs to occupy the historiographical scene not so much
as an arm of secular forces, but as a religious culture. In its American
usage the term took its rise in the 1820s from theological debates endemic to New England Protestantism and the controversies over Unitari-
anism. Liberalism was always as much, if not more, a religious vision of
emancipated souls as a political theory of individual rights and civil liberties or an economic calculus of the beneficence of free markets. In the
early republic, liberalism first cohered as a radical form of Protestantism
that then over the next half century readily edged beyond Christianity
itself.

It might be said, only half in jest, that liberals in the second third of
the nineteenth century came to define themselves as spiritual, but not
religious. Two categories, in particular, took on a significance that they
hitherto had not enjoyed: mysticism and spirituality. In colonial America,
few pilgrims were seeking "spirituality" *per se* (the term shows up in only

---

8. Herbert Asbury, *Up from Methodism* (New York, 1926). There are, of
course, various counterpoints to the historiography on evangelicalism. A leading
example is Christopher Grasso, "Skepticism and American Faith: Infidels, Con-
verts, and Religious Doubt in the Early Nineteenth Century," *Journal of the Early
Republic*, 22 (2002): 465–508.

one American title before 1800, and that in a collection of hymns in which the concept refers to a quality of corporate Christian worship, not individual interiority). Anglicans and Puritans had practices of piety; evangelicals pursued devout, holy, godly, or spiritual lives; "spirituality" meanwhile was not close to being a keyword in the early Protestant vernacular of salvation. At 1700 John Tillotson presented "spirituality" as an attribute of God (in a chain of attributes like goodness, omnipotence, patience, and eternity), not, as say, Bronson Alcott did in 1877 as an answer to "one's highest aspirations."[9] "Mysticism" lay still farther off the map (at 1800, no English work on either side of the Atlantic had carried the word in its title). By the eve of the Civil War, both had become highly elevated notions within liberal Christian and post-Christian circles; both had come to embody the very poetry and romance of religious experience.

In 1844 Unitarian Henry Ware Jr., an esteemed member of the faculty of the Harvard Divinity School, epitomized these transformations in an article for the *Christian Examiner*. Six years earlier another author in the *Christian Examiner*, still tarring mysticism with an enthusiast brush, had been able to answer negatively his own rhetorical question, "Is mysticism spirituality?" Ware's piece suggested the extent to which the ground was shifting in liberal circles. In lifting up mysticism for the considered attention of all "rational Christians," Ware indicated that "there is, perhaps, no one element of religion to which Ecclesiastical history has done so little justice." Predictably cautious in his reclamation, he remained dismissive of "rude and unenlightened" forms of mysticism, including the "Fetishism" of devotions aimed at "outward objects." (Certainly fetishism, a construct universalized in the French Enlightenment, is another category of cross-cultural comparison in lively circulation in the period that merits further examining, all the more given its Marxist and Freudian afterlives.) Ware wanted a rarefied mysticism that could serve as a basis for liberal spirituality. "Now," he averred, "as a higher stage in spiritual life has been reached, we find the mysticism of religious experience." "We have used the word mysticism in a wider than its usual signification," Ware concluded, rightly highlighting the innovations of the period, "but what is mysticism but the striving of the

---

9. John Tillotson, *The Remaining Discourses, on the Attributes of God* (London, 1700); A. Bronson Alcott, *Table-Talk* (Boston, 1877), 104.

soul after God, the longing of the finite for communion with the Infinite." "Without it," he claimed, "there is, and there can be no religion."[10]

According to historian Peter van der Veer, in his recent book *Imperial Encounters*, "a master concept like 'spirituality' is not epiphenomenal to 'real history' but rather productive of historical change." What van der Veer has in mind is the anti-colonial, nationalist uses to which both Vedantists and Theosophists put the construct of "spirituality" in late nineteenth-century India.[11] The basis for the changes that he documents lay in the liberal reinventions in the prior half century of mysticism and spirituality as cosmopolitan, universal essences that stand against the ravages of materialism. Similarly, how Old School Presbyterian notions of "the spirituality of the church"—politically productive in its very claim for an apolitical church—were developed in the South alongside and in tension with these northern liberal sentiments about "spirituality" would be another story worth telling.

So it is that cultivating Coleridge's habit of reflection might prove fruitful for those of us studying religion and the early republic. Not that historians have necessarily been remiss heretofore: Mark Noll on "virtue" and "liberty," Ann Taves on "experience," or Robert Cox on "sympathy" stand among various exemplars of scholars who have already well honed Coleridge's aid.[12] Still, critical terms have many avatars and buried genealogies. It is for historians to resurface the flux of shifting usages, ellipses, and reinventions. Totem and totemism, for instance, were words that arose in the fluid encounters of Anglo-American travelers with indigenous religious practices in the 1790s. Little more than a century later the terms had widened into constructs so compelling that they could

---

10. [G. E. Ellis], "Swedenborg's True Christian Religion," *Christian Examiner and Religious Miscellany*, 24 (1838): 262; Henry Ware Jr., "The Mystical Element in Religion," *ibid.*, 37 (1844): 309–11, 314, 316. For more on this genealogy, see Leigh Eric Schmidt, "The Making of Modern 'Mysticism,'" *Journal of the American Academy of Religion*, 71 (2003): 273–302.

11. Peter van der Veer, *Imperial Encounters: Religion and Modernity in India and Britain* (Princeton, 2001), 69.

12. Mark A. Noll, *America's God: From Jonathan Edwards to Abraham Lincoln* (New York, 2002), 214–16; Ann Taves, *Fits, Trances, and Visions: Experiencing Religion and Explaining Experience from Wesley to James* (Princeton, 1999), 47–75; Robert S. Cox, *Body and Soul: A Sympathetic History of American Spiritualism* (Charlottesville, 2003), 24–35.

serve as the underpinning of some of the most lurid imaginings of patricide, criminality, and guilt that western culture has conjured.[13] The very conception of "religion" itself changed dramatically in the aftermath of democratic revolution, especially in its political, moral, interior, and aesthetic framing. At the same time, the classification of the species of "religions" was also gradually elaborated and enlarged, allowing an ever growing number of Americans to enter plural worlds of comparison that proved, by turns, fearful and alluring. The enterprise of engaging the history of all religions beguiled many Americans in the early republic, and historians could do worse than to fall under that spell too.

---

13. See Eric J. Sharpe, *Comparative Religion: A History* (1975; rep., Chicago, 1987), 74, 199–201.

Questions, Suspicions, Speculations

DAVID S. SHIELDS

Prognosticating our understanding of the culture of the early republic inevitably produces false prophecy. There is something baldly whiggish in assuming that inquiries will be fruitful and knowledge enriched, something equally presumptuous in delineating matters that will matter most in years to come. Certain types of knowing prosper; others falter. Our grasp of the myriad instantiations of gender waxes, theological literacy wanes. Will insight outpace amnesia? Will the portraits painted of classes of persons be any freer of disfigurement than those of earlier historians whose representations have been revised. Each age has its own myopia. The one certitude is that inquiry will continue as restlessly as ever. This moment is no less troubled by questions than those of former investigators. Perhaps the least arrogant thing one can do when speaking to "what's next" is to capture certain of the emerging questions. How best to approach the future? With rules? Suppositions? Questions? Questions predispose, yet are open enough to permit the unanticipated finding. Suppositions may not. So—a prognosis in the form of questions.

1. Given the religious impetus of wars in the 21st century, will the inquiry into early American culture recover religion as a category of historical meaning as telling as race, gender, and class? Or will we continue to perform the characteristic gestures of the hermeneutics of suspicion, regarding religion as a mask for economic, political, or social interests?
2. Given the application by some scholars of postcolonial analysis

David S. Shields is McClintock Professor of Southern Letters at the University of South Carolina. A historian of literary and learned culture, he edits the journal *Early American Literature* and is presently compiling the Library of America's volume of early American poetry.

upon the culture of the republic, and given their strong investment in its tropes of "national imaginary" and "national memory," will "recollection," "circulation," and "space" so supplant "event," "change," and "time" in their reflection that it ceases to be history?

3. As the internal, continental sensibility promoted by Alan Taylor vies with the global (transatlantic and transpacific) emphases of the recent generation of scholars, will this tension so dominate inquiry that other sorts of cultural and geographical framing disappear? In particular, will the comparative hemispheric analysis of the culture of the Americas that burgeoned during the Pan-American heyday after World War II recede into inattention?

4. As numbers of scholars take up Benedict Anderson's national imaginary often to highlight the rhetorical character of the United States at a time when sections, parties, interests, classes, and sects fissured the body of the state, will there be a countervailing inquiry, "material nationality," to explore the increasingly regularized and mechanized character of material, aesthetic, and social production during the early national period? Will such a counter inquiry come from historians of the market, or from cultural historians following Laura Rigal's explorations of the "federalizing" of American material and institutional practices?

5. The present moment has seen cultural studies converge with material culture studies in reconstructions of "visual culture" and "the acoustic world" of times and places. Each of these inquiries emphasizes a mode of sensate apprehension, rather than an integral phenomenology of being or an aesthetics of the whole body. Visual culture, for instance, does so to explore the social construction of "the visual" and to explore how art and modes of visual representation destabilize epistemology. Has the concentration on the visual and the audible renovated the old Platonic privileging of the "spiritual" intangible senses over touch, smell, and taste. Is there a historical propriety to this privileging of sight and sound during the period of the early republic—is there some merit to the old claim that the eighteenth-century ear was supplanted by the nineteenth-century eye as the organ that most adduces meaning? What then are we to make of the increasingly somatic turn of aesthetics from sensibility in the eighteenth century to sensitivity in the early nineteenth century to sensation in

the mid nineteenth century? And what of eating? Wasn't that sometime resident of the early republic, Brillat-Savarin, author of the *Physiology of Taste*, the truest prophet of the emerging world system of any among his generation when he said that the economy of the globe was being organized around consumption—that the belly spanned the globe?

6. Now that the public and private spheres have become less dichotomized and more ramified in historians' understandings of the early republic, will the representations of citizens become more theatrical? Will the multiple arenas of social projection and civic presentation lead to portraits that reveal a modal performance of personality, with expressions and manners peculiar to each zone, and sometimes appropriately contradictory? Will sentimentalism—particularly in its increasing investment in the notion of sincerity—be seen as a compensation for the multiplication of forms of and venues for social and civic performance? How will gender and "gender roles" play out?

7. Is one's powerlessness in early American society registered in the restriction of the number of roles one could play? Or was power an obdurate insistence on the primacy of a single identity?

8. Given the Christian insistence on the integrity of "psyche" and its traditional critique of hypocrisy, how did belief work as a brake, block, or reaction to the theatricalization of personality?

9. A signal accomplishment of current historians has been the charting of race, gender, class, nation, and locality as categories of individual and communal self-understanding in the early republic. Yet there have been other categories of self-understanding that have been scanted in the academic practice of history. Will family be restored to its primordial place as a frame of identity in future historiography? Will history acknowledge the intense personal investment (then and now) in genealogy?

10. Familiarity during the last part of the eighteenth century meant extending the special favor shown to relatives to members of one's acquaintance, particularly fellow members of a class or set. It had particular associations with aristocratic special treatment in cases of law or matters of commerce and so was despised by Washington and the civic republicans of the founding generation. Yet one dimension of the sentimentalization of American culture after the turn of the century was the creation of a politics of sympathy that

made the citizenry into a brotherhood or sisterhood. Familiarity became demotic; it was divorced from its history of special privilege. Yet was its practice freed of the evasion of legal and moral obligation?

11. Will scholars determine when, under what circumstances, and why did personality eclipse character as the prevailing figure of individuality?

12. Why is there such a pronounced rejection of utility, commerce, common sense, and heterosexuality by second-generation Federalist men of letters? Why the celebration of dronishness, bachelorhood, and genius?

13. The early nineteenth century saw an international drive to create new technologies of visual reproduction; wood engraving, lithography, and photography contributed substantially to the expansion of illustration in printed and other matter. How market driven was this development? How much did it depend on an international cabal of technological innovators who worked not for the glory of mankind, but for themselves? To what extent is the aesthetic frontier of reproduction pushed by a wish to master mimesis?

14. Language during the first half of the nineteenth century becomes riven into a curious complex of trajectories: as John Howe has recently argued, the key terms of the political discourse—liberty, property, slavery, civilization, citizen—became contested and increasingly slippery. The sciences, following the lead of medicine, grew concerned with erecting denotative nomenclatures and creating realms of usage that sought transparency by displacing terms from common parlance. In the schools academic philologists sought meaningfulness in language by recovering a linguistic past where the grammatical, lexical, and figural capacities of a tongue shone with a primitive intensity; in radical religious sects (the Shakers most vividly) the common tongue evaporated entirely in episodes of inspired glossalalia that seemed nonsense to uninspired onlookers. Public entertainment became increasingly intrigued by humorous nonsense, with the minstrel lyric pioneering in the humor of non sequitur, hyperbole, and incoherence. Meanwhile an American vernacular expanded, ballooned by neologism, slang, borrowings from other tongues, until Americanisms became an inevitable matter of remark by English visitors. Did the

increasingly disparate forms of linguistic performance trouble attempts to articulate a national and normative *sensus communis* in English? Given the populations of non-English speakers in Louisiana, Florida, Pennsylvania, and Native-American territories, how did the myriad character of English contribute to the establishment of English linguistic hegemony on the continent?

15. During the Washington administration's attempt to foster national consciousness through the promotion of civic ceremony, the republican court, and the celebration of the governing class, Philip Freneau in a poem entitled "The Country Printer" presented a counter myth of national solidarity. He argued that the country printer and the country newspaper would be the glue of nationhood, educating the dispersed citizenry in the ideals of representative government, liberty, and the rule of law. The country printer brought the nation to the people, not the people to the nation. How accurate was Freneau's assessment about the power of print culture to consolidate the extremities and the head of the body politic? When did country newspapers take up the task of articulating the spirit of the locality? Was Freneau correct in seeing the printer as the chief mediator of national identity? To what extent was the lawyer, the minister, the banker, the elected representative, and the "country merchant" a more potent bridge between the halls of power and the hinterlands of the governed?

16. Sarah Josepha Hale, in an editorial in *Godey's* wrote that the glue that held the country together was the familiar letter written between women, binding families, neighbors, friends dispersed across the continent by the restless migration of the population. The sympathy invoked in these manuscript writings dissolved those barriers of section, party, religion, and class that print culture—particularly the periodical press (including *Godey's*)—had erected and reinforced. Literary history has fixed the novel as the prime medium of women's projection of a politics of sympathy and their engagement with the republic of letters. Could this association be less revelatory than recent scholarship has insisted? Will Hale's claim be tested? What would a literary history look like that tried to make familiar letters the textual web out of which significance is woven?

17. There has been a concerted attempt to understand the character of citizenry—what legal conditions existed determining natural-

ization and enfranchisement and documenting how groups of persons enjoyed or lacked incorporation into the body politic of the United States. But what of the rights and potencies that adhered to ex-patriots, citizens who operated beyond the bounds of the United States? Isn't one of the more fascinating features of this period the way American citizens moved into territories held by neighboring powers, engineered local revolutions, and sought the incorporation of these entities (Louisiana—Florida—Texas—California) into the United States? What gave the filibusters such a sense of entitlement once outside the United States that they as private individuals felt warranted in violating the sovereignty of colonies and states?

18. Much has been made of the cultural projection of the individual in several registers—as a consumer, political actor, creator of culture. Why in sport does team competition and recreation so dominate until late in the nineteenth century? Do the German gymnophysist and later physical culture movements precondition the rise of individual sport?

19. Is it sport or the stage that has the greater influence in making the cultivation and display of the body a cultural fashion? How do the emergence of the circus strong man and the theatrical sensation of the "British Blondes" relate to the representation of the body by the antebellum Athenaeum sex lecturers treated by Patricia Cohen? When does the theatricalization of the male Indian as virile body take place?

20. One marker of elite and/or urbane culture in the early republic was an interest in various kinds of aesthetic historicisms (Greek or Egyptian Revival architecture, literary medievalism à la Walter Scott or Longfellow). Should this be regarded as an Old World nostalgia embraced by a class that felt themselves politically displaced from the center of commercial culture? Or was it a sign of cosmopolitan solidarity with elites across the Atlantic? An atavistic reclamation of durable values of "civilization" being eroded by an emerging mass market value system?

21. To what extent is the claim made by an array of cultural commentators from Joseph Dennie to Nathaniel Hawthorne that American culture was commercial, instrumental, and tasteless—a jeremiad that bespeaks an interest determined by education rather than class? How does the emergence of an increasingly specialized sci-

entific-medical contingent of the educated population challenge the preoccupation with taste and aesthetics among the learned? When does the genteel distrust of commerce vanish from the community of natural scientists?

22. Ballyhoo, huckstering, and early advertisement all presume that *homo economicus* is something more than a rational actor. When did salesmen and cultural promoters come to understand that imagination and sentiment governed decisions of the wallet? Was this understanding customary, and merely being amplified, or was it the result of the pragmatics of life in the post consumer-revolution market? Are there failed campaigns that could reveal the whys and wherefores of the commercial appeal to pathos?

23. There exists a general recognition that this period frames a change in popular interest from the natural spectacle (exotic animals, sapient pigs, Niagara Falls, western canyon lands) to the technological marvel (hot air balloons, steam paddle boats, locomotive engines). To what extent is the human creativity implicit in technology eclipsed by the technological object itself? Why is the personality cult surrounding explorers more potent than that of inventors? Is the inventor supplanted by the witness, who imagines himself guiding the balloon, piloting the steamboat, conducting the train? Is part of the compelling power of the technology the promise that the witness could manipulate it? To what extent do women participate in these fantasies of technological empowerment?

24. The overseas mission movement in the Protestant churches documents a burgeoning global consciousness in the early republic. How does this evangelical globalism relate to the international diplomacy of the United States government? How does it reflect the entrepreneurial globalism of overseas merchants? How does it relate to earlier Christian evangelical campaigns?

25. Cheap print, lecture networks, and commerce popularized medical findings about the internal workings of the body. How did the altered grasp of the functioning of the body influence people's sense of how political bodies thrive or languish? While it is common to speak of the monarch's two bodies in the early modern period, do we grasp the multiplicity of bodies inhabited by subjects in the American republic: physical body, moral body, body

of Christ, body politic? How do the slaves' bodies differ from those of the freed person?

26. The invisible world, once presided over by spirits in the understanding of Christians, became the abode of suprasensual entities discovered by scientific investigation. How did the changing nature of the realm beyond the senses affect people's self-understanding, particularly apprehensions of limit and place?

27. Every society has elements of the economy and human activity organized around the illicit. Where in the early United States was illicit activity most organized. Did campaigns that challenged legal actions as illegitimate (for example, abolitionists' defiance of Fugitive Slave Law) borrow techniques of performance from other sectors of illicit activity?

28. How did political and cultural drift toward irreconcilable differences between northern wage-labor and southern slave-labor societies strain the faith in a providentially-ordered world governed by God's grace, the reconciling power of Jesus Christ, the possibility of redemption, and the escape from a captivity to sin and selfishness? Was this soteriological faith supplanted by a vision of militant Christianity engaged in a cosmic war between irreconcilable powers?

Since early antiquity persons have complained that conversation with the learned gives rise to a proliferation of questions rather than satisfying answers. Perhaps Solomon did not appreciate the benefits of being pointed in specific directions; there is comfort in orientation.

Afterword:

The Quest for Universal Understanding

JOHN LAURITZ LARSON AND
MICHAEL A. MORRISON

So where are we going? We're going global, it seems, but also deep into the peculiar meanings of things locked in time and place and their own particularity. If there are trends to be discovered in the preceding essays, they seem to us to lie in these two contradictory directions. On the one hand, future scholarship seems destined to incorporate broader landscapes and multiple perspectives. Analytical specialization leading to claims of uniqueness or exceptionalism (to trot out a red herring), will not gratify the yearning for inclusion and multivocal representation that exercises so many historians and literary scholars. Much of what these authors call for is synthesis and accommodation to the multiplicity of readings that our sources can be made to sustain. At the same time, historians remain by definition students of particular times, places, events, and persons. Particularity itself is what distinguishes our craft from social science and literary studies. The synthetic narratives demanded by our cutting-edge historians must be rooted in detailed knowledge, informed by rigorous theoretical formulations, and assembled out of carefully scrutinized documentary evidence—or else we will not find it persuasive.

That's a tall order. Notice how the essays insisting on global inclusion all seem to rely on first-person perspectives to establish their point of view? Notice how environmental historians (if our sample is representative) retreat from the grand, inclusive declension narratives sketched out by William Cronon, Donald Worster, and Richard White, searching instead for particular deviations and more textured accounts of how we got from here to there in one place or another? At the polar ends of a spectrum of social relations stand slavery and freedom, yet all four essayists on that subject pull our attention to the messy middle. It could drive a philosopher mad trying to determine whether we want a grand unified theory of all things human and divine or an encyclopedic database in hypertext, searchable for any string of characters yet preserving undiminished the contextual information we associate with unexcavated shards of pottery. With characteristic aplomb we seem to want both. With the breathtaking confidence of postmodern hubris, we expect to have it.

We can imagine bright, ambitious graduate students and newly minted Ph.D.'s ruffling their feathers about this time and protesting that it is easy to ask and impossible to do what this collection of essays implies. As editors and scholars, each of us has rejected articles (and had articles rejected) for being too broadly synthetic, too breezy, not firmly anchored in the documents. Similarly, we have rejected articles (and had articles rejected) for being too narrowly stuck in the sources, for not engaging the literature, for not answering the "So what?" question. It is especially perverse when both complaints are lodged against the same manuscript (believe it or not this happens), but it is not hard to imagine being caught in the switches between inclusive synthesis and particularity—all the while being roasted for over- (or under-) theorizing the argument. What's a poor historian to do? How can we be all things to all people, addressing all questions (each in particular detail), while nevertheless clarifying that hierarchy of significance without which interpretation does not occur.

Part of the problem lies in the explosion of the quantity of historical literature since the early 1960s. There was a time, half a century ago, when major professors could hand out a reading list of fifty titles that, augmented with the article literature of half a dozen journals, constituted the corpus of a field. But with the expansion of higher education in the 1960s, the sheer number of historians working (and getting tenure by writing books) more than doubled. The simultaneous expansion of the parameters of the discipline to incorporate new social history, new economic history, women's history, black history, radical history, history of technology, and many others introduced subspecialties whose books eventually found their way back onto everybody's lists, so that the core lists ran to hundreds of titles by the late 1970s. Journals proliferated and with them articles—some of them damn good, too. The demands of tenure coupled with paperback publishing exploded the market for monographs, and soon everything that once was an article came out as a book from a decent university press. By the turn of the century, graduate mentors (such as the two of us writing here) began to wonder how on earth new students could ever master the conversation into which their own research was expected to fit.

The fact that we are interested in many new things can hardly be faulted. The days when history comprised war, diplomacy, and politics are over; in fact, some American Studies programs, born of frustration with that narrow template in the 1940s and 1950s, have collapsed as historians themselves reabsorbed cultural, literary, and interdisciplinary interests that once had been banished by the older model. But the expansion of our mandate makes life very difficult for readers and writers who would draw together the threads of our discipline. Every host or hostess knows that a table of six or less can converse together all through dinner; larger groups will split up into smaller clusters, and nobody will have heard the same conversation. By encouraging students and scholars to ask all kinds of new questions, we have opened the table to far more participants, and we must learn to accommodate their divergent goals, objectives, and experiences. The benefits of this explosion of participation are obvious: things we never thought we could know are now being explored in new and creative ways. The down side, however, shows up in the output of books and articles that has grown exponentially over the past generation, and the fragmentation of the resulting conversation.

The practical solution to the cacophony has been to carve out subfields and erect barriers—setting this or that body of literature outside one's zone of expertise. But the authors in this collection insistently press us to cross those barriers and reintroduce alternative perspectives that we carefully excluded the first time through. Our economic historians demand that we consider the role of religion, attend to entrepreneurial biographies to the second and third generation, trudge from farmhouse to farmhouse in search of variations, and look for class conflict *within* the hearts of tortured liberal Americans as well as between packs of ruthless competitors. Continentalists remind us there were millions of people in residence before the "conquest" began. Globalists then raise the ante by calling for comparisons with other places—whether like or unlike the ones we already know. Environmentalists insist on attention to the flora and fauna whose welfare shaped and depended on the behavior of *homo sapiens*. Social and cultural critics badger us to think about race theory, power dynamics, gender, sexuality, and the cultural construction of concepts like "deviancy" and "normal." As if to make fun of the polar extremes, Bernard Herman forces us to meditate for pages on the un-scenic "Mrs. Lewis" in George Washington's yard; then David Shields asks whether Alan Taylor's "continental sensibility" threatens the "comparative hemispheric analysis" once-fashionable in the immediate postwar decades? How are we to incorporate this bewildering multitude of scales, frames of reference, points of view?

Some readers of these essays have asked, What becomes of politics? More trenchantly, what happens to the master political narrative without which the early American republic is, well, not necessarily the early American republic at all? We believe, to the extent that politics served as a system for negotiating power, it will stay germane to any stories we tell about the history and culture of the period. At the same time, to the extent that formal politics—that is, the electoral system of filling offices—did *not* serve as the primary site for negotiations of power, we are not surprised to find its role diminished. Taking the long view, there is no doubt that popular governance is a central issue in American life from before the Revolution into the present day. However, much of what today lies clearly in the realm of political debate fell outside those limits two hundred years ago. Relations between husbands and wives, parents and children, masters and servants, employers and employees—most of these did not rise to the level of public political consideration. When viewed in terms of power relations and individual welfare, it may be the case through much our period that private, domestic, and sexual prerogatives most forcefully shaped the lives of common men and women. Some legal and political historians in fact are noticing the ways in which conflicts within these private realms gradually enlarged the purview of government starting in our period and running right on into the twentieth century.

Does the potential eclipse of political history endanger the "early republic" as a field? We suspect not. Even when taking a radically inverted perspective, as Dan Richter does in *Facing East from Indian Country* (2001), historians can hardly ignore the force of political markers such as the Revolution that erected (at least in their own minds) an independent political nation of white men in North America. The first several decades of the nineteenth century will always be a time of U.S. nation building no matter from what angle it is viewed. However, in addition to the "rise of the common man," that period also marks the "eclipse of Alta California," and the "demise of the Woodland Indians," the "decline of the traditional workshop," the "advance of massive deforestation," and the "era of emancipation" (when viewed from the North and the rest of the British Empire).

In the end, we should not be surprised if scholars interested in alternative perspectives find the political master narrative to be less helpful as a framework for ordering their work. If past trends hold, we would expect the urge to synthesize will keep old markers—such as the "Age of Jackson"—around for ages to come. Considering the ideological climate in the popular culture, we can expect standardized high school proficiency exams to continue requiring a basic familiarity with political "heroes," wars, and major political events. But some really great histories have ignored and will continue to disregard those frameworks with interesting results, and those results that fascinate research scholars will gradually infiltrate even the lowliest textbooks.

Enough of this problemitizing. Three things seem likely to be true in the coming generation. First, new historians will have to prove their training and talent by writing at least one and possibly two or three original monographic works. These will have to be based on original research in primary sources (the character of which may shift and expand), and they will have to find argumentative traction in the existing article and monographic literature of some field of specialty. Monographs may not continue to appear as stand-alone books, but students would be ill-advised to imagine a day when they do not have to write them. Second, editors, readers, publishers, students, hiring, promotion, and tenure committees all will demand engagement with a broader audience than the ones on which the success of the monographs rely. This may be achieved through teaching, public speaking, or different kinds of writing, but almost nobody will escape the pressure to "engage." Third, the wasteland, or better, demilitarized zone that exists between the communities of specialization and the repertoire of reasonably intelligent "normal" human beings—already wide and desolate—will grow ever wider. We cannot pursue the rigorously analytical and the broadly inclusive at the same time without creating a literature that requires some prior knowledge to comprehend fully. The price of admission to the table, measured in formal training or dedicated self-study, will be measured, like the price of fine dining, in two, three, or four Michelin stars.

If all these things be true, how do we proceed? It seems to us essential to follow the exciting and divergent strands suggested by the essays in this collection. We are working in a period of centrifugal, not centripetal, forces, even while we crave consilience. Therefore we must sustain intramural conversations with more and more different kinds of historians, who are asking different kinds of questions, using different kinds of sources, and producing very different kinds of writing—some of it perhaps unlike anything we have seen to date. This requires enormous effort, especially on the part of older dogs for whom new tricks come hard. As we grow academically we will become more confused and less certain about what we understand; at the same time we must guide youngsters through their graduate studies and archival research and allow them to enjoy the resulting certainty (it will dissolve soon enough) that comes from knowing *your thesis* inside out. Some of this is contrary to the natural inclination of senior scholars.

It is entirely possible that within a generation we will need to establish new forms of writing and academic discourse designed to improve the look of that demilitarized zone between specialists and "real people." Most highly technical and complicated disciplines already have given rise to several layers of mediating discourse that bridge the gap between leading scientists, for example, and the voters whose tax dollars they must secure. Interdisciplinary programs in molecular biology and biochemistry or biomedical engineering—disciplines that overlap enormously these days yet historically are housed in separate schools in land grant universities—intentionally force into regular conversation persons whose success depends on symbiotic understanding. Because we pretend to use nothing but the King's English to convey our insights, historians have gotten away with paying no attention to mediating discourses. We suspect this will not serve another generation. We are likely to need both new forms of writing to facilitate conversations among specialists within the discipline, and also more generalized and user-friendly forms aimed at nonprofessional but intelligent readers.

The discussion of new forms of academic writing brings us to our final observations regarding the future of this—or any—field of history. As long as most historians work for academic institutions, they will be judged, tenured, and rewarded for producing quality scholarship. Academic careers are fed by precisely the narrow and arcane productions that cost us our audience and send intelligent readers into the arms of Tom Brokaw, David McCullough, and Stephen Ambrose. As we develop a need for synthetic and intermediate writing even within our own community of scholars, it will become essential to find a way to credit and reward those who attend to the whole conversation, and not just the highly specialized leading edge. Web publications and the collapse of hierarchical peer-review gateways along the "information highway" already have forced our hands on this question. Deprived of easy shorthand markers for quality scholarship (rejection rates, press reputations), evaluators may have to do it the old-fashioned way: read the work and think.

We hope you have found food for thought, encouragement, and inspiration from the collection offered here. The intentions of the authors and editors, while honorable, are entirely provocative and in no way meant to dictate terms to the future. Students and colleagues are invited to approach these essays with whatever enthusiasm, appreciation, or hostility comes naturally to them. The result, whichever way, must be the one desired: to ponder, based on the extraordinary recent scholarship on the early American republic, where we are going next?

Index